PUNISHMENT AND INCARCERATION: A GLOBAL PERSPECTIVE

SOCIOLOGY OF CRIME, LAW AND DEVIANCE

Series Editors: Mathieu Deflem
Jeffrey T. Ulmer (Volumes 1–5)

Recent Volumes:

Volume 6: Ethnographies of Law and Social Control – Edited by Stacey Lee Burns, 2005

Volume 7: Sociological Theory and Criminological Research, Views from Europe and United States – Edited by Mathieu Deflem, 2006

Volume 8: Police Occupational Culture: New Debates and Directions – Edited by Megan O'Neill, Monique Marks and Anne-Marie Singh, 2007

Volume 9: Crime and Human Rights – Edited by Stephan Paramentier and Elmar Weitekamp, 2007

Volume 10: Surveillance and Governance: Crime Control and Beyond – Edited by Mathieu Deflem, 2008

Volume 11: Restorative Justice: From Theory to Practice – Edited by Holly Ventura Miller, 2008

Volume 12: Access to Justice – Edited by Rebecca Sandefur, 2009

Volume 13: Immigration, Crime and Justice – Edited by William F. McDonald, 2009

Volume 14: Popular Culture, Crime and Social Control – Edited by Mathieu Deflem, 2010

Volume 15: Social Control: Informal, Legal and Medical – Edited by James J. Chriss, 2010

Volume 16: Economic Crisis and Crime – Edited by Mathieu Deflem, 2011

Volume 17: Disasters, Hazards and Law – Edited by Mathieu Deflem, 2012

Volume 18: Music and Law – Edited by Mathieu Deflem, 2013

SOCIOLOGY OF CRIME, LAW AND DEVIANCE
VOLUME 19

PUNISHMENT AND INCARCERATION: A GLOBAL PERSPECTIVE

EDITED BY
MATHIEU DEFLEM
University of South Carolina, Columbia, SC, USA

United Kingdom – North America – Japan
India – Malaysia – China

Emerald Group Publishing Limited
Howard House, Wagon Lane, Bingley BD16 1WA, UK

First edition 2014

British Library Cataloguing in Publication Data
A catalogue record for this book is available from the British Library

ISBN: 978-1-78350-910-2
ISSN: 1521-6136 (Series)

CONTENTS

LIST OF CONTRIBUTORS

Lisa Adams	Faculty of Health and Community Studies, MacEwan University, Edmonton, Alberta, Canada
Elena Azaola	Centre for Research and Higher Studies in Social Anthropology, Tlalpan, Mexico
Mary S. Corcoran	School of Sociology & Criminology, Keele University, Keele, UK
Hayley Crichton	Department of Sociology, Faculty of Arts, Memorial University, St. John's, Newfoundland, Canada
Tom Daems	Leuven Institute of Criminology (LINC), University of Leuven, Belgium
Mathieu Deflem	Department of Sociology, University of South Carolina, Columbia, SC, USA
Zelia Gallo	Department of Law, London School of Economics and Political Science, London, UK
Shinichi Ishizuka	Ryukoku University Law School, Fushimi, Kyoto, Japan
Roy F. Janisch	Department of History, Philosophy, & Social Sciences, Pittsburg State University, Pittsburg, KS, USA
Aleksandr Khechumyan	Department of Criminology, Max Planck Institute for Foreign and International Criminal Law, Freiburg i. Br., Germany
K. Joe Laidler	Sociology Department and Centre for Criminology, University of Hong Kong, Hong Kong, SAR of China

Maggy Lee Sociology Department and Centre for Criminology, University of Hong Kong, Hong Kong, SAR of China

Willem F. M. Luyt College of Law, Department of Corrections Management, University of South Africa, Brooklyn, Pretoria, South Africa

Rose Ricciardelli Department of Sociology, Faculty of Arts, Memorial University, St. John's, Newfoundland, Canada

Ashley T. Rubin College of Criminology and Criminal Justice, Florida State University, Tallahassee, FL, USA

Serkan Tasgin Center for Criminological Research (SAMER), Karaköprü/Şanlıurfa, Turkey

INTRODUCTION: THE PRISON WORLD

More than a hundred years ago, French sociologist Emile Durkheim observed that the evolution of punishment in modern society was such that it became less severe, at least in modern societies that were no longer autocratic, and that over time the deprivation of liberty became the most typical form of punishment (Durkheim, 1901). The reason for this generalization of the prison as the ultimate sanction of crimes was according to Durkheim related to its potential to reform the prisoner and thus allow for re-integration of the offender back into society upon completion of a penalty of some duration and a prison stay with some distinct form of transformation.

The conception of the prison as a system of corrections, rather than detention alone, was philosophically inspired by Enlightenment ideas, especially as they were manifested in the utilitarian schools of philosophy and criminology (Foucault, 1975). Based on principles concerning human conduct as guided by an economic rationality principle to seek pleasure and fulfillment while avoiding pain and sacrifice, the notion was defended that punishment should be more lenient only at the cost of greater and appropriate intervention aimed at changing the conditions of behavior. A more efficient economy and technology of punishment was therefore proposed that would allow for a calculable exercise of power over the very soul of the offender. What on the surface appears as greater humanity or civilization in punishment more profoundly betrays a calculation of efficient means. The prototypical expression of this form of punishment was a new form of prison, radically different from the dungeon of old. Jeremy Bentham introduced its architecture as the so-called Panopticon, a technology of incarceration that is based on principles of visibility and economy geared toward reform of the prisoner by means of isolation, work, and an adjustment of the length of the penalty based on behavioral progress.

This 18th-century disciplinary prison system was based on the notion that criminal conduct was a choice, the result of an individual weighing of the anticipated costs and benefits of crime (Deflem, 2008). In the historical development of criminology, this idea found expression in the so-called

Classical School, whose representatives defended the notion of a prison as a system of corrections that was designed both to deter, by increasing the cost of crime, and to reform, based on self-reflection over the prisoner's choices (penitence). Over the course of the nineteenth century, the ideas of the Classical School were criticized by the emergence of a new, scientific approach to crime and criminal justice. In this so-called Positivist School of criminology, criminal behavior is conceived of as having certain identifiable causes (biological, psychological, and/or social) that had to be considered to deal with crime as an effect. Based on these new ideas rooted in the sciences of crime, the prison system as a system of corrections came to be redesigned in order to cure or rehabilitate on the basis of a treatment of the causes of crime.

The history of rehabilitation in the modern prison is by now well known (Garland, 2002; Simon, 2001). While the ideal of rehabilitation became increasingly popular after World War II, it would soon be sharply criticized and gradually dismantled, especially following fiscal crises in the 1970s along with the appearance of a new politics of crime and crime control based on populism and, arguably most importantly, a new culture of punishment that is oriented at retribution based on the notion that crime is the result of a choice. What appears under the influence of this neo-Classical culture of control is an exponential growth of the prison as a system of detention – and virtually nothing but detention. The panopticon has been replaced by the maximum-security prison.

The rise and rise of the prison, typically discussed (and criticized) under the heading of "mass incarceration," has especially affected the United States, where incarceration rates are of incomparable magnitude, even though an increase in imprisonment rates has also marked other (Western) societies. There are good reasons, therefore, to concentrate our penological focus on the United States. Yet, what this hyper attention among scholars towards the US has also brought about is a relative lack of concern for or at least knowledge of the conditions of punishment and incarceration in other parts of the world. This book is therefore most centrally conceived in terms of its aspiration to bring together in one volume a series of analyses on the conditions of prisons and imprisonment in a variety of countries around the world. At the same time, these country-specific investigations also unravel a variety of mechanisms, conditions, and implications of punishment from different and informed social-science perspectives.

The chapters can be briefly summarized to offer a comprehensive overview of what this book as a whole has to offer. Starting with countries from the European continent, Zelia Gallo discusses the role of judicial actors in the case of contemporary punishment in Italy. Zalo reveals that the judiciary in Italy has had a dual role in fostering both punitiveness as well as moderation in punishment. Turning to the situation in Turkey, Serkan Tasgin focuses specifically on the juvenile justice system. Tasgin argues that the leniency of the Turkish juvenile justice system is associated with high rates of recidivism. For England and Wales, Mary S. Corcoran adopts an economic-criminological perspective to concentrate on the market rationalities in the contemporary penal administration. She concludes that the drift towards increased privatization places additional strains on an inadequate regulatory system. Turning to the situation in Belgium, Tom Daems invokes the work of René Magritte to examine the recent history of strip searches in the prisons of this small country in the European Union. Based on the work of Stanley Cohen, Daems shows how Belgian prison administrators can circumvent legal restrictions on strip searches.

Turning to the American continent, co-authors Rose Ricciardelli, Hayley Crichton, and Lisa Adams unravel the evolution of Canadian corrections up to its current punitive rhetoric and the concrete impact the system of corrections has on conditions of confinement and program implementation. The authors show that punishment in Canada has been greatly shaped by social and political pressures of increasingly more punitive "tough on crime" policies. Elena Azaola analyzes the confinement conditions that women doing time for federal offenses nowadays face in Mexico. Based on interviews with female inmates, Azaola shows that anti-drug policies have increased the female imprisonment rate with very little positive consequences.

Three chapters of this book deal with punishment in the United States. Focusing on the historical condition, Ashley T. Rubin uncovers different periods of prison development over time. She shows that the penal landscape especially developed in diverse directions after the Civil War years. Roy F. Janisch subsequently focuses on the special problems faced by native American prisoners. Janisch argues that federal laws and bureaucratic actions have contributed to a disproportionate incarceration of this historically important minority category. Also focusing on a special category of inmates, Aleksandr Khechumyan adopts a human rights perspective to analyze the conditions faced by inmates who are terminally ill. Conceiving of terminal illness as an element related to the principle of proportionality of punishment, Khechumyan suggests that terminal illness of the offender should be observed not only when sentence is passed but also during imprisonment.

Covering yet more parts of the world, the final three chapters of this book take us to Africa and Asia. In the context of newly democratic South

Africa, Willem F. M. Luyt examines the influence of sentencing practices on the inmate population, especially since the end of Apartheid. The author is hopeful that scholars in other emerging democracies can learn from the South-African situation. In Japan, Shinichi Ishizuka discusses how the increase in reported crime over the past years has brought about a tightening of the criminal justice system. However, Ishizuka argues, changes in reported crime actually reflect changes in Japan's crime control policies. Finally, bringing in the issue of gender, Maggy Lee and K. Joe Laidler examine Hong Kong's prison system from its colonial past to its contemporary state as an autonomous region of China. The authors reveal the peculiar problems that are placed on Hong Kong's prisons because of a sharp and rapid growth in female imprisonment. Collectively, then, these chapters will shed an important light on the realities of punishment and incarceration across the world.

Mathieu Deflem
Editor

REFERENCES

Deflem, M. (2008). *Sociology of law: Visions of a scholarly tradition.* Cambridge: Cambridge University Press.

Durkheim, E. ([1901] 1983). The evolution of punishment. In S. Lukes & A. Scull (Eds.), *Durkheim and the law* (pp. 102–132). New York, NY: St. Martin's Press.

Foucault, M. ([1975] 1977). *Discipline and punish: The birth of the prison.* New York, NY: Pantheon.

Garland, D. (2002). *The culture of control: Crime and social order in contemporary society.* Chicago, IL: University of Chicago Press.

Simon, J. (2001). Fear and loathing in late modernity: Reflections on the cultural sources of mass imprisonment in the United States. *Punishment and Society*, *3*(1), 21–33.

LEGITIMACY AND PUNITIVENESS: THE ROLE OF JUDICIAL ACTORS IN ITALIAN PENALITY

Zelia Gallo

ABSTRACT

Purpose – *In this chapter I discuss judicial contributions to Italian penality. I look at the penal incentives produced by interactions between judicial and political classes, and ask whether judges and prosecutors have been forces for punitiveness or moderation. I discuss the relevance of the Italian case for broader analyses of Western penality.*

Design/methodology/approach – *My chapter offers a political-sociological account of judicial contributions to punishment. I analyse the penal incentives created by different national institutional set-ups, specifically addressing judicial contributions to penality using a framework developed by Joachim Savelsberg and Nicola Lacey. The framework examines judicial structure in the institutional context looking at the penal implications of bureaucratisation of the judiciary and the capacity for co-ordination between judges and politicians. I include judicial legitimacy as an additional dimension in this framework.*

Punishment and Incarceration: A Global Perspective
Sociology of Crime, Law and Deviance, Volume 19, 1–29

ISSN: 1521-6136/doi:10.1108/S1521-613620140000019001

Findings – *I conclude that the Italian judiciary have been forces for punitiveness* and *moderation. Their contributions can be systematised by looking at the waxing and waning of judicial legitimacy, and the consequent expansion and contraction of judicial powers. I claim that judicial legitimacy is also relevant to other ('non-Italian') analyses of judicial contributions to contemporary Western penality.*

Originality/value – *By adding legitimacy to investigations of judicial contributions to penality I provide an organising principle with which to analyse the penal role of Italian judicial actors. I thus allow Italy to be kept in conversation with existing comparative models, without assuming that it either conforms to the models entirely, or that the models should otherwise be eschewed. I use the Italian case to demonstrate the relevance of legitimacy when analysing judicial contributions to Western penality, arguing that changing legitimacy affects the terms and effect of interaction between judicial and political classes.*

Keywords: Italy; judiciary; legitimacy; punitiveness; Western penality

INTRODUCTION – PUNITIVENESS, JUDGES AND LEGITIMACY

Part of the contemporary criminological attention to Western 'punitiveness' has focused on the role of the judiciary in promoting or resisting pressures in favour of penal escalation. The hypotheses advanced by Joachim Savelsberg (1994, 1999) and Lacey (2008, 2011, pp. 91–97) are eminent examples of such work, interrogating judicial contributions to national penality. The authors offer a particularly fruitful approach to the question because they offer *institutional* analyses – looking at the judiciary in context – which allow a *systematisation* – explanation rather than mere description – of the judicial role in penality. Savelsberg's and Lacey's analyses also form part of the body of criminological literature that has attempted to question the applicability of 'punitiveness' and 'penal escalation' across contexts, by pointing to the existence of penal divergence across Western democracies (Cavadino & Dignan, 2006; Tonry, 2007; Lacey, 2008).

My argument is set within this context. This chapter is concerned with theorising about the contributions of judicial actors to national penality, using the Italian scenario as a case study with which to analyse these contributions across Western polities. With regards to Italy, I ask, 'what role have judicial actors played in Italian penality?' and 'have judicial actors been forces for moderation or for punitiveness?'. In keeping with Savelsberg's and Lacey's accounts I attempt to give systematic answers to such questions, with the added aim of factoring insights from the Italian context back into the authors' theses. I thus offer an institutional analysis of judicial contributions to Italian penality – one that looks to institutional set-ups and the penal incentives they sustain (Lacey 2008, 2011; Loader & Sparks, 2013) – providing a 'mid-level' analysis, set below 'macro' theories which explain punishment by 'global' shifts (De Giorgi, 2006; Garland, 2001; Wacquant, 2009), but above particular, empirical case studies. In formulating analyses at the level of nations and national institutions, I aim to synthesise 'macro' and 'micro' analyses, particularising the macro, and providing a theoretical framework to be tested by future micro-level studies.

My argument is that Italian judges and prosecutors – 'judicial actors', 'judges' or 'magistrates'[1] – have had a variable effect on Italian penality (between 1970 and 2008[2]). They have produced pressures in favour of punitiveness *and* of moderation, and have thus contributed to Italian penality's fluctuation between repression and leniency. These variable contributions can be explained by analysing the structure of the Italian judiciary, the institutional framework in which judges and prosecutors are ensconced, and the waxing and waning of judicial legitimacy. I argue that *legitimacy* is the key to understanding the acquisition, deployment of and limitations to judicial powers over the decades. Acquisition, deployment and limitations can then be understood in terms of pressures towards punitiveness or moderation.

Savelsberg's and Lacey's accounts are the starting points of this chapter. The authors are concerned with gauging whether judges will be agents for penal punitiveness and dynamism or, by contrast, for penal moderation and stability. Their hypotheses centre on the interaction between judicial and executive branches, with a view to the potential for co-negotiation of penal policy. They also investigate the institutional distance existing between public opinion and judicial decision-making, to understand whether a margin exists for judges to resist putative 'populist punitive' demands (Lacey, 2008, pp. 93–95; Savelsberg, 1994, 1999). My chapter specifically addresses interactions between judges and politicians, attempting to establish how these interactions have shaped judicial positions on punishment in Italy. However, Savelsberg's and Lacey's theses can only be a starting point in this chapter, as the Italian context forces a modification of their comparative models. Here, I propose to include *judicial legitimacy* into our analyses.

My chapter thus investigates how changing judicial legitimacy in Italy helps us understand the role that judges and prosecutors have played in national punishment. Implicit in this approach is the suggestion that judicial legitimacy be factored into other accounts of penal evolution.

The chapter is structured as follows. I first define the terms *legitimacy* and *punitiveness*. I then give a brief background to my discussion of judicial legitimacy, detailing the trends in Italian penality and providing a stylised profile of the Italian judiciary. I subsequently summarise the arguments advanced by Savelsberg and by Lacey and explain why judicial legitimacy is a necessary addition to their conceptual framework where we are concerned with tracing judicial contributions to Italian penality. I then explain the significance of legitimacy to our understanding of judges' role in Italy. I conclude by speculating on the broader implications of the Italian case.

LEGITIMACY AND PUNITIVENESS

Legitimacy

The notion of legitimacy is one of considerable theoretical complexity (see Tankebe & Liebling, 2013). In this chapter I adopt a definition of legitimacy that addresses two issues: 'the legality of law enforcement' (Bottoms & Tankebe, 2012, p. 166) – here conformity of judicial action to the law; and the 'ability' for judicial action 'to be [...] justified' ('Legitimacy': OED, accessed 2009). This definition encompasses both the idea of legitimacy as grounded in *legal validity* (Beetham, 2013, p. 20) and the idea of judicial action as *substantively* justified (Beetham, 2013, p. 20; Coicaud, 2013, p. 43). My discussion touches on legality insofar as I discuss the conformity of judicial action to judges' constitutional role and to their legal powers; it touches on substantive legitimacy because it addresses the extent to which judicial action was seen as justified and justifiable by the political class (see Beetham on normative justifiability and de/legitimation, 2013, p. 20; also Guarnieri & Pederzoli, 2002, pp. 68–69; Loader & Sparks, 2013, p. 113).

The notion of 'legitimacy', as applied to the Italian context, encompasses two questions: *were Italian magistrates acting within their remit?* and *how was their action received?* As such, my definition is in line with Bottoms and Tankebe's (2012) idea of legitimacy as *dialogic*, which is constituted through *claims* to legitimacy, and *responses* to such claims: here I focus on the 'dialogue' between judges and politicians. Casting legitimacy as a dialogue allows me to factor into my analysis the idea that there can, and have, been disagreements as to the 'values' to which judicial action conforms. It also allows an investigation of legitimacy as a state that is both constituted and expressed within given institutional set-ups (see Loader & Sparks, 2013, pp. 113–114).

I further distinguish between external and internal legitimacy. Legitimacy is *external* where it concerns an evaluation of judges and judicial action by politicians and the public (see Beetham, 2013, p. 19). It is *internal* where it concerns *judicial* evaluations of judges and judicial action. In the latter case articulation legitimacy interrogates judicial self-conception and the role judges have felt free to adopt, particularly in matters of law and order (see Bottoms & Tankebe on 'power-holder' legitimacy, 2012, p. 150; also Friedman, 1997, on 'internal legal culture'; on judicial self-conception and its penal consequences see Montana, 2009, 2012). This chapter addresses only issues of *external* legitimacy and only in relation to the political class.[3]

Punitiveness

In this chapter I evaluate punitiveness using the proxy of prison rates – such that high prison rates are an indication of punitiveness. I use low prison rates, and the possibility of deflation in imprisonment, as proxies for leniency. This is not to suggest that prison rates exhaust the issue of punitiveness and leniency (or that they are necessarily mirror images; see Nelken, 2011, p. 111); penality is more than just imprisonment (Blumstein, Tonry, & Van Ness, 2005, pp. 353–364; Nelken, 2010; Tonry 2007). However, prison rates remain a highly convenient measure of punishment, particularly for comparative purposes (Nelken, 2005, p. 221), as they are an easily available measure, consistent across Western polities (because they are collected on the same basis).[4]

JUDICIAL CONTRIBUTIONS TO PUNISHMENT – NATIONAL AND THEORETICAL CONTEXTS

The National Context – Italian Penality, Italian Judges

In order to analyse the role of judicial actors in Italian penality we need to know what it looks like. Firstly, we see that Italian prison rates between 1970 and 2008 do not present any unequivocal trend (Fig. 1). They do

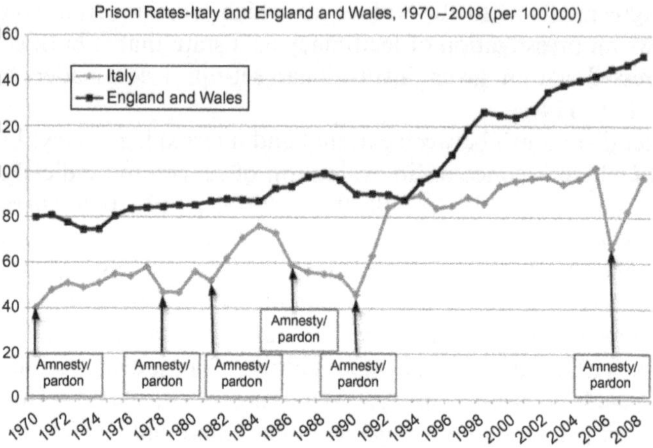

Fig. 1. Prison Rates in Italy and England & Wales Compared from 1970 to 2008, Including Italian Clemency Provisions. *Sources*: *Italy*: author's elaboration from ISTAT – *Annuari di Statistiche Giudiziarie Penali* (1970–2008) and ISTAT – Demo, Geodemo (accessed 2009); *England and Wales*: author's elaboration from HMSO (1980); Home Office (1984; 1986; 1987); White et al. (2000); Home Office (2003); Berman and Dar (2013); Office for National Statistics (1970–2000) Population Statistics.

show an overall upward tendency, most visible if discontinuous readings are taken, but they mainly progress in peaks and troughs (Cavadino & Dignan, 2006, p. 142). This undulating motion can partly be attributed to the pardons and amnesties cyclically passed in Italy (by presidential decree and, after 1992, by parliament), in an attempt to reduce the population detained. The 1990s see a marked increase in prison rates, but the shape of Italian prison rates overall suggests that Italy displays punitiveness (here represented by the background increase, and 1990s peak, in rates) *and* moderation (here represented by amnesties, which typify but do not exhaust the aspects of Italian leniency). This conclusion is also supported by comparisons with prison rates in England and Wales and Germany:[5] Italy has seen neither the penal escalation associated with England and Wales, nor the penal moderation associated with the more archetypal representations of Germany, as in Lacey's account of comparative penal variation (Lacey, 2008; Savelsberg, 1994, 1999). In Lacey's analyses Germany is indeed seen as a typical co-ordinated market economy, with institutional structure and political economy thought to incentivise penal moderation. By contrast, in so-called 'liberal market economies' such as the United Kingdom, the institutional structure and political economy are thought to incentivise penal punitiveness (Lacey, 2008, 2011).

As far as Italy is concerned, I claim that prison rates reflect broader tendencies at work: given the shape of Italian prison rates, Italian penality can thus be characterised as *fluctuating between repression and leniency*.

What position do Italian magistrates occupy in this scenario? What is the structure of the judiciary, and what is the institutional framework in which judicial actors are ensconced? Looking at the bureaucratisation of the judiciary as a key to understanding judges' interaction with the political class on matters of law and order (Lacey, 2008, pp. 93–97; Savelsberg, 1994, 1999) – I first note that the Italian judiciary is bureaucratic. It is akin to the judiciaries of nations such as France and Germany (Guarnieri & Pederzoli, 2002, p. 54) more than to the judiciary of England and Wales, where, by contrast, judges are not trained as civil servants but are lawyers, only later appointed to judicial posts. For example, Italian judges are tenured civil servants considered as part of the state's bureaucracy (similar to Germany: Lacey 2008, pp. 96–97; Savelsberg, 1994, p. 913), are selected by national examination and are presumed to have generalist approaches to their job (Guarnieri & Pederzoli, 2002, pp. 66–67).

However, the Italian judiciary is bureaucratic *with caveats*, as the judicial structure has been modified in post-war decades. Importantly, Italian judges and prosecutors are entirely independent of other government branches (rather than being accountable to the executive) and are self-governed by their Higher Council (*Consiglio Superiore della Magistratura:* Articolo, 104–105 Cost.). Moreover, progression within the Italian judiciary is premised on seniority alone: like self-government, this rule is intended to maximise judicial independence. The total independence of the judiciary is complemented by the rule on obligatory prosecution which – in theory – mandates that criminal proceedings should be initiated wherever there is evidence of a crime (Articolo, 112 Cost.; on the practical application of the rule see Montana, 2012; Nelken & Zanier, 2006; for criticism of the Italian model see Di Federico, 1998).

The Italian judiciary is heterogeneous, and thus encompasses different penal philosophies and political outlooks (Nelken, 2010, p. 42). These differences are crystallised in the various factions, known as *currents*, of the judges' professional association (*Associazione Nazionale Magistrati*), whose politicisation is explicit and understood as part of the judicial structure (Cotta & Verzichelli, 2007, pp. 240–243; Guarnieri & Pederzoli, 2002, p. 54). The judicial 'currents' have diverse 'political orientations', and 'somewhat different conceptions of the role' of the judiciary '[within] society' (Cotta & Verzichelli, 2007, p. 242). This heterogeneity has played a part in the late development of judges' professional culture (Della Porta, 2001, p. 11). A judicial 'esprit de corps' only truly flourished after 1990, in response to the conflict that developed with the political class, particularly over matters of political corruption. Partly because of the judicial-political conflict, judges have begun to see themselves as the last bastions of legality (Della Porta, 2001, p. 16), with the conflict between judges and politicians strengthening Italian judges' perceptions of their role as guardians of the Constitution (Borgna & Cassano, 1997, p. 55; Montana, 2012, p. 116). This means that it is the judiciary's role to listen and, in some sense, 'represent' all citizens, not just the majority (Della Porta, 2001, p. 16; Guarnieri & Pederzoli, 2002, p. 76; Righettini, 1995, pp. 227–265), even where this implies independent interpretation of legality, and even where it requires judges to uphold the Constitution *against the political majority* (Ferrajoli, 1994, p. 66; Morisi, 1999, p. 141).

In sum, the Italian judiciary is highly independent, though integrated within the national bureaucracy, heterogeneous and politicised, capable of adopting numerous stances on criminal justice matters *and vis-à-vis* the political class. What do our institutional analyses now suggest about the Italian judiciary's contribution to punishment?

The Theoretical Context – Institutional Models, Judicial Structure and Penality

The models developed by Savelsberg and Lacey, in their comparisons of the United States and Germany (Savelsberg, 1994, 1999), and of Germany and England and Wales (Lacey, 2008) are used to draw hypotheses on two particular dimensions of judicial action. First, the susceptibility of penal decision-making to public opinion; and second, the relationship between judicial and political classes and its effect on judges' action in the penal sphere. Both dimensions reflect judges' institutional organisation, which is 'likely to have distinctive implications for the environment in which penal policy is developed and implemented' (Lacey, 2008., p. 94). They also incorporate the broader political and economic context in which judges act (Hall & Soskice, 2001; Lacey, 2008), which has important implications for the manner in which different institutional actors interact over criminal justice matters. Lacey has observed, for example, how in polities with majoritarian electoral systems such as the United Kingdom, the importance of 'floating voters' swayed by 'law and order' has created the conditions for criminal justice matters to become important electoral issues (2008, pp. 66–71). This has consequently limited politicians' willingness to negotiate penal policy with judges, that is discuss with a willingness to be influenced by judicial opinion, if and where the latter manifests reservations on the appropriateness of a 'law and order arms race' (2008, p. 173).

Considering the second dimension of the analysis – the type of relations existing between judicial and political actors such as government and the civil service (Lacey, 2008, p. 95; also Downes, 1988) – a stylisation of Savelsberg's and Lacey's arguments leads to the following theoretical conclusions. At its simplest, the relationship between judicial and political actors can be expected to affect decision-making in the criminal justice field. For example, from her analysis of Germany and the United Kingdom, Lacey hypothesises that a system in which judicial and political actors are willing to negotiate may, under the right circumstances, provide incentives for penal moderation. Each level of negotiation can be seen as a space for debate over the purpose and appropriate quantity of punishment and, *given the right contingencies* – a judiciary devoted to rehabilitation, a political class interested in re-socialisation of deviance – each level of negotiation provides an opportunity for the development of penal moderation (see also Savelsberg, 1994, p. 925). Thus it seems that where judges are willing to negotiate policy issues with the (rest of the) bureaucracy, this helps to develop moderate policies that have political support if – for example – the judiciary are repositories of attitudes in favour of a moderate use of punishment.

This scenario is more likely to be prevalent in a nation such as Germany, whose institutional set-up is premised on 'co-ordination', including co-ordination between judicial and executive branches (Cavadino & Dignan, 2006, pp. 101–112; Lacey, 2008, p. 95; Lappi-Seppälä, 2008). In Germany, it is the judiciary's status as members of the state bureaucracy that presumes and incentivises this type of negotiation. By contrast, in the United Kingdom the role of the judiciary and the judiciary's understanding of its role, generally, preclude 'negotiated co-determination of criminal policy' (Lacey, 2008, p. 95). In England and Wales this may be because judges, though independent, are nonetheless not bureaucratic. This means they are considered (and consider themselves) to be *autonomous* of the political sphere: co-operation with legislative and executive is therefore thought to be improperly political (Lacey, 2008, p. 95). On the flip side, this culture of judicial independence also allows politicians to write off judges as out of touch (Lacey, 2008, p. 96) and thus makes co-ordination highly unlikely, particularly with the increasing politicisation of 'law and order' issues. It is also significant that in England and Wales, there has been a decline in respect for professional/judicial expertise over criminal justice matters (Lacey, 2008, pp. 72–74). By contrast, in other polities (Germany, Scandinavia) persisting respect for expertise has been crucial in stabilising penal policy and maintaining existing moderation (Downes, 1988; Lappi-Seppälä, 2007). In England and Wales the clash between judicial and political spheres has, in some instances, been so severe that it has led 'the government [...] to regard the judiciary as [...] irksome and irresponsible [...] to be thwarted as often as possible by legislative and other means' (Lacey 2008, p. 96). Overall, this reduces the margin available for existing discussions on 'penal moderation' to cross the judicial/executive boundary. This dimension encompasses the impact of *bureaucratisation* and *coordination* on judicial action. The hypothesis is that a bureaucratised judiciary, ensconced within a co-ordinated system in which there is persisting respect for judicial expertise, increases the likelihood of penally moderate attitudes, where these attitudes are already prevalent within the system.

To sum up: to understand judicial contributions to punitiveness or moderation, it is useful to adopt an approach that focuses on the incentives and opportunities created by the judicial structure and institutional context. This approach allows for some systemisation – with different institutional features acting as rough predictors of punitiveness/moderation – and provides margins for comparative divergence in punishment and in judges' penal role. The relationship that exists between judicial and political classes is a crucial component of this analysis. Looking at judicial-political relations, and their evolution within given institutional contexts, sheds light on the avenues that exist for collaboration or conflict to develop over criminal justice matters. Bureaucratisation appears to be a good predictor of collaboration between the judiciary and executive and, in institutional contexts that already incentivise penal moderation, it has also been a predictor of persisting moderation.

The Importance of Judicial Legitimacy

Looking at this analysis, we note that Italy and its judiciary pose something of a challenge. Not only is the Italian judiciary bureaucratic *and* independent, but it has also interacted with the political class in a number of ways, ranging from more or less formal collaboration, through collusion – particularly with corrupt politicians (Della Porta, 2001; Nelken, 2010, p. 43) – to virulent conflict. Italy thus falls *between* the axis of bureaucratisation/independence, and presents more variables than allowed for by the co-ordination/conflict axis. This suggests that institutional variables that, in Germany or England and Wales, have yielded pressures for moderation or punitiveness may have produced different penal effects in the Italian context. Indeed, one final assumption that can be drawn from the works of Lacey and Savelsberg is that we should not expect the dimension of 'judicial-political relations' to produce the same effects in all national contexts (see also Lappi-Seppälä, 2008, p. 315). The shape of Italian penality suggests as much, with its fluctuation between repression and leniency.

Is it then possible to systematise judicial contributions to Italian penality, or are we forced to eschew the comparative models? I claim that the models *can* be useful to our understanding, provided we add one more layer to their analysis: that of judicial legitimacy. The penal effects of institutional collaboration or conflict will indeed depend upon the *terms* on which judges and politicians clash or co-operate, and it is here that a consideration of legitimacy advances our analysis. Judicial legitimacy, for example, becomes the key to understanding how and why Italian judges have produced pressures for punitiveness *and* for moderation. With its effects on judicial powers, it acts as a key organising principle in a context that has not displayed the penal coherence presumed in the contrast between punitiveness and moderation, or the systemic institutional coherence presumed in those comparative models in which Italy features as a hybrid (Molina & Rhodes, 2007). Judicial legitimacy is thus also the key to contextualising our theoretical models, explaining Italy's variability relative to their predictions, whilst re-affirming the fundamental importance of their focus on judicial structure in 'institutional context'.

Legitimacy sheds light on the *type* and *terms* of interaction between judicial and political branches in Italy, and on the penal effects thought to follow from such interaction. Simplifying the relations between judges and executive/legislative in Italy, I note that at times and for certain judges the relationship with the political class can be characterised as one of three types of interactions: 'role substitution'; 'collusion' or 'conflict'. Each type of interaction can be understood as embodying a particular conception of il/legitimate judicial action. For example, the conflict that developed between the Italian judiciary and the political class as of the late 1980s, following judicial investigations into political corruption, expresses a particular criticism of judicial activism as *illegitimate* because it was guided by inappropriate aims. It expresses a particular judicial self-conception of this activism as legitimate but also *necessary* to protect the judiciary and legality. Here I will be concentrating primarily on judicial and political collaboration and conflict (on collusion see Della Porta, 2001).

Significantly, with a fluctuation of (external) judicial legitimacy in Italy, we witness both an expansion and a contraction of judicial penal powers that, I argue, has contributed to the co-existence of repression and leniency. In the next section I address this variation of legitimacy. I look first at *high* judicial legitimacy, represented and bolstered by 'judicial surrogacy', analysing its potential punitive effects. I then turn to a decline in judicial legitimacy and the outbreak of conflict between judges and politicians. Having noted how high and low legitimacy both derive from the same institutional structure, I proceed to detail the legislation that followed from conflict, and its effect on judicial action in the penal sphere. Though I am here focusing on the Italian situation, I argue that my discussion illustrates a broader point, namely that legitimacy will be relevant in understanding penal incentives that derive from judicial-political relations in other national contexts, for example England and Wales and Germany.

JUDICIAL LEGITIMACY – WAXING AND WANING

Waxing: Collaboration, Judicial Surrogacy and the Punitive Potential

The Italian judiciary has experienced fluctuating external legitimacy over the years. Legitimacy varied across time, socio-political groups and according to the different issues judges were called upon to resolve. To understand this varying legitimacy in Italy, I start by investigating the phenomenon known as 'judicial surrogacy' (Violante, 1998, p. lvi, my translation). 'Judicial surrogacy' indicates that judges in Italy have acted as 'surrogates', even as 'substitutes', for the political class (Della Porta, 2001, p. 16). This does not necessarily point to improper judicial expansion into the executive or legislature's remit. As Nelken (2009, p. 301) states: 'penal rules and judicial interventions are often relied on as a substitute for political and policy-led decision making' in Italy, and this is done within constitutional rules. In fact surrogacy was often expedient in the nation's otherwise 'blocked' political system, where incessant political conflict has stood in the way of timely reform. Issues that might have been resolved by legislative means or policy change, for example those pertaining to labour relations, thus fell to be resolved by judicial means (Della Porta 2001, p. 5).

If this expansion of judicial activity is not exclusive to Italy (Guarnieri & Pederzoli, 2002, p. 4), the increasing role played by judges in countering terrorism and organised crime *is* more particular to the Italian context. Internal political terrorism and organised crime have been Italy's 'emergencies' between (roughly) 1970 and the first half of the 1990s. The judiciary have been key players in combating both phenomena: 'in the fight against terrorism and the Mafia, the magistracy exercised a proactive power, [acting] as a surrogate for a weak political will' (Della Porta, 2001, p. 5). 'Surrogacy' in this particular ambit endowed the judiciary with a certain level of legitimacy among the public and political class (Della Porta, 2001, p. 14; Nelken, 1998, p. 621; Pizzorno, 1997, p. 331). A similar effect followed during the 1980s and early 1990s, in the wake of judicial engagement against organised crime: the legitimacy following from this proactive engagement was reflected in the political sphere until it waned from the late 1980s.

These emergencies gave rise to an expansion of judicial powers, aimed at defeating both terrorism and organised crime. The expansion of judicial power at the hands of the political class, through legislation and executive decrees, can be taken as a testimony of politicians' trust and belief that judges were well placed to defend the Italian state from challenges to its authority. To be sure, political willingness to co-ordinate with the judiciary was also instrumental: it was easier to deploy judicial action than to devise political solutions to Italy's 'emergencies', and it allowed the government to placate the public anxiety that the emergencies provoked. By passing penal legislation against the 'emergencies' the government seemed to be taking action, though it effectively delegated resolution of the issues to judges and the penal system. Despite this instrumental side to political support for judicial 'surrogacy', judicial legitimacy *did* increase between 1970 and 1990 by reason of this delegation of responsibility to judges. This type of 'surrogacy' enhanced judicial standing amongst sectors of the political class by giving judges the power of effective action in an immobile political system. I claim that surrogacy is thus both *expressive* and *constitutive* of high judicial legitimacy.

How does this relationship between judges and the executive/legislative branches link to punishment? The 'waxing' of judicial legitimacy here is linked to the type and extent of powers granted by the political class to Italian judges, such as the powers devolved to the judiciary in order to face Italy's 'emergencies' (Ferrajoli, 1994, p. 70). We witness, for example, increased use of preventive custody (roughly remand in prison – Libro IV, Titolo I, c.p.p.) and an extension of its maximum period.[6] Commentators have noted that preventive custody was then often used to obtain 'co-operation' from repentant terrorists and later organised criminals (Ferrajoli, 1984, p. 281; Rinaldi 1992, p. 65–96; Stortoni, 1992; also Nelken, 2010, p. 18 for corruption cases). This is cited as a mechanism born during the 'antiterrorist emergency' that transformed into generalised practice (Rinaldi, 1992, p. 96 note 33). This analysis can be read as pointing to a broader phenomenon whereby emergency practices persisted *beyond* the emergency for which they were introduced: a 'halo effect' (La Greca, 2005, p. 48) with repression spreading outwards. The 'halo effect' may explain 'the paradox [in Italian penal policy] whereby campaigns against specific offenders such as political terrorists and organised criminals, turn into increased penalties for [...] those who are not [direct] targets [of the campaign] or [even for] offenders in general' (Pavarini, 1994, p. 59, 1997, pp. 84–85; Ruggiero, 1998, p. 216). The notion of a 'halo effect' lends support to the existence of a *punitive potential* within Italian penality – harshness present but not always manifest – here engendered by emergency legislation. Where the potential is realised it would be expected to lead to an increase in incarceration rates. Emergency powers have indeed been singled out as one potential cause of the penal expansion experienced by Italy across the 1990s (Ferrajoli, 1996, pp. 65–84).[7] What we see here, then, is high judicial legitimacy expressed in an expansion of repressive powers: with co-operation (of sorts) between judicial and political classes producing a punitive potential (Fig. 2).

The general attitude with which the emergency provisions were accompanied is also interesting: the 'devolution' of responsibilities to the judiciary, I argue, reconfigured the latter as *political* actors over and above the specific provisions (for penal judges this was not limited to their role as criminal justice officials). Judges were 'political' not in the sense of party-political actors (though some have subsequently stood in this position), but in the sense of being actors in fact entrusted with executing policy in the face of a weak political will, operating within the Italian polity *at par* with the executive and legislative. The implication is that judges were capable of acting in concert with, or in contrast to, the political class[8] and, as such, could be independent arbiters of what action was required to uphold 'legality' in Italy (for criticism of the punitive

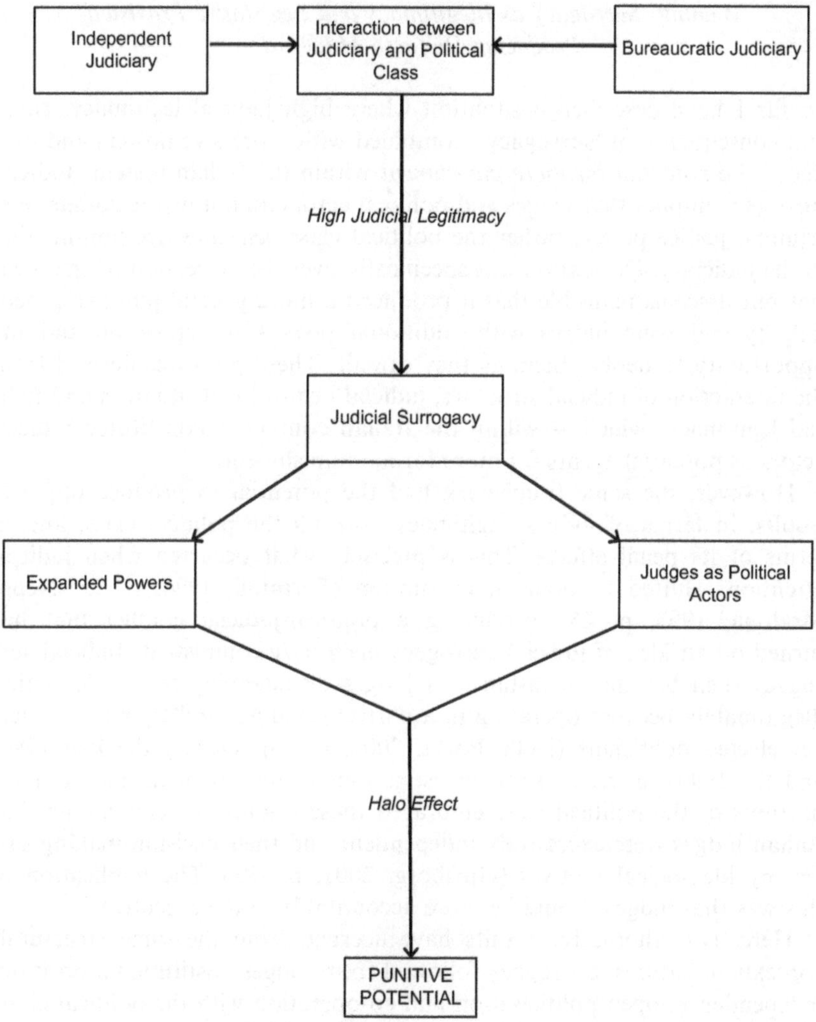

Fig. 2. Institutional Relations, Judicial Structure and Legitimacy – The Production of a Punitive Potential.

repercussions of this dynamic see Gamberini, 1992; Stortoni, 1992). This is also in keeping with the Italian judiciary's independence, which envisaged the judiciary *precisely as* a counterweight to its institutional counterparts (Foot, 2003, p. 65).

Waning: Surrogacy as Illegitimacy and Legislative Provisions Producing De facto Moderation

So far I have described a situation where high judicial legitimacy, cause and consequence of 'surrogacy', combined with repressive powers and produced the *potential for more punishment* within the Italian system. Judicial surrogacy implies that judges and political actors do not just negotiate over criminal justice policy, rather the political class *delegates* decision-making to the judiciary. Delegation was specifically over the repression of emergencies but it seems plausible that it produced a more general punitive potential, by endowing judges with additional powers of repression and the opportunity to deploy them as they saw fit. These pressures derived from the interaction of judicial structure, judicial institutional situation and judicial legitimacy, which – within the Italian context – constituted judicial actors as potential agents for more formal punishment.

However, the same framework had the potential to produce opposite results, in terms of judges' legitimacy *vis-à-vis* the political class, and in terms of its penal effects. This is precisely what occurred when judicial attentions shifted to political corruption (Ferrajoli, 1994, p. 75; Neppi Modona, 1993, p. 25), producing a political-judicial conflict that has turned on an idea of judicial surrogacy *negatively* conjugated. Judicial surrogacy then became an instance of judges overstepping their role, acting illegitimately because operating in a partisan manner and trying to undercut elected politicians (Della Porta, 2001, p. 15). During the late 1980s and the 1990s, in response to investigations against political misfeasance, portions of the political class embraced these arguments, contending that Italian judges were excessively independent and their decision-making driven by ideological motives (Ginsborg, 2001, p. 193). The implication of this was that judges should be more accountable to the executive.[9]

Here, two alternative results have accrued from the same structural-contextual features. Surrogacy followed from judges' institutional position: independence, open politicisation and co-operation with the political class, to the point of surrogacy. This judicial surrogacy expressed and bolstered judicial legitimacy. Crucially, where surrogacy was *not* over criminal justice matters (but, e.g. over employment disputes: Della Porta, 2001, p. 5; Reyneri, 2010, p. 135), it legitimised judges as broad political subjects. This set-up *simultaneously* paved the way for attacks against judicial legitimacy, whereby judges were perceived as politicised, biased and encroaching upon political functions. The interaction of structure and context constituted the penal judiciary as a political subject provided with powers of repression, and cast doubts on the motives behind their use.

These dynamics can further be understood by looking at the 1980s, a decade that provides apt illustrations of variable judicial legitimacy in Italy. On the one hand, during the 1980s the judicial class gained power and status by dint of its engagement against organised crime. This engagement increased the judiciary's 'reserve of legitimacy', testifying 'to a commitment to the State that politicians were unable to show' (Della Porta, 2001, p. 14). On the other hand, the late 1980s witnessed a series of legislative changes meant to impact on both judicial structure and role. In one interpretation, such changes testified to increasing political hostility to judicial investigations into corruption, directed against the independence of judicial action and the use of expanded judicial powers. The judicial powers that had been strengthened by the political class now became problematic when directed against politicians (Davigo & Mannozzi, 2008, p. 221; Ferrajoli, 1994, p. 75).

Proof of political hostility to the existing judicial structure and function can be sought in the 1987 referendum on judges' civil liability. In the referendum, 'members of the judiciary were called on to accept responsibility for civil liability in the cases in which they took part' (Della Porta, 2001, p. 7; Ginsborg, 2001, p. 194). Supporters of the referendum emphasised that the existing institutional set-up, including judicial independence, gave rise to judges' 'irresponsibility' and 'politicisation' (Bruti Liberati, & Pepino, 2000, p. 11, my translation). It left them with excess powers and excess discretion but limited accountability. The imposition of civil liability would curb this situation, presumably by deterring improper judicial action.

The referendum, which led to the introduction of civil liability, does not lend itself to straightforward interpretation. However, commentators such as Anna Chimenti have been explicit in stating that it marked the onset of conflict between judicial and political classes (1993, p. 84). For my purposes we can also refer to Della Porta's analysis of the campaign that accompanied the referendum. She contends that the campaign, led by the (then ruling) Socialist Party, expressed 'the hostility of both individual politicians and political parties' to judges' 'growing activism in bringing politicians to trial' (2001, p. 7). The referendum was an example of political 'attempts to reduce the power of the judges' (2001, p. 7) and, as such, prefigured political attacks of later decades in which the activism, and not the laxity, of the judiciary was criticised (Chimenti, 1993, p. 84). An interpretation of these interrelations is shown in Fig. 3.

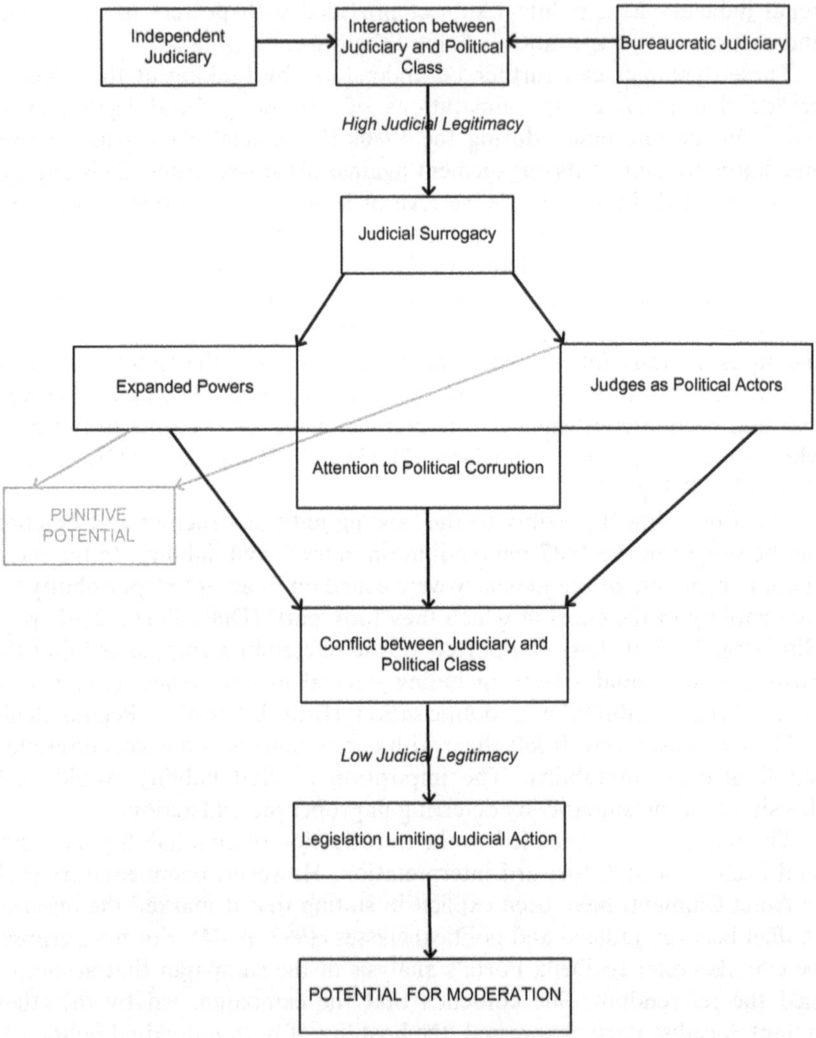

Fig. 3. Institutional Relations, Judicial Structure and Legitimacy – The Production of Potential for Moderation.

Similar sentiments can be traced in the 1989 reform of Italian criminal procedure, which attempted to graft adversarial elements onto Italy's existing inquisitorial system (Grande, 2000; Mirabella, 2012; Montana, 2012; Montana & Nelken, 2011; Pizzi & Marafioti, 1992). The reform has been interpreted as the expression of 'worries about [judicial] neutrality'

(Mirabella, 2012, p. 233), and concerns about a 'machinery of justice [...] unable to fully protect the defendant's right to a fair trial' (Grande, 2000, p. 230), to be assuaged by the increased separation between investigative and adjudicative bodies within the trial. Like the referendum, the 1989 reform is not easy to interpret, not least because it embodied a variety of concerns and interests. As Montana and Nelken note: 'the continued accuracy and validity of [Italy's] traditional inquisitorial models', which the reform aimed to change, was 'widely criticized *both* by academic commentators *and* – for their own reasons – by politicians' (2011, p. 287, my emphasis). Academic reasons included concerns with defendants' guarantees (criticism advanced also by progressive judges: Colombo, 1991; Ferrajoli ,1984, pp. 280–284; Neppi Modona, 1993, p. 25); politician's reasons included concerns with judicial activism. At the political level, it seems that judicial actors were no longer considered sufficiently 'trustworthy' to be in charge of an inquisitorial system (Mirabella, 2012, p. 252).

Ultimately, the 1989 reform did not achieve a policy graft, but created 'another type of non-adversarial model' within the Italian system (Davigo & Mannozzi, 2008, pp. 175–190; Grande, 2000, p. 230; Montana, 2012; Montana & Nelken, 2011). Judicial actors resisted their new role, where a more passive judiciary was presumed, and 'judicial activism [remained] highly prevalent in Italy's system' (Grande, 2000, p. 238). Whatever its effects, the reform emphasises the increasing conflict between the judicial and political class. It can partly be seen as a political attempt to influence judicial action via legislation. Here it is worth pointing to the difference between Italy and England and Wales, as the comparison highlights both the importance of judicial structure in the institutional context *and* the significance of judicial legitimacy in producing penal effects. In both cases we have structural similarity: an independent judiciary that, because of its independence, can and has entered into conflict with the political class (Lacey, 2008, pp. 94–97). The effect of this conflict has, however, had different results in Italy compared to England and Wales. In particular, in Italy, the conflict has been over judicial *activism* (Nelken, 2011, p. 109) and putative '*repressiveness*'. By contrast – and simplifying greatly – in England and Wales, putative judicial *leniency* has been a mainstay of political criticism of judges (Downes, 1988, p. 203). In Italy the executive has been concerned with limiting judicial activism and – with political misfeasance in mind – it has approved provisions that have had wider penal implications (the 1987 referendum affected *all* judges; the 1989 reform applied to criminal procedure *as a whole*). These provisions have acted to restrain penal expansion, whereas the conflict between judicial and political classes in England and Wales, which has hardened political distrust of the judiciary on penal matters, has provided an impetus for the political class to press on with the 'penal arms race' *despite* judicial opinion.

This difference between England and Wales and Italy is, as Nelken has observed, due to different contextual variables intervening to disturb our institutional models (2010, pp. 109–110). Yet we need not abandon these models: 'legitimacy' – as I define and use it – helps us explain penal divergence even in the face of apparent institutional similarity. In contrast to England and Wales, where the judiciary interpret their legitimate role as independent and aloof *vis-à-vis* the political class (Lacey 2008, pp. 95–96), or to Germany, where the lower level of institutional conflict casts legitimacy in terms of co-ordination between government and judiciary (Lacey, 2008, p. 95), in Italy, judges see their legitimate role as independent but also activist. This difference in interpretations of judges' roles determines the terms on which the political class critique/clash with the judiciary and the penal effects thought to follow.

In Italy the conflict between political and judicial classes peaked during the early 1990s with the events collectively described as *Tangentopoli*, wherein Italian magistrates launched a series of investigations into political corruption, with a primary focus on politicians belonging to the ruling parties. The term *Tangentopoli* has since been used to indicate the 'highways and byways of corruption' (Ginsborg, 2001, p. 257) of Italian public life that emerged during this period. Nelken has analysed *Tangentopoli* as the product of a confluence of disparate factors that permitted a political 'revolution' at the hands of the judiciary, conducted from within the law (also Montana, 2009, p. 491), and within the boundaries of constitutional propriety. '[It] [ultimately] led to the condemnation […] of […] a whole political class' (1996, p. 96) and this was possible, Nelken explains, because of the particular structure of the Italian magistracy. Judges' and prosecutors' independence from executive and legislative control was crucial in this respect, removing the investigations from political attempts to hinder their progress. So was the fact that 'each prosecutor [could benefit] from the same guarantee of independence as the judges', and that each prosecutorial office could enjoy a high degree of autonomy in its decisions (1996, p. 100). *Tangentopoli* contributed to the overhaul of Italian politics, and the demise of Italy's existing parties (and it is associated with the shift between a 'First' and a 'Second' Italian Republics).

Unsurprisingly, after *Tangentopoli*, judges' role as 'high counsellors' (Violante, 1998, p. lxvi) to politicians on matters of justice began to wane. Judges became the primary target of increasingly direct political attacks against the breadth and misuse of judicial powers (Nelken, 2003, p. 11).[10]

As in the 1980s, these attacks took legal and not just a rhetorical form, crystallising in political reforms with the potential of diluting judicial activism.[11] Here, again, we have a concentrated version of the dynamics described above where, by contrast to the effect it has had in Britain (Lacey, 2008, pp. 95–97), judicial-political conflict in Italy has contributed to *contain* rather than increase penal rates (Nelken, 2011, p. 109). 'Containment' has been achieved by means of political initiatives to curb judicial powers. These were to become particularly apparent in the late 1990s and early 2000s, with the introduction of procedural changes that lengthen the duration of the penal process. Nelken recounts, for example:

> The centre-left coalition [in power during the second half of the 1990s] had [...] been the author of a variety of stricter provisions to do with the validity of types of testimony, as part of the creation of 'just trials' [...]; these provisions were adding considerably to the difficulties of gaining convictions. (2003, p. 122; Articolo, 111 Cost.; also Davigo & Mannozzi, 2008, pp. 155, note 152)

A similar result followed from the so-called *Cirami* law, passed by the right-wing government of 2002, modifying article 45 of the Italian criminal procedural code (Legge 7 Novembre, 2002; Nelken, 2003, p. 116). The article allows 'defendants the right to take their case to the Supreme Court and ask for a delay of sentence while a decision [is] made as to whether the case should be removed from a whole tribunal area' (Nelken, 2003, p. 115). Referral can be requested on a number of grounds including – a motive introduced by the *Cirami* law – 'legitimate suspicion', 'a grave, objective local situation, representing a real threat of judicial bias, or a threat to the trial unfolding serenely' (Legittimo Sospetto: Treccani, accessed 2009). Referral may lead to the trial being transferred to another judge.

The *Cirami* law is significant as a concentrate of the sentiments that bloomed in the 1990s after *Tangentopoli*. It speaks of conflict between judicial and political classes, phrased in terms of potential judicial bias and thus illegitimate judicial action. Conflict was embodied in provisions, such as the *Cirami* law, capable of limiting judicial activity by enhancing procedural delays (Nelken, 2003, pp. 116–117). Nelken's research further testifies to a generalised political unease at judicial action at the time of the *Cirami* law: as I show, there is evidence that this unease also existed in preceding years (Davigo & Mannozzi, 2008, p. 192; Nelken, 2003, p. 122).[12]

The procedural changes of the 1990s and 2000s are thus indicative of the broader penal effects of political reactions to the judicial-political conflict. They increased the obstacles that must be surpassed before the statute of limitation applies and criminal proceedings are discontinued (Nelken, 2003, pp. 122–123). Nelken is not alone in observing that procedural changes have substantially slowed the pace of the Italian penal trial (2010, p. 64): legal delays have more than once been the subject of research and reform proposals (Grande, 2000; Paciotti, 2006). The Italian penal trial has been characterised as a series of 'overlapping norms that have created a cumbersome system [...] full of traps' (Diotallevi, Onida, & Scotti, 2006, p. 84, my translation; Nelken & Zanier, 2006). Where these legal delays have combined with limitation periods (*prescrizione*), they have also given rise to the practice among lawyers, whereby 'the ultimate aim of the defence is almost always, and explicitly, that of obtaining temporal dilations in view of the approaching *prescrizione*' (Nelken & Zanier, 2006, p. 160, my translation). It is logical to suppose that, by adding to Italy's already lengthy procedural delays, the set of procedural hoops introduced by political reform may have been used to reduce the total number of cases ending in a conviction, reducing penal escalation overall (Davigo & Mannozzi, 2008, p. 191; Nelken, 2011, pp. 109–110). Here, the conflict between judicial and political classes – expressed in terms of illegitimate (because politicised and excessive) judicial activism – has produced legislative changes that impacted upon national penality as a whole.

Interestingly, the 1990s also saw a number of executive decrees meant to *bolster* judicial powers against organised crime.[13] This emergency legislation has been described in terms of 'reform and counter-reform' (Annetta, accessed 2012; Davigo & Mannozzi, 2008, p. 188, my translation), a description that summarises the essence of varying relations between the Italian judiciary and political classes (for a similar point on procedural reform see Montana, 2012, p. 106). Politicians have been interested both in *enlisting* the judiciary in the fight against organised crime (Rinaldi, 1992, pp. 71–76) – expressing high judicial legitimacy and co-operation – while simultaneously remaining concerned with hampering judicial investigations into political misfeasance – expressing low judicial legitimacy and conflict. I suggest that these contradictory relations have had a wider impact on Italian penality, producing both a punitive potential and a potential for de facto moderation.

To sum up: judicial and political actors in Italy have interacted in a number of ways. Judges have been collaborators, even surrogates, for the political class, endowed with repressive powers and the independence (and self-perception) to deploy them. The high legitimacy marked by collaboration and surrogacy has engendered a potential for *more* punishment in Italy. Judges and politicians have also clashed, producing political attempts to limit judicial powers where the latter were directed against the 'wrong' targets. Attacks on the legitimacy of judicial action have led to legislation that, more or less explicitly, attempted to limit judicial investigations. To the extent that the legislation *has* limited judicial action (Nelken, 2010, p. 22), it has created the conditions for *less* punishment. Low judicial legitimacy has bolstered the (de facto) leniency that co-exists with repression in Italian penality. *Legitimacy* here acts as a key organising principle for us to understand the acquisition of, and limits to, judicial powers and their links to judicial-political relations. The concept thus bolsters theoretical models that have explained judicial contributions to penality by looking at the judicial structure in the institutional context.

CONCLUSIONS

In this chapter I have investigated judicial legitimacy in Italy as a means to understand judicial contributions to Italian penality. In particular I have focused on the relationship between the judiciary and the political class, and the penal repercussions that have followed from their changing interaction. I have argued that this interaction can be understood in terms of evolving judicial legitimacy – especially substantive legitimacy – whose highs and lows can be linked to the expansion and contraction of judicial powers. These powers can, in turn, be understood in terms of penal pressures. I have illustrated how periods of high legitimacy – manifest in political reliance on judicial action – have engendered a punitive potential, while periods of low legitimacy – manifest in conflict between judges and politicians – have contributed to a potential for de facto moderation. Judges, in their interaction with the political class, have thus been agents both for more and for less punishment, and have contributed to the variability of Italian penality. *Legitimacy* is the key organising principle that allows us to understand and systematise such contributions. It also helps contextualise existing institutional models, allowing for variation relative to their archetypes (Germany and England and Wales) and for different results to accrue from similar institutional set-ups, while emphasising the importance of their overall approach. The question now is whether, taking into account their usefulness in the Italian case, we should not also integrate questions of legitimacy into such models, and into our broader analyses of judicial contributions to penality.

NOTES

1. I deal with judges and public prosecutors together because of their institutional position in Italy. Judges and prosecutors are part of the same professional body and 'prosecutors enjoy the same independent status as judges': total formal independence from the executive and from 'institutional mechanism[s] to direct [...] prosecution' (Della Porta, 2001, p. 19; Guarnieri & Pederzoli, 2002, p. 118; Montana & Nelken, 2011; Nelken, 1996).

2. The year 1970 is my starting point, as the year is thought to mark the onset of 'late modernity' and/or 'post-Fordism' and thus the structural changes that have been linked to Western 'punitiveness' (De Giorgi, 2006; Garland, 2001). My analysis stops at 2008, before the global economic crisis, the Eurozone crisis and – in Italy – the political changes experienced since 2008. The end-date has been chosen in the belief that it is wise to let the dust settle before attempting any overall conclusions on how these 'crises' have affected politics, penality and their relevant institutions.

3. I should point out that I am interested in charting the answers *given*, by the political class and judges, to the questions 'were Italian magistrates acting within their remit?' and 'how was their action received?' I am therefore not providing a normative evaluation of judicial action in Italy.

4. By contrast, alternatives to imprisonment may vary significantly across contexts (Tonry & Farrington, 2005, p. 9). To the extent that, in contemporary Western Europe, the prison formally remains the most serious type of punishment available, and ideally a measure of last resort (Blumstein et al., 2005, p. 350), prison rates also provide indicative measures of how European nations have used their most extreme form of punishment. Of course prison rates cannot be de-contextualised: in the existing literature on contemporary penality, prison rates are seen as significant in and of themselves, but also because they express broader qualitative shifts in the intensity and meaning of Western punishment (see inter alia Garland, 2001; Wacquant, 2009). My analysis only starts from prison rates, but develops outward into a discussion of how interactions between different state institutions affect the significance and uses of formal punishment.

5. For Germany see Eurostat data (http://epp.eurostat.ec.europa.eu/portal/page/portal/statistics/themes).

6. This had already been reformed in 1974 and was further extended in successive years.

7. Ferrajoli argues that emergency laws extended judicial discretion, consequently 'lowering the level of procedural guarantees' overall (1996, p. 71). For similar observations on the use of preventive custody in *Tangentopoli* see Della Porta (2001, p. 14) and Neppi Modona (1993, p. 18). On pre-trial detention as Italy's 'chronic problem' see Cavadino and Dignan (2006, p. 145) and Ruggiero (1998, p. 223).

8. This 'reconfiguring', in conjunction with judicial heterogeneity, has allowed judicial actors to purvey pressures both for penal expansion *and* penal moderation. Judges and prosecutors have, for example, resisted pressures for more punishment where they have thought it necessary, even where this meant being guided by priorities 'different *both from those of the politicians and of the general public*' (Nelken, 2011, p. 109, my emphasis; Montana, 2012; Montana & Nelken, 2011).

9. This line of argument was partly bolstered by a period of explicit political engagement of certain judges during the 1970s (see Borgna & Cassano, 1997; Della Porta, 2001, p. 5; Guarnieri & Pederzoli, 2002, p. 76).

10. Epitomised in later years by the attacks of Prime Minister Silvio Berlusconi.

11. See the 1994 'Biondi decree' (Decreto Legislativo 13 luglio 1994 n. 480) that limited the use of preventive custody for a series of offences including forms of corruption then under investigation. It provoked 'such strong protest by judges, public opinion' and even a governing party, that it was withdrawn (Della Porta 2001, p. 7; see also Davigo & Mannozzi, 2008, pp. 159–173; Nelken, 2003; pp. 115–126).

12. They also persisted in successive years. See in particular laws passed since 2003 (Legge 20 Giugno 2003 n. 140; Legge 23 Luglio 2008 n. 124; Legge 7 Aprile, 2010 n. 51) which aimed to insulate certain institutional figures (such as the Prime Minister) from penal proceedings. The laws (or portions thereof) were declared unconstitutional; the last was abolished by popular referendum. The dialectic between political and judicial classes over their respective legitimacy also constitutes a contemporary, public concern: see Ferrajoli quoted in Coccoli (2013).

13. For example by subordinating re-educative benefits and alternative measures, for those detained for organised crime offences, to co-operation with the judiciary in 'anti-Mafia' investigations (Decreto Legge 8 giugno 1992 n. 306; Decreto Legge 13 maggio 1991 n. 152).

ACKNOWLEDGEMENTS

Many thanks to Jeremy Horder and Nicola Lacey for their comments on earlier drafts, and to Sean Deel for his insightful advice. My thanks also to The European Society of Criminology panel who listened to, and commented on, my argument when I first presented it in September 2013. All responsibility for the contents of this chapter and any errors it may contain are my own.

REFERENCES

Annetta, M. (2012). Dalla legge Gozzini alla legislazione di emergenza. Politica penale e professionalita' della magistratura di sorveglianza. Retrieved from http://www.altrodiritto.unifi.it/ricerche/misure/annetta/

Articolo 104. Costituzione della Repubblica Italiana.

Articolo 105. Costituzione della Repubblica Italiana.

Articolo 111. Costituzione della Repubblica Italiana.

Articolo 112. Costiuzione della Repubblica Italiana.

Beetham, D. (2013) Revisiting legitimacy, twenty years on. In J. Tankebe & A. Liebling (Eds.), *Legitimacy and criminal justice: An international exploration* (pp. 19–36). Oxford: Oxford University Press.

Berman, G., & Dar, A. (2013). *Prison population statistics*. London: House of Commons Library.
Blumstein, A., Tonry, M., & Van Ness, A. (2005). Cross-national measures of punitiveness. *Crime and Justice*, *33*(1), 347–376.
Borgna, P., & Cassano, M. (1997). *Il giudice e il principe*. Roma: Donizelli Editore.
Bottoms, A., & Tankebe, J. (2012). Beyond procedural justice: A dialogic approach to legitimacy in criminal justice. *Journal of Criminal Law and Criminology*, *102*(1), 119–170.
Bruti Liberati, E., & Pepino, L. (2000). *Giustizia e referendum*. Roma: Donzelli Editore.
Cavadino, M., & Dignan, J. (2006). *Penal systems a comparative approach*. London: Sage.
Chimenti, A. (1993). *1987* I referendum su giustizia e nucleare. *Storia dei Referendum* (pp. 77–88). Roma-Bari: Editori Laterza.
Coccoli, D. (2013). E la sinistra dimenticò la giustizia. *Left Avvenimenti*. Retrieved from http://www.left.it/2014/04/10/tabu-giustizia-la-sinistra-ventanni-immobilismo/15858. Accessed on April 12, 2013.
Coicaud, J. (2013). Justice and legitimacy: A brief theoretical inquiry. In J. Tankebe & A. Liebling (Eds.), *Legitimacy and criminal justice: An international exploration* (pp. 37–59). Oxford: Oxford University Press.
Colombo, G. (1991). The new code of criminal procedure. In F. Sabetti & Catn (Eds.), *Italian politics: A review vol. 5*. London: Pinter Publishers.
Cotta, M., & Verzichelli, L. (2007). *Political institutions in Italy*. Oxford: Oxford University Press.
Davigo, P., & Mannozzi, G. (2008). *La corruzione in Italia*. Roma-Bari: Editori Laterza.
De Giorgi, A. (2006). *Re-thinking the political economy of punishment*. Aldershot: Ashgate.
Decreto Legge 8 giugno 1992 n. 306 (convertito con modifiaczione dalla L. 07 agosto 1992, n. 356) (1992) in materia di 'Modifiche urgenti al nuovo codice di procedura penale e provvedimanti di contrasto alla criminalita' mafiosa.
Decreto Legge 13 maggio 1991 n. 152. (coordinato con la legge di conversione n. 203/1991) (1991) in materia di 'Provvedimenti urgenti in tema di lotta alla criminalita' organizzata e di trasparenza e buon andamento dell'attivita' amministrativa.
Decreto Legislativo. (13 Luglio 1994 n. 480). in materia di 'Riforma della disciplina sanzionatoria contenuta nel testo unico delle leggi di pubblica sicurezza, approvato con regio decreto 18 giugno 1931, n. 773', 1994.
Della Porta, D. (2001). A judges' revolution? Political corruption and the judiciary in Italy. *European Journal of Political Research*, *39*, 1–21.
Di Federico, G. (1998). Prosecutorial independence and the democratic requirement of accountability in Italy. *British Journal of Criminology*, *38*(3), 371–387.
Diotallevi, G., Onida, V., & Scotti, L. (2006). La giustizia penale. In E. Paciotti (Ed.), *I tempi della giustizia. Un progetto per la riduzione dei tempi dei processi civili e penali* (pp. 83–113). Bologna: Societa editrice il Mulino.
Downes, D.. (1988). Contrasts in tolerance. Post-war penal policy in the Netherlands and England and Wales. Oxford: Clarendon Press.
Eurostat. Eurostat statistics – crime and criminal justice. Retrieved from http://epp.eurostat.ec.europa.eu/portal/page/portal/crime/introduction. Accessed on October 2009.
Ferrajoli, L. (1984). Emergenza penale e crisi della giurisdizione. *Dei delitti e delle pene*, *2*(2), 271–292.
Ferrajoli, L. (1994). Per una storia delle idee di Magistratura democratica. In N. Rossi (Ed.), *Giudici e Democrazia* (pp. 55–79). Milano: Francoangeli.

Ferrajoli, L. (1996). La giustizia penale nella crisi del sistema politico. In E. Bruti Liberati, A. Ceretti, & A. Giasanti (Eds.), *Governo dei giudici – la magistratura tra diritto e politica*. Milano: Feltrinelli Editore.

Foot, J. (2003). *Modern Italy*. Basingstoke: Palgrave Macmillan.

Friedman, L. (1997). The concept of legal culture: A reply. In D. Nelken (Ed.), *Comparing legal cultures* (pp. 33–40). Aldershot: Dartmouth.

Gamberini, A. (1992). Emergenza, legislazione speciale e riforma penale. *Dei delitti e delle pene*, *2*(3), 53–56.

Garland, D. (2001). *The culture of control*. Oxford: Oxford University Press.

Ginsborg, P. (2001). Italy and its discontents 1980–2001. London: Penguin Books.

Grande, E. (2000). Italian criminal justice: Borrowing and resistance. *The American Journal of Comparative Law*, *48*(2), 227–260.

Guarnieri, C., & Pederzoli, P. (2002). *The power of judges: A comparative study of courts and democracy*. Oxford: Oxford University Press.

Hall, P., & Soskice, D. (Eds.). (2001). *Varieties of capitalism*. Oxford: Oxford University Press.

HMSO. (1980a). *Statistics of the criminal justice system England and Wales 1969–1979*. London: Her Majesty's Stationery Office.

HMSO. (1980b). *Statistics of the criminal justice system England and Wales 1969–1979*. London: HM Stationery Office.

Home Office. (1984). *Home office statistical bulletin 1984*. Surbiton: Home Office.

Home Office. (1986). *Home office statistical bulletin 1986*. Surbiton: Home Office.

Home Office. (1987). *Home office statistical bulletin 1987*. Croydon: Home Office.

Home Office. (2003). *Prison statistics England and Wales 2001*. London: Home Office.

ISTAT. (1970–2008). *Annuari di Statistiche Giudiziarie Penali*. Roma: ISTAT.

ISTAT. Demo-Geodemo. (October 2009). Retrieved from http://demo.istat.it/

La Greca, G. (2005). La riforma penitenziaria del 1975 e la sua attuazione. *Rassegna Penitenziaria e Criminologica*, *2*(3), 39–53.

Lacey, N. (2008). *The prisoners' dilemma*. Cambridge: Cambridge University Press.

Lacey, N. (2011). Why globalisation doesn't spell convergence: Models of institutional variation and the comparative political economy of punishment. In A. Crawford (Ed.), *International and comparative criminal justice and urban governance*. Cambridge: Cambridge University Press.

Lappi-Seppälä, T. (2007). Penal policy in Scandinavia. *Crime and Justice*, *36*(1), 217–295.

Lappi-Seppälä, T. (2008). Trust, welfare, and political culture: Explaining differences in national penal policies. *Crime and Justice*, *37*(1), 313–387.

Legge 7 Aprile 2010 n. 51. (2010). Disposizioni in materia di impedimento a comparire in udienza.

Legge 7 Novembre 2002 n. 248. (2002). Modifica degli articoli 45, 47, 48 e 49 del codice di procedura penale.

Legge 20 Giugno n. 140. (2003). Disposizioni per l'attuazione dell'articolo 68 della Costituzione nonche´ in materia di processi penali nei confronti delle alte cariche dello Stato.

Legge 23 Luglio n. 124. (2008). Disposizioni in materia di sospensione del processo penale nei confronti delle alte cariche dello Stato.

'Legitimacy'. (2009). Oxford English dictionary. Oxford: Oxford University Press. Retrieved from http://oxforddictionaries.com/definition/english/legitimacy?q=legitimacy. Accessed on October 2009.

'Legittimo sospetto'. (2009). *Treccani, enciclopedia Italiana*. Rome: Edizioni Treccani. Retrieved from http://www.treccani.it/enciclopedia/legittimo-sospetto/. Accessed on October 2009.

Libro IV Titolo I. Codice di Procedura Penale. Misure cautelari personali.

Loader, I., & Sparks, R. (2013). Unfinished business: Legitimacy, crime and democratic politics. In J. Tankebe, & A. Liebling (Eds.), *Legitimacy and criminal justice: An international exploration* (pp. 105–126). Oxford: Oxford University Press.

Mirabella, J. G. (2012). Scales of justice: Assessing Italian criminal procedure through the Amanda Knox trial. *Boston University School of Law*, *30*(1), 229–260.

Molina, O., & Rhodes, M. (2007). The political economy of adjustment in mixed-market economies: A study of Spain and Italy. In B. Hancké, M. Rhodes, & M. Thatcher (Eds.), *Beyond varieties of capitalism* (pp. 223–252). Oxford: Oxford University Press.

Montana, R. (2009). Prosecutors and the definition of the crime problem in Italy: Balancing the impact of moral panics. *Criminal Law Forum*, *20*(4), 471–494.

Montana, R. (2012). Adversarialism in Italy: Using the concept of legal culture to understand resistance to legal modifications and its consequences. *European Journal of Crime, Criminal Law and Criminal Justice*, *20*(1), 99–120.

Montana, R., & Nelken, D. (2011). The ambivalent role of Italian prosecutors and their resistance to 'Moral Panics' about crime. In S. C. J. S. X. Zhang & B. Rosemary (Eds.), *Routledge handbook of international criminology* (pp. 286–296). Oxford: Routledge.

Morisi, M. (1999). *Anatomia della Magistratura*. Bologna: Il Mulino.

Nelken, D. (1996). The judges and political corruption in Italy. *Journal of Law and Society*, *23*(1), 95–112.

Nelken, D. (1998). Il significato di Tangentopoli: La risposta giudiziaria alla corruzione e i suoi limiti. In L. Violante (Ed.), *Storia d'Italia Annali – Legge Diritto Giustizia* (pp. 597–632). Torino: Giulio Einaudi Editore.

Nelken, D. (2003). Legitimate suspicions? Berlusconi and the judges. In B. Jean & S. Paolo (Eds.), *Italian politics. The second Berlusconi government* (pp. 112–128). Oxford: Berghahn Books.

Nelken, D. (2005). When is a society non-punitive? The Italian case. In J. Pratt (Ed.), *The new punitiveness* (pp. 218–235). Cullompton: Willan.

Nelken, D. (2009). Comparative criminal justice: Beyond ethnocentrism and relativism. *European Journal of Criminology*, *6*(4), 291–311.

Nelken, D. (2010). *Comparative criminal justice*. London: Sage.

Nelken, D. (2011). Explaining differences in European prison rates. A comment on Lacey's 'The Prisoners' Dilemma'. *Punishment and Society*, *13*(1), 104–114.

Nelken, D., & Zanier, M. L. (2006). Tra norme e prassi: Durata del processo penale e strategie degli operatori del diritto. *Sociologia del diritto*, *2006*(1), 143–166.

Neppi Modona, G. (1993). Ruolo della giustizia e crisi del potere politico. *Quaderni di Sociologia*, *37*(5), 6–30.

Office for National Statistics. (1970–2000). *Mid–1971 to mid–2010 population estimates: United Kingdom; estimated resident population for constituent countries and regions*. London: Office for National Statistics. Retrieved from http://www.ons.gov.uk/ons/rel/pop-estimate/population-estimates-for-uk–england-and-wales–scotland-and-northern-ireland/population-estimates-timeseries-1971-to-current-year/rft—table-1-total-persons-constituent-countries-regions.zip

Paciotti, E. (Ed.). (2006). *I tempi della giustizia. Un progetto per la riduzione dei tempi dei processi civili e penali.* Bologna: Societa Editrice il Mulino.

Pavarini, M. (1994). The new penology and politics in crisis: The Italian case. *British Journal of Criminology*, *34*(Special Issue), 49–61.

Pavarini, M. (1997). Controlling social panic: Questions and answers about security in Italy at the end of the millennium. In R. Bergalli & C. Sumner (Eds.), *Social control and political order. European perspectives at the end of the century* (pp. 75–95). London: Sage.

Pizzi, W. T., & Marafioti, L. (1992). The new Italian code of criminal procedure: The difficulties of building an adversarial trial system on a civil law foundation. *The Yale Journal of International Law*, *17*(1), 1–40.

Pizzorno, A. (1997). Le trasformazioni del sistema politico italiano, 1976–92. In F. Barbagallo (Ed.), *Storia dell'Italia Repubblicana: III. L'Italia nella crisi mondiale. L'ultimo ventennio: 2. Istituzioni, politiche, culture* (pp. 301–344). Torino: Giulio Einaudi Editore.

Reyneri, E. (1989/2010). The Italian labor market: Between state control and social regulation. In P. Lange & M. Regini (Eds.), *State, market and social regulation. New perspectives on Italy* (pp. 129–145). Cambridge: Cambridge University Press.

Righettini, S. (1995). La politicizzazione di un potere neutrale. Magistratura e crisi italiana. *Rivista Italiana di Scienza Politica*, *XXV*(2), 227–265.

Rinaldi, S. (1992). Un dibattito dulla risposta istituzionale alla criminalita' organizzata. *Dei delitti e delle pene*, *2*(3), 57–99.

Ruggiero, V. (1998). The country of Cesare Beccaria: The myth of rehabilitation in Italy. In R. P. Weiss & N. South (Eds.), *Comparing prison systems: Toward a comparative and international penology* (pp. 207–232). Amsterdam: Gordon and Breach.

Savelsberg, J. (1994). Knowledge, domination and criminal punishment. *The American Journal of Sociology*, *99*(4), 911–943.

Savelsberg, J. (1999). Knowledge, domination and criminal punishment revisited: Incorporating state socialism. *Punishment and Society*, *1*(1), 45–70.

Stortoni, L. (1992). Criminalita' organizzata e legislazione di emergenza. *Dei delitti e delle pene*, *2*(3), 39–52.

Tankebe, J., & Liebling, A. (Eds.). (2013). *Legitimacy and criminal justice: An international exploration.* Oxford: Oxford University Press.

Tonry, M. (2007). Determinants of penal policy. *Crime and Justice, 36*(1), 1–48.

Tonry, M., & Farrington, D. (2005). Punishment and crime across space and time. *Crime and Justice*, *33*(1), 1–41.

Violante, L. (1998). I cittadini, la legge e il giudice. In L. Violante (Ed.), *Storia d'Italia Annali – Legge Diritto Giustizia* (Vol. 14, pp. xvii–lxxiii). Torino: Giulio Einaudi Editore.

Wacquant, L. (2009). *Punishing the poor: The neoliberal government of social insecurity.* Durham, NC: Duke University Press.

White, P., Cullen, C., & Minchin, M. (2000). *Home office prison population brief.* London: Home Office.

JUVENILE JUSTICE AND INCARCERATION IN TURKEY

Serkan Tasgin

ABSTRACT

Purpose – *In this chapter, I examine the juvenile justice system and incarceration practices in Turkey. The study focuses on the basic agents and the legislation of the juvenile justice system and the current status of juvenile incarceration. This study also reveals the problems of the functionality of the system. I conclude with policy recommendations for successful implementation of the juvenile justice system and prevention of recidivism.*

Design/methodology/approach – *I discuss concepts in the juvenile justice system of Turkey and highlight the function and problems of each agent of the system. I focus on problems of the juvenile justice system and its reflection on high rates of recidivism of juveniles.*

Findings – *Overall, the leniency of the juvenile justice system is associated with high rates of juvenile recidivism in Turkey. Infrastructure insufficiencies have limited the standardization of services and practices. The delayed response and perceived leniency of the justice system promoted juveniles' continuation on a crime trajectory.*

Punishment and Incarceration: A Global Perspective
Sociology of Crime, Law and Deviance, Volume 19, 31–52

ISSN: 1521-6136/doi:10.1108/S1521-613620140000019000

Originality/value – *Few scholars have examined the functionality of the juvenile justice system, its problems, and its reflection on high rates of juvenile recidivism in the Turkish case.*

Keywords: Juvenile justice; juvenile police; recidivism; juvenile courts; deterrence

INTRODUCTION

Turkey, a country located between Europe and the Middle East, had a total population of 76,667,864 in 2013. According to the 2013 census, 18,849,814 (24.6%) of the population was under the age of 19. Current projections indicate that the juvenile population in Turkey will continue to grow throughout the next decades. One child in five is working, and children living and working on the streets have become a social phenomenon particularly in big cities; one child in four lives in poverty and the number of children in need of protection has increased (UNDP, 2008). In addition, the images of the children that were represented in the media in the last decade have raised concerns about sexually exploited children, street children, forced child labor, children working as prostitutes and street sellers, and child beggars, glue-sniffers, and other criminals (İrtiş, 2010).

By 2009, young people under the age of 18 comprised approximately 32% of the total population and almost one third of them were between 12 and 18 (UNDP, 2008). Juveniles are responsible for 15% of all crimes and make up almost 25% of suspects in crimes against property in 2012 (McKinney & Salins, 2013). Potentially undermining the promise afforded by Turkey's growing youth population, the country is now facing a juvenile delinquency problem that has become increasingly visible in the last decade.

THE TURKISH JUVENILE JUSTICE SYSTEM

In Turkey, when experts talk about juvenile delinquency, they prefer to use the phrase, "*juveniles pushed into crime*" instead of juvenile delinquents, because they believe that delinquent acts result not from an exercise of agency, but solely from external influences. They assume that juveniles who break the law are victims and passive actors in their lives (Tasgin, 2012).

Until the late 1980s, Turkey did not adopt a separate justice system for juveniles. Before this time, juveniles in conflict with law were processed through the adult criminal justice system. Therefore, there were no difference between adults and juveniles at that time. A separate juvenile justice system was established in 1979 but was not implemented until 1987. In 1994, Turkey ratified the United Nations Convention on the Rights of the Child which recognized rehabilitation and diversion of juveniles (McKinney & Salins, 2013).

The Turkish Constitution which was prepared in 1982 did define a child, and the former Turkish Penal Code categorized juveniles' age to determine penal liability without defining who was a juvenile. The law which designed Juvenile Courts in 1979 defined minors as being under 15 years old but did not define a juvenile (Polat, 2010). However, according to the Turkish Penal Code which was revised in 2005, a juvenile offender is defined as a person under 18 years old who violates the law.

The Turkish Penal Code assesses juveniles in three different age categories in Article 31. The first paragraph states that, "The children having not attained the full age of twelve on the commission date of the offense, may not have criminal responsibility. Besides, no criminal prosecution may be commenced against such persons; but, it may be deemed necessary to take certain security precautions specific to children" (Kazankaya, 2013). That is, the first category involves juveniles younger than 12 years old at the time of the committed crime; they are not considered as being responsible for their acts. Whatever crime they commit, they cannot be punished. However, if they commit serious crimes, protective precautions can be taken such as being returned to their families or being placed with a foster family or in a children's home, which is a residential social service institution under the Department of Child Service. Juveniles below the age of 15 who are deaf and mute have the same rights as juveniles below 12 years old (Akbulut, 2013; Oto, 1998). The Seizure, Detention and Interrogation Code (SDIC) contains a special section for juveniles who are below 12 and juveniles below 15 who are deaf and mute. Article 19 of SDIC lays out the general principles for seizing, detaining, and interrogating juveniles and according to this law juveniles below 15 who are deaf and mute cannot be seized as a result of crime. However, they can only be seized for identification of who they are and detection of crime. They will be released immediately after the identification process.

The second paragraph of the article defines the second category that includes juveniles between 13 and 15. The article states:

> In case a person who attained the age of twelve but not yet completed the age of fifteen on the commission date of the offense does not have the ability to perceive the legal meaning and consequences of the offense, or to control his actions, he may not have criminal responsibility for such behavior. However, security precautions specific to

> children may be adopted for such individuals. If a person has the ability to apprehend the offense he has committed or to control his actions relating to this offense, then such person may be sentenced to imprisonment from nine years to twelve years if the offense requires heavy life imprisonment; from seven years to nine years if the offense requires life imprisonment. Two thirds of other punishments is abated and in this case, the imprisonment to be imposed for each offense may not be more than six years. (Akbulut, 2013; Kazankaya, 2013)

The criminal responsibility of those aged between 12 and 15 is determined by psychologists. They are examined by an expert to determine their capacity for being responsible for the crime. If they are determined to be able to understand the criminal nature of their activity and its consequences, they get less punishment than juveniles between 16 and 18. If their criminal offense requires life imprisonment, their punishment is reduced to between 9 and 12 years imprisonment and sentences for all other offenses are reduced to one third of the original punishment. They are sent to reformatories, juvenile training homes, or juvenile prisons, as determined by the courts. If their criminal activity is not serious, protective precautions may be applied as is the case for juveniles in the first category. If they are determined to be unable to consider the consequences of their criminal behaviors, they are routinely handled like juveniles in the first category (Oto, 1998; Polat, 2010).

The third category consists of juveniles between 16 and 18. The article states that, "*A person who attained the full age of fifteen but not yet completed the age of eighteen on the commission date of the offense is sentenced to imprisonment from fourteen years to twenty years if the offense requires heavy life imprisonment; and from nine years to twelve years if the offense requires life imprisonment. One half of the other punishments is abated and in this case, the imprisonment to be imposed for each offense may not be more than eight years*" (Kazankaya, 2013). The law does not require determination of criminal responsibility for juveniles in this category; they automatically receive less punishment than adults. For instance, if their criminal offense requires life imprisonment, their punishment is reduced to between 14 and 20 years' incarceration (Oto, 1998). All other offenses result in incarceration for half the length of time that would be used for adults. Youth aged 16 to 18 are incarcerated in juvenile prisons.

Deterrence-oriented laws and punishments are designed to reduce delinquency. However, there are mixed results from U.S. research on the deterrent effect of laws and punishment intended to reduce delinquency (Trojanowicz, Morash, & Schram, 2001). Consistent with this research and motivated by the European Union membership process, the Turkish criminal justice system became less punitive, less stigmatizing, and more lenient for juvenile offenders after a drastic policy change in 2005. Detention and incarceration are only used as a last option. There is no life imprisonment for juveniles for any kind of crimes. Youth are sent to juvenile prisons, juvenile training homes, or reformatories, where they are held separated from adult prisoners. However, even the shift to leniency and the suspension of trials did not slow the increase in numbers of juveniles being convicted or arrested. If the old penal code had been used, there would have been even more convicted or arrested juveniles between 2005 and 2008 (Solmaz, 2010).

There are different facilities for arrested juveniles. Reformatories and juvenile training homes are places where youth are diverted instead of being placed in prison. Reformatories and juvenile training homes are for juveniles who were sentenced for less serious criminal offenses. The main purpose of the three reformatories in Turkey, which have a total capacity of 360 youth, is to reintegrate juveniles into society. These facilities are considered to effectively rehabilitate juveniles. That is, having education opportunity at these places, juveniles become better educated, more socialized, and their familial and community relationship is better facilitated. In reformatories and juvenile training homes, juveniles are allowed to visit their homes once a month at the weekends and incarcerated juveniles' familial contact continues (McKinney & Salins, 2013). Juvenile prisons are for juveniles awaiting a court hearing or sentenced for serious criminal offenses (İrtiş, 2010).

There are three juvenile prisons in Turkey. They are located in Ankara, Izmir, and Elazig. These facilities can house up to 400 juveniles in total. Youth in other provinces are detained in adult prisons but are kept in different places in adult prisons. Youth can be detained in juvenile prisons until the age of 21 (McKinney & Salins, 2013). In juvenile reformatories, juvenile training homes, and prisons, juveniles are encouraged to attend different activities such as reading courses, elementary and high-school level distance education, and classes teaching handcraft skills. For instance, if convicted juveniles did not graduate from elementary or high schools, they are provided opportunities to finish their education. Most of the programs implemented in reformatories, juvenile training homes, and juvenile prisons focus on education or providing youth job skills instead of rehabilitation of the juveniles. When comparing these facilities, juveniles have better opportunities for their lives in reformatories and juvenile training homes instead of juvenile prisons; because, prisons cannot wholly draw on the resources of the community and juveniles do not feel attached to school due to not having daily routines around the school (McKinney & Salins, 2013).

In order to rehabilitate juveniles, the causes of their delinquency need to be identified and addressed. The lack of information about causation or pathways which youth follow into delinquency stands in the way of developing and delivering effective rehabilitation. Consistent with this view, a criticism at a conference sponsored by the Turkish Justice Department was that, instead of identifying causes of delinquency and related needs, the focus was on education and, after release, monitoring youths' behavior (Acar, 2004).

BASIC AGENTS OF THE JUVENILE JUSTICE SYSTEM

Social Services and Child Protection Agency

The Social Services and Child Protection Agency is a governmental social aid services that includes not only children but also elderly, disabled, women, and family. Under child protection services, there are child adoptions, foster family, child houses, and youth centers which take care of children who are in need of protection. According to the Child Protection Law, social services and child protection agencies should take the necessary measures immediately with regard to events referred to it. These agencies should place the juvenile under the care of governmental or private organizations. These agencies should be notified by law-enforcement agencies, health and education institutions, administrative authorities, and nongovernmental organizations. This organization helps youth having trouble with justice. That is, when juveniles complete their sentences in prison and believe that they will not have enough protection outside; after release, they can be taken under the shelters of social services and child protection agencies (Yamak & İnci, 2010). Although this organization operates within all (81) provinces of Turkey, its capacity to help children coming from the judicial system does not meet the needs. Due to lack of enough personnel, budget issues, and other tasks an organization's capacity to deal with juvenile offenders can be curtailed. For instance, if there are court orders to be taken under care by the Social Service Agency for juvenile offenders, most of the juveniles never come to the Agency because addresses of these juveniles are not effectively recorded by police and courts thereafter. Moreover, if a counseling measure is decided by the court for juvenile victims, a social service agency should do it. However, a social service agency does not have any authority to bring the counselee before the social worker, and social workers report this situation back to the court. Moreover, there is no clear understanding of what should be included in these counseling sessions that are decided by courts and social services.

Juvenile Bureau of the Public Prosecutor

The Child Protection Act (CPA) is a main legal document which designs how a juvenile justice system works. According to the CPA Article 15/1 juvenile cases should be conducted by the public prosecutor himself and not the police. When a police officer arrests a juvenile, he or she must immediately inform the public prosecutor (Atilgan & Atilgan, 2009; McKinney & Salins, 2013). Therefore, the public prosecutor is the chief figure in the juvenile justice system. He has an authority to interrogate juveniles and he conducts the investigation. Although the law emphasizes the importance of the public prosecutor in juvenile cases, due to the limited number of public prosecutors in cities, mostly the juvenile police division conducts the juvenile cases and conveys the prepared investigation to the public prosecutor. Then, the public prosecutor only takes the statement of the juvenile and handles the case. We can see that the juvenile police division is the chief figure in practice in the juvenile justice system.

Juvenile Police Division

Article 31/1 of the CPA asserts that juvenile cases must be investigated by the juvenile division of police where applicable. The juvenile police division was founded in 2001 with the Juvenile Police Division Code (JPDC). CPA states that police officers who work at the juvenile police division should have trainings on specific issues such as rights of the children, social work, child development, psychology of children, and juvenile delinquency. Therefore, juvenile police divisions are present in all provinces of Turkey and officers who work at this division are recruited using special selection procedures. When compared to other police divisions, officers working at juvenile police divisions have higher education levels and mostly receive a specialized in-service training program provided by the Turkish National Police. Juvenile police division officers must work in plain clothes and they have to conceal their weapons in the presence of juveniles due to the sensitivity of their work and responsibilities. This division had several subdivisions such as offices of social work, missing children, crime prevention, investigation, and administrative affairs. In each division, different tasks concerning the juveniles are handled. Because juvenile division officers cannot take the statement of the juvenile offender, they mostly focus on juvenile victims. Therefore, instead of juvenile offenders, missing and found children, juvenile victims, and children who are in need of protection are the focus areas of the division. While some countries such as New Zealand have juvenile police divisions, this model largely remains unique to Turkey (McKinney & Salins, 2013).

Juvenile Courts

The first law enacted for the establishment of the juvenile courts was in 1979 although the efforts to establish juvenile courts started around 1945 in Turkey. The law required to establish juvenile courts in cities where the population is over 100,000. In 1987, only four juvenile courts were founded (Erukcu & Akbas, 2012). In 2005, with the new version of the CPA, new regulations were implemented and old regulations were abolished regarding the operations and the establishments of the juvenile courts. This act not only regulated operations regarding juvenile offenders but also regulated operations for juveniles who are in need of protection. Therefore, one of the most common activities of the juvenile courts is decisions for supportive and protective measures for the juvenile victims or juvenile offenders with limited or no criminal liability. Article 25 of the CPA regulated the operations and establishment of juvenile courts in Turkey and divided juvenile courts into two types: Regular Juvenile Courts and Juvenile Serious Delinquency Courts. There are 92 juvenile courts in 39 provinces and only 7 courts are juvenile serious delinquency courts.

Regular Juvenile Courts

There is always one regular juvenile court in each city of Turkey. In big provinces such as Istanbul or Ankara where the population is high, there can be more regular juvenile courts. This court consists of only one judge and prosecutors cannot be present during the trials in these courts; however, they can appeal against the court decisions to a superior court. These courts are congruent with the Criminal Courts and Criminal Courts of Peace in an adult criminal justice system. These courts are authorized to trial offenses that are committed by juvenile offenders that are punishable with 10 years or less of punishment (Atilgan & Atilgan, 2009).

Regular juvenile courts exercise the fundamental principles of CPA. The first fundamental principle is that penalty of imprisonment and measures that restrict liberties are the last resort for juveniles. Therefore, regular juvenile courts usually take protective and supportive decisions for less serious juvenile offenders, which is the second fundamental principle of the Act. For instance, counseling precautions helps juveniles' parents and informs them about raising children. Education precaution helps juvenile offenders to continue their education and attend school regularly. If juveniles do not go to school, they can be sent to job training centers to learn about certain jobs they prefer. Health precaution refers to helping juveniles who are in need of health services such as quitting drug use. These measures ensure that social responsibility is shared (Erukcu & Akbas, 2012). Keeping juveniles separate from adults at the institutions is the third fundamental principle, and the fourth principle is to take measures to prevent detection of juveniles' identities in transactions related to juveniles (Kazankaya, 2013).

Juvenile Serious Delinquency Courts

There are more judges in these courts. One judge is a chief and two other judges are the member judges for trials. These courts are established by the approval of the Higher Board of Judges and Prosecutors which is the highest institution for judges and prosecutors. This Board considers the geographic location and the juvenile delinquency workload of the courts. As mentioned above, if the population is high and there is heavy workload, there can be more than one juvenile serious delinquency court in one city. These courts are similar to Higher Criminal Courts in an adult criminal justice system which deals with serious offenses. These courts are authorized to trial offenses that are committed by juvenile offenders which are punishable with 10 years or more of punishment (Atilgan & Atilgan, 2009).

In case of no regular juvenile court or juvenile serious delinquency court, the trial of the juvenile delinquents are held by the general courts until the establishment of juvenile courts in that jurisdiction. However, these regular courts must implement the legal regulations of the CPA on the trial of juvenile offenders. Both courts may take judicial measures for juvenile offenders as mentioned in Article 20 of CPA:

- Not to leave the borders of determined area
- Not to go certain places
- Not to get in relation with offenders

- Not to leave the country
- To appear before certain authorities in certain times
- To comply with the calls of certain persons or institutions regarding job training or education
- Not to operate certain vehicles and leaving driving license if necessary. (Polat, 2010)

Among those judicial measures, the most common judicial measure is to appear before certain authorities at certain times. That is, most of the time juvenile offenders are required to go to police stations once in a week and sign a document indicating that they were present. If juveniles do not comply with any of the judicial measures, then, the court may order for detention in a correctional facility.

Judges in Juvenile Courts

Judges that are assigned to both courts are trained by the Ministry of Justice. These judges follow a special curriculum on laws related to juveniles, child development, social work, and child psychology. Then, before their assignment to juvenile courts, they work as intern judges at courts. However, most of the time, judges are assigned to juvenile courts based on their preference. Most of the time, their previous experiences are not considered for their assignment to juvenile courts. For instance, if they mostly worked at adult criminal courts and were experienced at dealing with serious adult offenses, they can be assigned to juvenile courts. This causes disappointment among judges who do not want to work at juvenile courts. Moreover, when they are assigned to juvenile courts, they are not provided adequate in-service training on issues related to children. That shows how articles of the CPA related to determination and education of judges of juvenile courts are not fully implemented as directed by the law (McKinney & Salins, 2013).

Social Work Offices

Article 33 of the CPA proposes that besides judges and public prosecutors, juvenile courts should employ social workers to juvenile courts. These social workers should at least have bachelor's degree related to issues regarding children and family. They should conduct social examinations of juvenile offenders, accompany juveniles during the interrogation, and conduct other duties determined by the CPA (Akbulut, 2013; McKinney & Salins, 2013). However, this article is not fully implemented. That is, the numbers of social workers that are employed to juvenile courts or prosecutorial offices are inadequate and in most cases, they do not accompany juveniles during the interrogations. Instead, the public prosecutor interrogates the juvenile by himself. In these circumstances, social workers that are working at local social services are called to prosecutorial offices. However, due to lack of enough social workers at local social services and their heavy workload, they cannot come to trials or prosecutorial offices. That mostly causes delays in juvenile trials and the system loses its efficiency eventually.

GENERAL PRINCIPLES AND PROBLEMS OF HANDLING JUVENILE OFFENDERS

As in all criminal cases, police become aware of juvenile crimes from the victim's complaints, parental complaints, direct order from the public prosecutor to police, witnesses' testimonies, police encountering the crime, and others. However, handling juvenile offenders is quite different from handling adult offenders. In principle, in order to seize individuals, a court order or the public prosecutor's written command is necessary. In case of emergency circumstances, police can seize individuals without a court order or the prosecutor's written command. In the first two circumstances, the police must seize juvenile offenders as civilian police and not as uniformed police officers whenever possible. If the police encounter the crime which is committed by the juvenile, he/she can be also arrested by uniformed police officers. In all criminal cases, offenders must be handcuffed so as not to harm themselves or others. However, if a juvenile is seized, he/she cannot be handcuffed. They cannot be tied with any tools. In those circumstances, the police must take necessary security measures to prevent the juvenile's escape, or prevent posing a danger to his or someone else's life or physical safety (Atilgan & Atilgan, 2009). This issue is a mostly encountered problem when arresting juveniles because, in some cases, juveniles may be stronger than officers and it may be difficult to control them by other means. Sometimes, juveniles can escape from the juvenile police division, prosecutor office or court room due to not being handcuffed.

After seizing the juvenile, an official report is prepared regarding the seizure and if the juvenile is taken into the custody, the public prosecutor's written command must be taken. Like all criminals, juvenile offenders are taken to the medical doctor for health examination to officially document the state of the suspect's health before they enter jail. When the juvenile is arrested, he/she must be provided a legal representative which is also demanded by the "European Convention on the Exercise of Children's Rights." Therefore, the Criminal Procedural Code arranged this principle under the Article 150/2 with the following section:

> If the accused or suspect is a child does not have an attorney, or somebody who is handicapped to the degree that he/she cannot defend himself/herself alone, or deaf and mute, an attorney shall be assigned without seeking for their request.

SDIC articles also mentions the same issue and states that if a juvenile does not want a legal guardian, an attorney will be assigned immediately. Moreover, the juvenile's family may also bring another advocate if they prefer. Overall, arrested juveniles always have an advocate during the criminal procedures.

The CPA mentions how juveniles will be kept in detention. According to Articles 16/1 and 2 when a juvenile is taken into custody, he is put into the jail in the juvenile police division. If there is no jail in the juvenile police division, then the juvenile is kept separate from other adult offenders in jail (Akbulut, 2013). These jails are quite different from other jails where adult offenders live. For instance, the walls are mostly covered with cartoons, cartoon figures such as Mickey Mouse, or castles, flowers, and others. Families of the juveniles are informed about the juvenile's situation by police. The regular detention period for every suspect is 24 hours. Within 24 hours, every suspect must be taken to the prosecutor. During detention, the police cannot interrogate the juvenile. However, when the juvenile is arrested, the police conduct an initial interview with the juvenile to learn about basic issues about the crime. The police can document this interview in a report but some legal experts claim that this procedure is against the law. Therefore, the police are reluctant to conduct an initial interview with the juvenile so that sometimes the speed of the investigation may be delayed.

Prosecutors are responsible for taking statements of the juvenile. While the prosecutor is taking the statement of the juvenile, it has to be video recorded and a social worker and an advocate must accompany the prosecutor (Akbulut, 2013). However, due to a lack of personnel at the social worker's office, most of the time social workers are not present during the interrogation. The same problem is also present at juvenile police divisions.

When the police take the statement of juvenile victims, social workers, social service experts, psychologists, or pedagogues must be present at juvenile police divisions. However, due to lack of personnel and their workload with other agencies, interviewing juveniles at juvenile police divisions is a mostly difficult issue in juvenile investigations. The family of the juvenile may also be present during the interrogation unless there is a legal obstacle or their presence will be against the child's benefits.

If a juvenile commits a crime with adults, prosecution of these cases changes. SDIC Article 19/b and CPAP Article 7/1 rule that if juveniles commit crimes together with adults which are listed in the Juvenile Courts Act, investigation files are separated from adults and both investigations are conducted separately. That is, the juvenile goes to the juvenile's prosecutor and the adult goes to the adult's prosecutor. If there is a compulsory situation for merging adults and juvenile files, the trial will be carried out in general courts (Akbulut, 2013).

Overall, we can see that police officers do not have full investigative power for juvenile cases. They are not allowed to interview juvenile offenders so that police cannot know who are the other suspects, where is the crime tool, and other facts. They have to wait for the next day for the prosecutor's interviewing of the juvenile offender. Sometimes the prosecutor may want to see the offender several days later. In these cases, the juvenile is turned to his/her families and they are informed of the date of the proceedings at the prosecutor's office. However, in most of the cases, families do not bring their children and when the police demand to find these juveniles; it becomes very difficult to find them. That causes a great deal of delays and problems in juvenile cases.

Another problem with juvenile cases is the limited number of prosecutors in cities. Due to lack of manpower, police cannot bring the juvenile offenders to the prosecutors' offices because they have to deal with other adult cases also. For instance, in Şanliurfa, which is the ninth largest city of Turkey, there are only two prosecutors to handle juvenile cases. However, due to the heavy workload of prosecutors, they only accept juvenile cases on Tuesdays and Thursdays. That causes accumulation of juvenile cases and delays in juvenile investigations, a good deal of time loss, wrongful convictions, or unjust decisions. Moreover, the police start the investigation, prepares most of the paperwork except for the juvenile offenders' statement. The police conduct their proceedings at the crime scene, interview witnesses and victims, and obtain first-hand information about the case. The police cannot do anything related to criminal cases without the prosecutor's approval. The police inform the prosecutor about the case over the phone. Sometimes, he can forget giving some details. Under these circumstances, when the prosecutor interviews the juvenile offender, he does not have full knowledge of the case and cannot ask specific questions to the juvenile offender and he also has other duties such as attending cases in courts and prosecuting other crimes.

Rehabilitation initiatives were limited due to high numbers of convicted juveniles, lack of personnel, and a lack of cooperation among agencies which negatively affected the effectiveness of initiatives (Kırımsoy & Çavdar, 2005). In terms of judicial decisions, it can be stated that infrastructure insufficiencies have limited the standardization of services and practices. Reports from psychological and social evaluation of youth are a cornerstone of judgments that promote rehabilitation, but are generally not completed. İrtiş (2010) found that such reports were hardly ever prepared, and when they were, they did not fulfill the required criteria. In addition, due to lack of time, judges did not thoroughly read even those reports that were prepared in accordance with the required criteria. Thus, judges did not know the factors that led children to deviance and crime, and their judgments were based only on the nature of the offense itself. This approach eliminates the possibility of interventions that might prevent delinquency or reduce recidivism.

Juveniles are released from Turkish reformatories, juvenile training homes, or prisons either after serving all of their time or on parole. Upon being released, there is no official institution to supervise or help them. Therefore, they are free to return to the same social context that may have contributed to their delinquency. According to the Juvenile Court Act, juveniles might be on parole for a time ranging from six months to three years. However, in most cases, courts order six months of parole. Usually social workers are appointed to prepare reports for paroled juveniles once every two months and to submit them to the juvenile court. Those reports are used to identify behavioral changes of juveniles, and to present evaluation of their family issues, school participation, and working conditions if they are employed. Based on this information, the social workers recommend whether or not it is necessary to extend parole (Erukcu & Akbas, 2012). Uluğtekin and Acar (2005) examined 926 parole reports of 219 juveniles and stated that parole reports were not helpful to guide supervision and to help youth upon release from prison or reformatories. They found that although the report specified many types of information to be collected, most sections were left blank, which made it difficult to identify change in juveniles' circumstances. Therefore, we do not have valid data on juvenile offenders on parole. As seen above, the juvenile justice system lacks the information needed to guide rehabilitation efforts for convicted juveniles either in reformatories or prisons or when they are on parole.

CAUSES OF JUVENILE DELINQUENCY AND INCARCERATION

There are different pathways which lead juveniles to commit crime. A family's low socioeconomic status as well as the family's structural background was associated with juvenile's living in squatter areas where juveniles meet delinquents. Lack of attachment to the parents, witnessing domestic violence at home, beating as parental discipline, and lack of parental supervision were four important dimensions of the family process affecting juveniles' lives, including their delinquency. Due to those circumstances, juveniles prefer to spend time with their delinquent peers. Lack of interest in schools, truancy, drop out, repeating grades, and expulsion are school-related influences on a juvenile's life and delinquency (Hancı, Eşiyok, Şimşek, & Ulukol, 2005; Öğel & Aksoy, 2007; Öntaş & Akşit, 2008; Türkeri, 1995). Due to lack of attachment to school, juveniles think that there is no normal future for them and associate with delinquent peers around them. Peer influence has the greatest influence on juvenile delinquency. Having delinquent peers substantially affects the routines of juveniles. When juveniles do not feel close to their parents and spend most of their time with their delinquent peers, it changes their routines and they spend their time in bachelor's houses, use drugs together, and do not continue their schooling (Günçe & Konanç, 1983; Mangır, 1992; Subaşı, 1979; Yavuzer, 1981). Due to lack of parental supervision, youth spend most of their time with their delinquent friends which exacerbate their engaging in crime and drug use. Therefore, having delinquent peers changes routine activities of juveniles by detaching them from their parents and school. They spent most of their time free from supervision of their parents and in bachelor's houses, which put them at high risk of using drugs. Then, their lives end up in juvenile prisons (Tasgin, 2012).

These issues raise the question of what is the current condition of juvenile delinquency. According to the data displayed in Table 1, which was gathered from the Turkish Statistical Institute and General Directorate of Police, a rise in the number of arrested juveniles in conflict with the law can be seen. Most offenses are committed against property (burglary from workplace, theft, auto theft, motorcycle theft, destruction of property, and

Table 1. Comparison of Crimes Committed by Juveniles between 2011and 2013.

Crime Type	2011 Suspect	2012 Suspect	2013 Suspect
Assault	39,257	43,014	47,056
Burglary from workplace	11,174	11,023	12,387
Drug abuse	7,439	8,167	11,451
Theft	22,245	20,940	18,115
Motorcycle theft	2,116	2,629	5,610
Destruction of property	7,374	6,269	5,247
Threat	5,000	5,077	4,663
Theft from auto	3,140	3,256	3,461
Extortion	3,887	3,799	3,862
Insult	4,897	4,261	2,529
Child sexual abuse	1,826	1,943	1,935
Gun violence	1,921	1,572	1,465
Resistance to police officers	1,209	1,260	1,458
Auto theft	1,435	1,300	1,162
Kidnaping	724	727	614
Molestation	616	565	444
Pickpocketing	572	490	402
Rape	603	729	620
Homicide	268	294	299

theft from auto). There is a certain increase in offenses against individuals especially in the category of assault.

As displayed in Table 2, there is an increase in the number of arrested juveniles and juvenile victims. The number of juvenile victims is almost close to the total number of adult victims.

Table 3 shows the age group of arrested juvenile offenders between 2011 and 2013. The number of arrested juveniles increases when juveniles get

Table 2. Total Number of Offenders and Juvenile Offenders between 2011 and 2014.

Offender or Victim	Total Number of Offenders			Juvenile Offenders		
	2011	2012	2013	2011	2012	2013
Suspect	1,142,233	1,210,903	1,217,278	125,625	128,189	133,170
Victim	283,753	295,251	308,244	189,428	198,871	206,127
Total	*1,425,986*	*1,506,154*	*1,525,522*	*315,053*	*327,060*	*339,297*

Table 3. Comparison of Age Groups of Juvenile Offenders between 2011 and 2013.

Age Groups of Juvenile Suspects between 2011 and 2013				
Age groups	2011	2012	2013	Total
0–12	6,521	6,531	3,995	17,047
13–15	30,561	31,191	33,569	95,321
16–18	88,538	90,451	95,611	274,600

older. This highlights the fact that juveniles are less detained when they are younger than 15 which shows the leniency of the system. The most affected age group for juveniles is that of 16 to 18-year-old juveniles. Juveniles start offending in their early ages and they continue to commit crimes when they grow up. The reason of having a large number of arrested juveniles between ages 16 and 18 is that they are not diverted to other facilities or there is no mediation option for their crimes.

Table 4 displays the top 15 cities of Turkey where the number of arrested juveniles and juvenile victims is high. Istanbul, Izmir, and Ankara have the highest number of arrested juveniles and juvenile victims.

Table 4. Top 15 Cities where Juvenile Offenders and Victims Are More Prevalent.

City Name	Juvenile Offender	Juvenile Victim	Total Number of Juveniles
Adana	4,069	6,675	10,744
Ankara	6,601	12,011	18,612
Antalya	3,078	4,521	7,599
Balikesir	2,485	3,175	5,660
Bursa	6,941	8,618	15,559
Diyarbakir	2,543	3,203	5,746
Gaziantep	2,680	7,233	9,913
Istanbul	16,761	16,686	33,447
Izmir	10,133	11,877	22,010
Kayseri	3,218	6,093	9,311
Kocaeli	2,419	3,944	6,363
Konya	4,581	9,309	13,890
Manisa	3,023	3,954	6,977
Mersin	3,204	5,980	9,184
Şanliurfa	2,189	3,386	5,575

HOW MUCH OF A DETERRENT IS THE JUVENILE JUSTICE SYSTEM?

A deterrent effect of the Turkish Juvenile Justice System is questionable. According to the Turkish Penal Code, judges decrease the overall one sixth of the punishment given by the court. Execution of Punishment Law requires that all offenders can be detained for only two thirds of the punishment. Then, offenders can be on parole for their remaining punishment. Moreover, for some offenses whose punishments are between 1 and 3 years such as burglary and theft, offenders can be on probation without being sent to the prison. Probation service was modeled after the National Probation Service for England and Wales. As of May 2011, 7,179 juveniles benefited from the 133 probation services throughout Turkey (McKinney & Salins, 2013). Therefore, most of the time, offenders are arrested and released due to a change in the legal system. Then, due to not being sent to prison, offenders start to think that nothing is happening to them even if they are arrested (Dolu, Büker, & Uludağ, 2012). The same thing is also prevalent for juvenile offenders. Their punishments are more lenient than adult punishment. Therefore, juvenile offenders are less punished than adult offenders. Then, committing crime becomes the rational choice for juvenile offenders as they are not being punished.

The most common theme relevant to the influence of the juvenile justice system on juveniles' lives is its leniency. In 2005, the Turkish Penal Code and Turkish Criminal Procedure Code were changed. This change was criticized for reducing penalties. Although most criminal acts resulted in criminal proceedings, the length of time for the trial process and delays in the process led to periods of no response after youth were arrested. Juvenile offenders thought that nothing would happen to them due to their age; therefore, they continued committing crimes and escalated their lawbreaking. Therefore, perceived leniency led juveniles to commit more crime because they did not experience any punishment. The lack of response promoted youths' continuation on a trajectory of crime. The slow process of juvenile proceedings worsens youth's delinquency. When juveniles are in the prison, they have upcoming sentences from their previous crimes, which they never anticipated being held responsible for. Therefore, the slowness in processing disrupts juveniles' dreams for their future. If juveniles decide not to commit a crime again due to the effect of incarceration and want to start a good life, due to upcoming punishments from their waiting cases, they enter prison (Tasgin, 2012). Due to the perceived leniency of the juvenile justice system, juveniles recidivate at incredible rates as displayed in Fig. 1 below.

As displayed above, 31,260 juveniles committed crime twice; 17,812 juveniles committed crime between 3 and 5 times; 6,449 juveniles committed crime between 6 and 15 times; 1,000 juveniles committed crime between 16 and 30 times; 227 juveniles committed crime between 31 and 50 times; and lastly 76 juveniles committed crime between 51 and 143 times. The most common offense types are displayed in Table 5.

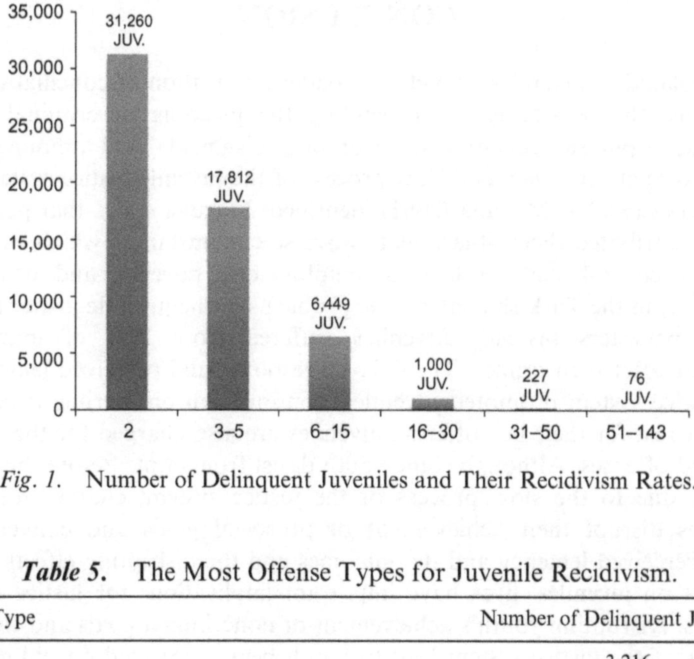

Fig. 1. Number of Delinquent Juveniles and Their Recidivism Rates.

Table 5. The Most Offense Types for Juvenile Recidivism.

Crime Type	Number of Delinquent Juveniles
Assault	3,216
Burglary	4,249
Destruction of property	975
Threat	1,314
Theft from auto	662
Drug abuse	651
Motorcycle theft	254
Extortion	206
Children's sexual abuse	77
Total	*11,604*

Acar (2004) stated that robbery, assault, and theft were the most common offenses committed by Turkish juvenile offenders. Consistent with the literature, as displayed in Table 5, the most common offense type for juvenile recidivism is burglary and assault. The reason for assault and burglary being the most common offense type is that the below and above punishments for these two offenses are too lenient for juveniles. When juveniles commit these two offenses, they rarely enter prison and when they enter prison, they are released within a month.

CONCLUSION

Laws related to juveniles provide a broader application of conciliation and introduce the possibility of suspending the pleading of criminal cases, decrease in punishments or suspension of punishments, and announcement of the verdict. Leniency and slow process of the juvenile justice system create "persisters," as Maruna (2001) identified. Maruna states that persisters mostly attributed their situations to adverse circumstances which were out of their control such as lack of employment, poverty, and drug use. However, in the Turkish context, the problems in the juvenile justice system create persisters instead. Juveniles suffered from lack of immediate response after their crimes. The delayed response and perceived leniency of the justice system promoted juveniles' continuation on a crime trajectory. After arrest for their last offense, juveniles are also charged for their accumulated offenses. Although some youth desist from crime before they enter prison, due to the slow process of the justice system, charges for prior offenses disrupt their achievement of prosocial goals and conventional lives. Perceived leniency and its outcomes and the disrupting effects of old charges on juveniles' lives have important implications for justice system policies. Disrupting youth's achievement of noncriminal goals and the slow process of the justice system lead to youth being convicted on old charges even after they desist from crime. The initial leniency of the justice system limits juveniles' awareness of future consequences, and this lack of awareness promotes their continuity in criminal involvement. Therefore, juveniles in Turkey recidivate many times and do not benefit from the lenient juvenile justice system. Some of them may be charged even years later after they forget their crimes.

Severity of the punishments is not clear in the Turkish juvenile justice system. Due to leniency in juvenile punishments, juveniles recidivate and think that nothing will happen to them even if they continue breaking the law (Dolu et al., 2012). Therefore, juveniles should be informed about possible future consequences of recidivism.

Most of the time, due to heavy workload, understaffed courtrooms and prosecution offices, juvenile cases remain pending in the courtrooms for years. During this time, due to not being punished, juveniles continue to break the law. Therefore, celerity of the punishment should be an ideal in the juvenile justice system (Dolu et al., 2012). The number of judges and prosecutors should be increased in order to deal with juvenile cases.

REFERENCES

Acar, Y. B. (2004). *Cinsel suçtan hükümlü çocukların yaşam öyküsü çalışması ve grupla sosyal hizmet uygulaması.* [*The study of life history of juveniles convicted of sexual offense and social work practice with group.*] Unpublished doctoral dissertation, Hacettepe Üniversitesi, Ankara.

Akbulut, B. (2013). Child in criminal legislation and children's apprehension and detention. *Marmara University Journal of Law Research, 19*(2), 541–586.

Atilgan, A., & Atilgan, E. U. (2009). Çocuk hakları paradigması ve çocuk ceza yargılamasına hakim olan ilkeler açısından Türkiye'deki düzenleme ve uygulamaların değerlendirilmesi. [Paradigm of juvenile rights and the evaluation of principles that are prevalent in juvenile justice system.] Ankara: Ihop.

Dolu, O., Büker, H., & Uludağ, Ş. (2012). A critical assessment of the deterrent capacity of the Turkish criminal justice system. *Ankara University Journal of Law School, 61*(1), 69–106.

Erukcu, G., & Akbas, E. (2012). A critical review of child court practice in Turkey. *Journal of Human and Social Science Researches, 1*(3), 135–153.

Günçe, G., & Konanç, E. (1983). Child abuse in Turkey. In J. E. Lavitt (Ed.), *Child abuse and neglect research and innovations* (pp. 135–149). Boston, MA: NATO ASI Series.

Hancı, İ. H., Eşiyok, B., Şimşek, F., & Ulukol, B. (2005). Cezaevinde bulunan çocukların temel özellikleri ve suç tipleri [Demographics and offense types of juveniles in prison]. In E. Akyüz, S. Uluğtekin, Y. B. Acar, & Ö. C. Öntaş (Eds.), *3. Ulusal çocuk ve suç sempozyumu: Bakın, gözetme ve eğitim* (pp. 399–405). [*National violence and juvenile symposium: Care, supervision, and education.*] Ankara: Yorum Matbaacılık.

İrtiş, V. (2010). Understanding juvenile penal justice in Turkey: An attitude both punitive and lax, expressing a will for solidarity. In F. Bailleau & Y. Cartuyvels (Eds.), The criminalization of youth: Juvenile *justice* in Europe, Turkey, and Canada (pp. 231–262). Brussels: Vubpress Brussels University Press.

Kazankaya, C. (2013). Kollugun el kitabi. [The handbook of police.] Ankara: Murat.

Kırımsoy, E., & Çavdar, Y. (2005). Adalet Bakanlıgı'na bağlı kurumlarda bulunan çocuklara yönelik bir sivil toplum çalışması: "Eğitsel, Sportif, Sanatsal ve Sosyal Etkinlikler Projesi" [Civil Society initiative towards juveniles in justice institutions: Educational, sportive, and social activities project]. In E. Akyüz, S. Uluğtekin, Y. B. Acar, & Ö. C. Öntaş (Eds.), *3. Ulusal çocuk ve suç sempozyumu: Bakın, gözetme ve eğitim* (pp. 101–109). [*National violence and juvenile symposium: Care, supervision, and education.*] Ankara: Yorum Matbaacılık.

Mangır, M. (1992). Ankara kalabalık çocuk ıslah evinde bulunan suça yönelmiş çocukların işledikleri suç türleri ile uyum düzeylerinin bazı değişikliklere gore incelenmesi. [Examination of incarcerated juveniles by their offense types and their compliance.] Ankara: Ankara Üniversitesi Z.F. Yayınları.

Maruna, S. (2001). *Making good: How ex-convicts reform and rebuild their lives.* Washington, DC: American Psychological Association.

McKinney, B., & Salins, L. (2013). A decade of progress: Promising models for children in the Turkish juvenile justice system. *UCLA Journal of Islamic and Near Eastern Law*, *12*(1), 13–53.

Öğel, K., & Aksoy, A. (2007). Substance abuse among incarcerated and convicted juveniles. *Journal of Dependence*, *8*, 11–17.

Öntaş, Ö. C., & Akşit, B. T. (2008). Crime reasons from the eyes of juvenile offenders: A study conducted in a detention center in a capital city. *European Journal of Social Sciences*, *6*(1), 33–46.

Oto, R. (1998). Suç, çocuk ve isnat yeteneği. [Crime, juveniles, and their capability.] Kamu Hukuku Arşivi, Ankara: KhukA.

Polat, H. (2010). A survey on penal liability of mentally disturbed and the properties of their judgment process according to the Turkish law. *Union of Turkish Bar Association Review*, *23*(90), 64–101.

Solmaz., Y. (2010). Türk çocuk adaleti sistemine genel bakış. [A general look at the Turkish juvenile justice system.] *Proceedings from Çocuk Adalet Sistemi*, Ankara, Turkey.

Subaşı. (1979). Psikososyal açıdan çocuk suçluluğu. [Psycho-social perspective of juvenile delinquency.] Ankara: Ankara Üniversitesi Egitim Bilimleri Fakültesi.

Tasgin, S. (2012). *Assessing an age-graded theory of informal social control: A qualitative study exploring pathways to youth incarceration in Turkey.* Unpublished doctoral dissertation, Michigan State University, Lansing.

Trojanowicz, R. C., Morash, M., & Schram, P. J. (2001). *Juvenile delinquency: Concepts and control* (6th ed.). Upper Saddle River, NJ: Prentice Hall.

Türkeri, S. (1995). Çocuk ıslahevleri ve çocuk cezaevlerindeki çocukların suç işleme nedenleri açısından incelenmesi. [Juvenile reformatories and the assessment of incarcerated juveniles for causes of delinquency.] Ankara: Ankara Üniversitesi Sosyal Bilimler Enstitüsü.

Uluğtekin, S., & Acar, Y. B. (2005). Türkiye'de çocuk mahkemeleri ve gözetim raporları araştırması temelinde Türkiye'de gözetim sisteminin değerlendirilmesi [Juvenile courts in Turkey and examination of parole system]. In E. Akyüz, S. Uluğtekin, Y. B. Acar, & Ö. C. Öntaş (Eds.), *3. Ulusal çocuk ve suç sempozyumu: Bakın, gözetme ve eğitim* (pp. 157–183). [*National violence and juvenile symposium: Care, supervision, and education.*] Ankara: Yorum Matbaacılık.

UNDP. (2008, September 13). *Human development report: Youth in Turkey.* Retrieved from http://planipolis.iiep.unesco.org/upload/Turkey/Turkey_NHDR-2008-Eng.pdf

Yamak, O., & İnci, B. S. (2010). The analysis of child protection services from a systems perspective. *International Journal of Social Sciences and Humanity Studies*, *2*(2), 103–112.

Yavuzer, H. (1981). *Psiko sosyal açıdan çocuk suçluluğu.* [*Juvenile delinquency from psychosocial perspective.*] Unpublished doctoral dissertation, Istanbul Üniversitesi, Istanbul.

THE TRAJECTORY OF PENAL MARKETS IN A PERIOD OF AUSTERITY: THE CASE OF ENGLAND AND WALES

Mary S. Corcoran

ABSTRACT

Purpose – *This chapter reviews the economic turn in criminology to contextualise the prominence of market rationalities in penal privatisation and outsourcing in England and Wales. It illuminates how fiscal crisis and austerity have provided opportunities for transferring state penal assets and powers to private interests on an unprecedented scale. A series of scandals relating to fraud and mismanagement by private companies have revealed regulatory gaps and wilful oversight on the part of legislators. These factors virtually guarantee that state regulators will continue to be disadvantaged in asserting the public interest.*

Design/methodology/approach – *The chapter brings together the literatures on prison privatisation with theoretical critiques of neoliberal influences on state disaggregation. It applies those insights to recent trends and controversies surrounding the privatisation of prison and probation services in England and Wales.*

Punishment and Incarceration: A Global Perspective
Sociology of Crime, Law and Deviance, Volume 19, 53–74

ISSN: 1521-6136/doi:10.1108/S1521-613620140000019002

Findings – *The race to privatise more prisons and resettlement provisions in England and Wales is placing additional strains on an already inadequate regulatory system, which virtually guarantees that future scandals and crises relating to private sector custodianship will recur.*

Originality/value – *This chapter explores the under-appreciated criminogenic and governmental challenges to the regulatory environment which are brought about by outsourcing.*

Keywords: Marketisation; privatisation; prisons; probation

INTRODUCTION

The influence of market forces is a prominent and much discussed feature of the way in which advanced capitalist societies have addressed crime, soaring economic inequality, unemployment and social exclusion. Several scholars have made connections between increased imprisonment, social inequality and the emergence of market societies, especially in those states which have most eagerly adopted neoliberal models of political administration (Albert, 1997; Wacquant, 2000, 2009). Often referred to as the Anglo-American capitalist economies (such as the United States of America, the United Kingdom, Australia or New Zealand), they have gone furthest in deconstructing their state bureaucracies and apportioning ancillary areas of security and corrections to non-state parties.

In England and Wales,[1] the state's near-monopoly of criminal justice services is being replaced over time by a competitive 'mixed' market in which a growing number of penal functions are open to acquisition by private corporations and non-governmental organisations (NGOs) such as charities and community enterprises. Today, the penal service industry in England and Wales comprises networks of 'core' institutions of police, courts, prison and probation systems, which remain for the time being in public ownership, and a growing satellite shadow state comprising for-profits and NGOs who are contracted to provide 'complementary' facilities for offenders such as housing; drugs and alcohol misuse services; electronic tagging and monitoring, employment and training programmes, for example. This chapter reviews the accelerated pace and scale of outsourcing by the current government under the precept of fiscal responsibility at a time of economic austerity. It concludes by arguing that the lure of the 'mixed social economy' has been given an added impetus by fiscal restructuring in the wake of the banking crisis (2007–present). Recent scandals surrounding the activities of the largest security corporations have also revealed significant, if under-appreciated, gaps in oversight and governance which challenge the regulatory structure and defence of the public interest.

POLITICAL ECONOMY AND CONTEMPORARY PENALITY

Several influential commentaries have subscribed to a broad consensus that the scale and organisation of punishment have been transformed in recent decades. These radical changes are most visibly manifested in the increased rates of incarceration globally since the 1990s, with some of the most pronounced increases occurring in advanced capitalist economies (Gottschalk, 2006; Walmsley, 2013). One of the main points of that consensus is the belief that changes in the political economies of these countries are exacerbating punitive attitudes in a late-modern era defined by globalisation and adjustment to insecurity (Garland, 2001; Pratt, 2008; Wacquant, 2000, 2009). For example, parallels have been drawn between economic restructuring and growing social inequality in advanced capitalist countries which is manifested in penal responses towards disenfranchised groups, migrants, the unemployed or precariously employed, minority social groups and subaltern youth (Annals of the American Academy of Political and Social Science, 2014; Dorling, 2011; Standing, 2011; Wilkinson & Pickett, 2009).

More specifically, it is contended that we have witnessed a convergence of market and correctional rationalities as penal developments in several countries are conditioned, even determined, by the need to 'adapt to ... transnational market forces' (Leys, 2001, p. 1). In this scenario, the influence of capital and business interests has swept through Western correctional systems, altering them out of recognition in some important respects. Governments have transferred assets and powers to for-profit corporations and latterly, to NGOs, to undertake an increasing proportion of criminal justice activities. Public agencies are increasingly exposed to the laws of competition, supply and demand, and consequently obliged to adopt business-like practices and outlooks in order to become players in deregulated service markets (Rynne, Harding, & Wortley, 2008). Justice and penal services, such as offender supervision in the community, drugs and alcohol programmes, electronic monitoring and prison transport, are repackaged as commodities which can be auctioned off in the open market to prospective suppliers. At the core of this network is the state whose controlling hand slows down, speeds up, colludes with or creates the conditions in which penal services markets can flourish.[2] One outcome of this phenomenon is that punishment by the state is said to be giving way to *state-sponsored punishment*, where corrections are no longer the sole province of the state, but whose functions are increasingly co-produced alongside non-state interests such as for-profit businesses and NGOs (Corcoran, 2011; INCITE, 2007).

These changes have been hypothesised as signifying the pervasive influence of 'market-driven politics' (Leys, 2001, p. 5), which, having become established in the policy agendas of several countries, are reshaping the public services in elder care, health and education and latterly, justice and corrections. According to this formulation, the rise of contemporary market societies can be traced to the closing decades of the 20th century, when governments in several countries acceded to the economic and political dominance of the neoliberal political ideology (Harvey, 2007; Leys, 2001). Neoliberalism has many variations (Bonefeld, 2012), but these broadly converge on a political project which promulgates a freely operating economy as a guarantor of political and social liberty (Hayek, 1960/2009), and where government regulation represents an illegitimate interference in society. Because the sanctity of the market precedes state authority, the proper role of government is to foster the conditions for markets to operate, unhindered by distortions such as a big government, consumer or worker protection or unionisation, for example. Secondly, there is a stress on optimising the scope of market agents to provide public goods and services on the purported grounds of their superior efficiency, cost, productivity and effectiveness in meeting consumer demands. Thirdly, the failures and inefficiencies of public criminal justice agencies are claimed to derive to a large degree from the fact that they are state monopolies (Carter, 2003; Le Grand, 2007). If necessary, the imbalance between the economy and bloated state sectors should be corrected by turning over some functions exercised by them to the market.

The complexity involved in formulating a conceptual framework for marketisation raises questions as to its precision or importance for examining why it has become pivotal to both political rhetoric and structural reform in England and Wales. The relationship between neoliberalism as a political project and marketisation as a governmental regime and set of practices for implementing programmatic aims are not mutually reductive (Lippert & Walby, 2014). However, these are closely intertwined to a degree that marketisation can be justifiably regarded as a means towards neoliberal goals. At an essential level, privatisation is quantifiably measurable according to the proportion of the penal service industry that is produced or managed by non-state agents (Albertson & Fox, 2012). Marketisation connotes deep political change as governing elites install the primacy of 'market testing' as both a cultural norm and defining rationality for the distribution of social goods. The 'market test' implies that there is no inherent exemption to the application of competitive principles, which should ideally apply to all potential areas of service consumption. Counter-arguments that corrections might constitute moral, ethical or social exceptions to the general rule are not accepted as a prima facie basis for protecting them from privatisation (Coyle, Campbell, & Neufeld, 2003). It is assumed that legality and rights are not incompatible with market interests as adequate checks can be put in place, for example with the state retaining responsibility for the 'highest risk' offenders while outsourcing the rest of the correctional field. From this perspective, marketisation entails the penetration of private interests into an erstwhile public sphere of interest by a range of strategies, including:

- Conflating stubbornly high rates of imprisonment and reoffending with the inadequacies of criminal justice agencies, and by extension, with the failures of public service models.
- Encouraging the involvement of for-profit and NGO providers as essential actors in crime prevention and security.
- Converting goods or services produced by the state into commodities which can be contracted out to other parties.
- Developing competitive service markets which will foster bidding wars among potential providers, irrespective of sector.
- Developing systems of co-production between adjacent private and public competitors. This includes 'inter-agency' partnerships where private and public services 'share' the same clients, or jointly occupy the same premises, with workforces discharging separate elements of the same process, such as arrest (police function) and custody (outsourced security officer function).
- Responding to lobbying from for-profit and NGO interests to deregulate service markets.
- Applying managerial techniques for measuring and evaluating performance by public agencies, allied to a punitive culture of league tables and 'naming and shaming' the 'failing' ones (Clarke & Newman, 1997) and exploiting negative data to further privatise them (Le Grand, 2007).

- Moderating the rules or specifying different targets, outputs and governance for new entrants to the market.

> Here, the whole range of market politics come into play, involving both inter-firm cooperation (to get a field opened to private accumulation, or strategic alliances to carve up the market) and competition (to be first into it) and using political influence, cash, market power and social connections to get the rules changed or to have the breaking of them ignored. (Leys, 2001, p. 84)

Not all scholars agree that trends in punishment can be attributed to overarching theories about neoliberalism or market forces. Lacey (2008, p. 55) warns against economically deterministic theories which 'erroneously transpose[...]' the experiences of the most obviously neoliberal polities into 'an account which purports to have global implications'. Others point to countries with neoliberal characteristics that have not embarked on more punitive trajectories (Cavadino & Dignan, 2006). There are important qualifications to the broad argument, therefore, the most obvious being that national systems are as much shaped by legal and political structures and cultural factors shaping public leniency or punitiveness, as by economic determinants (Pratt, 2008). Although not impervious to global trends, several countries such as France, Germany, the Nordic and Scandinavian countries and Israel have applied indigenous constitutional or policy mechanisms to moderate or check the pace of global convergence (Brown, 2013; Pratt & Erickson, 2013). Undoubtedly, commodified security and justice has been borne on the tides of globalisation, through transnational policy transfers, exchanges of expertise and flows of capital and profits. But a more nuanced approach suggests that these influences are unevenly distributed and dependent on local as well as geopolitical factors. Equally, however, it is evident that states differ in their capacity or political will to restrain or encourage such trends.

OUTSOURCING PUNISHMENT

In England and Wales, the transfer of assets and the development of co-produced corrections evolved over three decades and via different models for establishing a mixed social economy. This process has been characterised by a plethora of methods and means for 'externalising' state services that vary in levels of opacity and complexity. However, one consistent factor is that asset and managerial transfers have been justified by successive governments, of both the centre-Right and centre-Left, on the basis that they will deliver the elusive formula of greater efficiency, cheaper costs and better quality services. The principal mechanisms are discussed below.

Contract Managed Prisons

The first wave of externalisation was directly imported from the United States in the early 1990s to address chronic overcrowding and poor prison conditions (Pozen, 2003, p. 253). This model involved the construction of prisons from public funds but where the operational contract was awarded for up to five years. Legislation was enacted to allow for the contracting out of publicly operated prisons and juvenile detention centres (*Criminal Justice Act*, 1991, ss. 84–89) (H. M. Government, 1991). The first publicly built but privately managed prison in Europe, the Wolds, was opened in 1992. Another variation of this model entails 'market testing' which pitches the public prison service and private corporations in competition to manage prisons which are still in public hands. This has lowered costs and reduced staffing levels (Panchamia, 2012, p. 3).

The 'contract managed' business has proven to be comparatively insecure for profit-making companies, as the contracts are of comparatively short tenure and subject to re-tendering on completion of the contract term. Because the asset still belongs to the state, a handful of these prisons have shifted back and forth between public and private management. The Wolds, for example, was taken back into public management after the prisons inspectorate issued two reports criticising 'deteriorated performance ... poor behaviour ... [and] limited work and training provision' (H. M. Inspectorate of Prisons, 2012, p. 5). A more cynical interpretation was that this transfer was a public sanction from the government following the widely publicised failure of the prison's contractor, G4S, to fulfil its contract to provide security for the Olympics in London in 2012, as discussed below.

Design, Finance, Construction and Management (DFCM)

This involves commissioning new prisons through competitions inviting for-profit companies to submit tenders to design, construct, finance and manage the entire process. These are fully capitalised by the contractor through Private Finance Initiatives (PFIs). PFIs are sophisticated financial instruments which allow consortia of construction companies, facilities management companies and banks to finance the whole process from construction to operation for periods between 15 and 25 years. In use since the 1990s, PFIs are mutually advantageous for both governments and operators. They are favoured by the state because capital programmes funded by PFI do not appear on the schedule for public debt. Therefore, governments have been able to service the public appetite for prison-building programmes (for which demand has also been politically manufactured) without raising taxes in the short term, while deferring final payment to the end of the term of contract. Equally, they are favoured by for-profit companies because they allow them to retain ownership of the asset for the duration of the contract (Pollock, 2004, pp. 52–60), before cashing in at inflated rates of interest from the state. Since 1991, 11 prisons in England and Wales have been capitalised in this way by private sector contractors. Additionally, 5 out of 10 detention or 'immigration removal centres' are operated in this manner by private contractors.

The United Kingdom has the highest proportion of privatised prison estates in Europe, holding 16 per cent of the prison population (Prison Reform Trust, 2013, p. 71). Insofar as they are comparable with public prisons, their cost effectiveness, safety, regimes and rehabilitative effects are no better and no worse than public prisons (National Audit Office, 2003), contradicting dubious claims as to their inherent superiority. Fourteen prisons in England and Wales are operated by three companies: G4S (which operates 5), Serco (5) and Sodexo (4). These also dominate the market for maintenance and ancillary services in other areas. The public prison system still takes £7 (USD$11) of public money for every £1 (USD$1.68) that the private prison system takes, but that proportion is increasing as every new prison that has opened since 1991 has been financed by private capital (Justice Committee, 2009, figure 1).

Outsourcing

This approach involves contracting out ancillary services such as prisoner transport, catering and hygiene, prisoner education, drugs and alcohol programmes as these are the most 'market ready' elements. In 2007, further legislation was enacted to remove the remaining legal restrictions on NGO and charitable sector agencies with a view to recruiting them as correctional suppliers. Charitable involvement is politically critical to making privatisation publicly acceptable. The legislation also allowed for probation personnel and property to be transferred to 'third parties'.

Mixed Markets

The current, favoured model envisages a penal landscape populated by a constellation of public, private and charitable providers which are kept in constant competitive motion. The United Kingdom is distinctive in Western Europe because of the high proportion of public spending which is allocated to for-profit and NGO providers. About half of the £187 (USD $300) billion of government expenditure on goods and services is contracted out (Public Accounts Committee, 2014, summary). Approximately £1.5 (USD$2.50) billion is spent annually on services to prison and probation agencies (CCJS, 2014, p. 25). For-profit companies receive approximately £428.1 million annually (Prison Reform Trust, 2013, p. 73). By contrast, charities received less than two per cent of Ministry of Justice expenditure on service contracts between 2010 and 2012 (CCJS, 2014, p. 20). Even these figures can only be indicative as contracts under the value of £25 thousand pounds (USD$41 thousand) are not counted and charities tend to win smaller contracts.

Counting the Cost of Imprisonment

The appeal of extra capital and flexible workforces provided by for-profits and NGOs is explicable in the context of long-term structural strains on the prison and probation systems. The reasons why, and with what effects, incarceration levels have doubled in Britain since 1993 have been widely analysed, and it would be redundant to detail them here. Suffice to say that projections that the prison population will continue to grow into the next decade bear considerable cost implications (Justice Committee, 2009: para. 64; Ministry of Justice, 2012, table 1).[3] Spending on probation and servicing prisons (as capital build has largely been deferred 'off the books') is estimated to reach £4 (USD$6.7) billion for 2014, although this is lower than in previous years. Nevertheless, these services alone account for over half of the entire budget for the Ministry of Justice (Ukpublicspending.co.uk). Three quarters of that expenditure is absorbed by prisons, with the rest spent on probation services (Justice Committee, 2009, para. 63). Community-based interventions, largely operated by NGOs, are allocated about £40 (USD$67) million, a tiny proportion of overall correctional expenditure (Justice Committee, 2009, para. 12).

With inflation and more expensive essential utilities and food, the costs of running the prisons will rise even if the prison population stays stable (Albertson & Fox, 2012, p. 189). As fixed costs cannot be easily reduced, even when camouflaged by the private sector's contribution, government has sought to claw money back through scaling back employment in police, prisons, probation and the courts, reducing wage costs and service conditions of public sector officers and putting more public services out to contract (H. M. Treasury, 2013, para. 2.42)

From a governmental vantage point, managing the prison population trends presents two urgent areas for reform. The first relates to providing new prison places to absorb the projected increase in prisoner populations. The second relates to the high rates of re-imprisonment of mainly non-violent, repeat offenders within a year of release. This is to be achieved while 'bear[ing] down the costs of the criminal justice system' (Ministry of Justice, 2013a, p. 3). The rationale that increased state spending on public systems has so far failed to reduce reoffending. This has prompted 'a wholesale realignment of our prison service' to designate resettlement to 'a new mix of providers':

> It is clear that in order to invest in extending and enhancing rehabilitation we need to free up funding through increased efficiency and new ways of working. I want to bring the best of the public, private and voluntary sectors to help us achieve this and we will design a competition process which allows a range of organisations … to bid to deliver services. (Ministry of Justice, 2013a, foreword)

A prominent exemption from the spending review is the prison-building programme, which is declared to be a vital infrastructural investment for regenerating the economy (H. M. Treasury, 2013). In 2010, the incoming coalition government continued the prison expansion plans of the previous administration 'in order to get ahead of the curve of the increase [in the] prison population' (Justice Committee, 2009, para. 37). Their tendering competition for eight prisons 'represents a massive acceleration in the pace of contracting out and will be the largest privatisation programme in the history of the sector' (Panchamia, 2012, p. 3). Several public local prisons have been closed, but this is not a progressive development, as their replacements will be large 'Titan' prisons holding up to 2,000 inmates (Ministry of Justice, 2013b). Prison expansion is facilitated almost entirely by private capitalisation, greased by substantial subsidies from the state (Hansard, 2012, col. 366W). Funding for further prison building has been 'more or less guaranteed by the Treasury' (Justice Committee, 2009, para. 30). Government remains 'wedded to a prison-building agenda' despite the fiscal savings and better rehabilitative results that can be gained from investment in non-custodial programmes (*ibid.*).

In the context of recession, struggling public services and proclamations about relaxing the stranglehold of state bureaucracy on enterprise, the idea of a social market economy is politically attractive. The fundamental question for government is how to promote security and consensus for authoritarian criminal justice measures in conditions of economic shock, financial crisis, social strife, poverty and crime. The message is also more persuasive when it is delivered as the only feasible option. The construction and articulation of crime and punishment in cash terms has produced a historical opportunity to shrink the state by passing off this political choice as a necessity. Crime and punishment have been reframed as fiscal burdens, which sustains the political momentum for the state to seek market solutions and approaches. Despite its rhetoric of radical change, this government wants it both ways: to reconcile the upward trajectory of prison expansion that began in the decades before the economic crisis, while masking the social fallout of its economic policies by demonstrating firm management of the casualties of those same policies.

Transforming Rehabilitation: A New Correctional Cartography

Since 2010, the United Kingdom government, a coalition of radically neoliberal Conservatives and centrist Liberal Democrats, has set in motion an ambitious programme for reconfiguring the economy in an uncompromisingly marketised direction. This is focused on 'reducing the public deficit', 'cut[ting] public spending' and stimulating the economy by 'growing the private sector' (H. M. Government, 2013; H. M. Treasury, 2013). Those aims are embodied in the 'Transforming Rehabilitation' programme, which is unabashedly promoted as a project for orchestrating the transfer of the public probation infrastructure to the market from June 2014. To this end, England and Wales have been carved up into 21 'contract package' areas, each of which will be outsourced to Community Rehabilitation Companies (CRCs) and operated by private sector and charitable organisations. According to the Minister of Justice, this will resolve entrenched recidivism in ways that public agencies never could:

> Reoffending rates in this country are shamefully high and we must revolutionise our approach to reforming offenders – we need to stop recycling people around the system. … I know we can deliver better rehabilitation for offenders, a smarter system of detaining and educating teenage offenders, a cheaper and better prison system and a criminal justice system that commands public confidence – and at the same time bring costs down. (Grayling, 2012)

The CRCs will be vehicles for discharging 70 per cent of resettlement functions currently undertaken by the public probation service. The regional Probation Trusts, which were abolished in 2013, will be replaced by a centralised National Probation Service, who will have responsibility for about one third of all offenders classified as 'high risk'. The remaining two thirds of offenders, who are subject to 'low' and 'medium' risk community orders and prison licenses (parole) will be transferred to the oversight of the new companies. This model hinges on splitting probation into a residual public sector and a prime business terrain comprising private sector companies, charities and social enterprises.

It is difficult to fully capture the convoluted arrangements that are being put in place in order to assemble the mosaic of new providers into a coherent framework for taking over the greater part of resettlement. Successful rehabilitation companies will acquire the rights to run the contract areas for up to 10 years. The published list of approved 'primary' contractors comprises multinational for-profit companies, large charities and a couple of mutual (employee-owned) ventures led by ex-probation managers (Ministry of Justice, 2013c). The eventual winners will subcontract to two lower 'tiers' of providers comprising 'secondary' medium-sized businesses and charities, and 'tertiary' community providers. Public probation staff have been provisionally allocated, to either the shadow National Probation Service or, involuntarily, to the prospective CRCs.

An observable sense of urgency, which some interpret as panic, has arisen in the government as the race to privatise has revealed complex legal, human rights, public safety, operational and funding problems (British Journal of Community Justice, 2013). In turn, these have been addressed by the implementation of even more intricate and cumbersome formulas that are compounding problems they are meant to resolve. For example, the *Offender Rehabilitation Act* (2014) extends retrospective, compulsory parole supervision to all prisoners serving sentences of up to one year (many of whom had previously not been bound by such licenses) as well as extending the period of mandatory community supervision for those serving up to two years. This is estimated to add 65,000 to the pool of those on probation (parole), all of whom will be subject to mandatory drug tests and recall to prison for breach (violation) of license. These will be 'customers' of the new rehabilitation companies. Although it is strenuously defended as a progressive development because it extends a minimum period of one year's 'care and supervision' to those at the highest risk of reoffending, this has been achieved by effectively increasing their sentences. Moreover, the Ministry of Justice's (2013d, p. 9) own internal impact study estimates that 'breaches of those offenders brought [under] license conditions will increase by one third', incurring additional costs of up to £27 (USD$45) million per year.

It has taken successive governments decades to drive through the endorsement of private profit as a key component of probationary provision against considerable opposition, not only from the labour movement or sections of the political left, but academics, public administrators, lawyers and professionals. Although charities are described as full 'partners' in CRCs, they retain justifiable suspicions that their role, status, influence and income will be vastly outweighed by for-profit contractors (Corcoran & Hucklesby, 2013). The case for privatising the probation service has been widely discredited and it is apparent that the motives lie elsewhere. The fate of the probation system in England and Wales is determined by the political will to outpace the electoral clock by putting much of it into private domains before the next election, scheduled for May 2015.

'A MULTIPLE TRAIN CRASH'

Unsurprisingly, there has been a corresponding series of widely publicised cases involving mismanagement and allegations of dishonesty and fraud by large, transnational security corporations. Evidence periodically emerges about poor conditions, lack of constructive regimes, riots, hunger strikes and deaths in custody, although these are not unique problems to private sector prisons. However, the scale and reach of private security companies came into public focus in July 2012, when the media reported that G4S, which had been contracted to provide 'on the ground' security for the Olympic Games in London, had failed to provide enough staff. G4S had delayed recruiting and training staff until days before the opening of the games to save costs, obliging the government to deploy 4,700 military personnel to make up the shortfall. G4S was further damaged when the press reported that, as the deadline approached, its security training programme was cursory and weighted to maximise the number of trainees passing the course. Nick Buckles, the chief executive of G4S, subsequently defended the company's intentions not to waive its management fee of £57 million (which it subsequently forfeited), despite admitting total responsibility before the Parliamentary Home Affairs Committee. The Chief Executive of the London Olympic organising committee was blunter:

> We signed a contract with the biggest security company in the world, whose biggest customer was the UK government. They continually reassured us they had the capacity to deliver. It was obviously a huge disappointment … This is all about their poor performance in a very strong contract. (Guardian, 2012)

In June 2013, reports from a regulator, the National Audit Office, and two parliamentary bodies, the Justice Committee and the Public Accounts Committee, criticised the 'unnecessary' sale of the courts interpreter service to Capita, after which the service had almost collapsed (Guardian, 2013). The Chairman of the Justice Committee concluded:

> The Ministry [of Justice] is putting out to contract 70% of rehabilitative services under the transforming rehabilitation proposals, £450 (USD$755) million in custodial services over the next six years and a large part of criminal legal aid, all of which will be the subject of contracts. I do not need to spell out that if things go wrong in those areas as they have in court interpreting, we face a multiple-train crash (Hansard, 2013, col. 296WH).

The warning was prescient. In July, investigations into the electronic monitoring contracts held by Serco and G4S showed that they had overcharged for tagging criminals who were either dead, already in prison or never tagged in the first place. The companies were initially placed under 'administrative supervision', which entails subjecting their contracts to a 'forensic audit'. This is a non-criminal investigative procedure for tracing the payments-and-delivery trail. Participation was voluntary and G4S refused to cooperate. The main sanction for any misdemeanours under this process is removal from the list of approved contractors to the government.

In August 2013, Serco, which had cooperated with the voluntary 'forensic audit' of its electronic tagging contract, became the subject of a separate criminal investigation for alleged fraud in its prisoner transportation contract in London. By November 2013, the timetable for further privatisation seemed to be in disarray when three prisons were withdrawn from outsourcing because two of the potential contenders were in disgrace (Telegraph, 2013). In December, the review of all contracts held by Serco and G4S found 'potentially significant' errors or irregularities in three more contracts for the Work Programme for putting the long-term unemployed into the workforce (Guardian, 2013).

The Serious Fraud Office, which has criminal investigatory powers, started an investigation into G4S and Serco's operation of the tagging contracts in late 2013. Major fraud investigations typically take several years, and this one is likely to extend beyond the period of the parliamentary election in 2015. In the meantime, the Ministry of Justice was compensated by Serco (£68/USD$114 million) and subsequently rewarded with approval to bid for future public contracts (BBC, 2013). G4S, which was slower to cooperate, eventually agreed to pay £109/USD$182 million in March 2014, but remained suspended from the list of approved contractors (Telegraph,

2014). In April 2014, G4S was restored to the approved contractors list after paying up (Independent, 2014).

THE STATE OF THE MARKET

Despite the contrived narrative that outsourcing will lead to diversity, the penal service market is monopolistic and concentrated. Apart from the state, ownership of the penal services industry is overwhelmingly in the hands of four transnational security companies (TNCs): Atos; Capita; G4S and Serco. G4S and Serco between them account for 40 per cent of the Ministry of Justice spending on prisons and probation (CCJS, 2014, p. 25).

Additionally, their dominance is consolidated by cross-ownership of strategic interests ranging from private prisons, Immigration Removal Detention Centres, prisoner transport and ancillary services, to a point where the 'government is exposed to huge delivery and financial risks should one of these suppliers fail' (Public Accounts Committee, 2014, Q7, p. 8). These companies have evolved complex chains of horizontal and vertical subsidiaries, allowing the parent company to extend its interests via alliances, joint ventures and internal subcontracting. In the course of the *Parliamentary Inquiry into Contracting out Public Services to the Private Sector* (2013), the Comptroller General, Amyas Morse, noted that the exponential growth of the Big Four security companies had occurred in less than a decade through the predatory acquisition of newly privatised services and businesses. The key consequences of this were that; (a) the speedy expansion of the major corporates in Britain meant that they lost the capacity to control their burgeoning subsidiaries; (b) they had undertaken new ventures in areas where they lacked experience and (c) the parent companies had elaborate systems of internal shadow companies which allowed them to engage in tax avoidance (Public Accounts Committee, 2013, Q. 46–50).

Monopolisation is also a feature of the charitable sector, with a few 'Big Players' dominating the landscape. In England and Wales, two thirds of the value of service contracts issued by the central government between 2011 and 2012 went to three charities (CCJS, 2014, p. 20). Over time, the majority of smaller NGOs are being drawn further into the orbit of the big providers as their best hope for funding increasingly relies on securing a place as a subcontractor to them.

These factors contribute to a hazardously skewed market in which government and large providers (both for-profit and charitable) are embedded in mutually over-reliant relationships. Government is overexposed to the leverage that large providers can exert because they are seen to be 'too big to fail'. This caucus is also 'too big to exclude' from the list of approved contractors, despite misdemeanours. Conversely, the few corporations and charities that dominate the market are themselves over-dependant on government contracts as their source of income, and therefore susceptible to changes in fiscal policy. England and Wales has barely progressed from the state of concentrated ownership and control of correctional facilities that privatisation was meant to diversify. Austin Mitchell, parliamentary member of the Public Accounts Committee, summarised:

> The nub of the argument … is that [we have] replace[d] public monopoly with an oligopoly – that is to say, a small handful of big organisations like yourself which are big enough to dominate the bidding and then, when they are incumbent, are too big to be replaced. (Public Accounts Committee, Evidence 9, Q. 52)

Accountability

The lack of openly accessible data about expenditure on criminal justice services reaches into the core of recent political controversies about problems in the oversight and governance of contracts. Outsourcing is an opaque process and neither contracting parties, official and corporate, are obliged to disclose details of their negotiations or choices. Information about the levels and destinations of governmental spending on outsourced services in Britain is inaccessible or non-existent. It emerged from the Public Accounts Committee inquiry (2013) that the government did not maintain central records of the contracts it awards. Researchers rely on information which is painstakingly collated from the masses of raw 'transparency data' that are released in several different locations by the Treasury, Ministry of Justice and the Home Office (CCJS, 2014). Comparative assessments as to benefits of outsourcing services or keeping them in public hands are not publicly available. Audits related to the values and risks associated with privatising probation services were withheld from public consumption on the grounds that publication 'could put contractual negotiations at risk and prejudice the effectiveness of the competition' (Ministry of Justice, 2013d, p. 3).

Seeking information under Freedom of Information legislation is a complex and capricious process which allows officials considerable discretion about what to release, sometimes in a heavily redacted form, to the applicant. According to the House of Commons Public Accounts Committee, 'the government has used commercial confidentiality as an excuse to withhold information' with respect to contracts to private providers (Public Accounts Committee, 2014, p. 5). Members of parliamentary inquiries do not have an automatic right to order disclosure relating to investigations into irregularities, and have complained that materials arising from investigatory audits have been withheld from them (Public Accounts Committee, 2013, Q39, p. 6). The final report of the Public Accounts Committee's inquiry into *Contracting out public services to the private sector* (2014, p. 5) concluded that:

> There needs to be far greater visibility to government, parliament and the public about suppliers, performance, costs, revenues and profits ... We expect to see all government bodies that contract out functions and public services, and the contractors themselves, having transparency, not commercial sensitivity, as their default position. (Public Accounts Committee, 2014, p. 1)

These investigations have revealed areas where systems for state administration and oversight were overwhelmed by the too rapid growth of outsourcing, which had exposed 'fundamental weaknesses in how some government bodies have contracted for public services from private contractors' (Public Accounts Committee, 2014, col. 777/3). Although this work has retrospectively shed light on official mismanagement and corporate manipulation, it is much more circumspect in apportioning responsibility in the wake of highly publicised scandals. Even watchful parliamentary scrutineers concluded that both government *and* contractors were *equally* culpable in recent cases. Departments had 'not always [been] sufficiently vigilant of contractors' operations and delivery of services to users'. Whilst it was 'scandalous' that G4S and Serco had 'overcharged by tens of millions of pounds' for electronic tagging, it was equally 'shocking' that the Ministry of Justice had failed to notice the discrepancy for eight years.

> Government needs a far more professional and skilled approach to managing contracts and contractors, and contractors need to demonstrate the high standards of ethics expected in the conduct of public business. (Public Accounts Committee, 2014, summary)

PLAYING (AND LOSING) THE MARKET GAME

What is lost in the midst of all this detail is that this ineffectuality is ultimately a consequence of accumulated *political* decisions. Post-facto investigations, however revelatory, are weak counterweights to the institutional leverage that has accrued to a few major providers as a result of the concentration of resources, bargaining power and political influence they wield. Just as problematic is the nexus of elitism and hierarchy surrounding political and corporate interests that pervades the outsourcing phenomenon, and which preserves their decisions from accountability. These signify deeper structural problems that originate in policy but are deflected by a preoccupation with technocratic, short-term fixes. Political elites wilfully ignore the bureaucracy, intricacy, wastefulness and escalating hidden costs associated with privatisation programmes. The rate and scale of outsourcing to private and charitable providers have outstripped the capacity of government agencies to monitor, manage, investigate and prosecute possible fraud and deception. Regulatory agencies that have the responsibility for investigating corruption or mismanagement have themselves suffered debilitating cuts to their resourcing and personnel. Consistent with the neoliberal credo of 'light touch regulation', the prosecutorial framework is used as a last resort. The collapse of lengthy and complex cases involving misdemeanours in the finance sector has established a culture of hesitancy about undertaking criminal proceedings. Fines for poor performance are visibly minuscule in comparison with the profits that companies gain.

Even if regulatory systems were strengthened, they are not designed to curb the structural advantages of major corporations in manipulating supply, prices and performance targets. Despite assurances that providers fear damage to their reputations more than financial sanctions, they also know that the termination of contracts involve punitive costs to the public. The *Deregulation and Contracting Out Act* (1994) guarantees substantial compensation to for-profit companies if a future government tried to overturn existing contracts, thus weakening the state's capacity to seek redress for poor performance. Governments have been averse to deterring potential private financiers by guaranteeing that the public sector will repay losses and assume ownership of the project in the event of the termination of a contract.

CONCLUSION

The rules of the market have become integral to the polity and economy of the United Kingdom. The ascendance of an imaginary market is exemplified by the central place that economic frames of reference now occupy in criminological, as well as policy, thinking. As such, the debate about the private capitalisation of criminal justice is played out on the terms of the naturalised and unquestioned legitimacy of business rules and games in public administration. State regulators can merely 'catch up' with the superior gaming tactics of market players. The normalisation of competition, 'risk' and creative destruction has subsumed the hidden politics, ethical and social costs of privatisation as legitimate subjects of analysis or critique. This is not to say that problems such as fraud, cheating, incompetence or deadlock have not been interrogated as significant matters of public interest. However, serious failures and scandals arising from the performance of private companies are portrayed as predictable and manageable side effects of competition, which are amenable to technical correction.

Recent political thought suggests that, in the wake of an economic crisis, we might be entering an era of 'post-neoliberal politics' in which the extremes of an unregulated free market will secede to some level of state regulation. Prison privatisation is being partially reversed in the United States and Australia, which have introduced moratoria on some areas of outsourcing. England and Wales is travelling in the opposite direction in hastening the transformation of the state towards a 'competition state … a market enforcing and embedding state' (Bonefeld, 2012, p. 635). For some observers, this confirms the surrender of politics to the market. Rather than the state receding, however, a more paradoxical relationship between politics and business is developing as new laws and demands to regulate the consequences of sweeping market reforms have 'to be directed to the state simultaneously as *both implicated actor and potential accomplice*' (Karstedt, 2007, p. 5: emphasis added). Viewed like this, such demands imply that the policing of markets will itself become a significant activity, requiring the kind of resourcing and political commitment that are not forthcoming.

NOTES

1. The 'United Kingdom' refers to the whole jurisdiction of Great Britain and Northern Ireland. It encompasses three different penal systems: England and Wales; Scotland; and Northern Ireland. We focus on England and Wales as the pace and scale of marketisation is the most pronounced there.
2. Although marketisation and co-production are evident in all areas of justice, from policing to the courts, this chapter focuses on developments in the prison and probation services.
3. Estimates of future prison numbers vary widely. By the end of June 2018 the demand for prison spaces is projected to be between 80,300 and 90,900.

REFERENCES

Albert, M. (1997). *Capitalism against capitalism*. London: Whurr Publications.

Albertson, K., & Fox, C. (2012). *Crime and economics: An introduction*. Oxford: Routledge.

Annals of the American Academy of Political and Social Science. (2014). Special edition on *Detaining democracy? Criminal justice and American civic life*, *651*(6).

BBC online. (2013). Serco to pay government back £68.5m over tagging, 19 December, 2013. Retrieved from http://www.bbc.co.uk/news/uk-25448674

Bonefeld, W. (2012). Freedom and the strong state: On German ordoliberalism. *New Political Economy*, *17*(5), 633–656.

British Journal of Community Justice. (2013). Special edition on *Probation: Peering through the uncertainty*, *11*(2–3).

Brown, D. (2013). Prison rates, social democracy, neoliberalism and justice reinvestment. In K. Carrington, M. Ball, E. O'Brie, & J. Tauri (Eds.), *Crime, justice and social democracy: International perspectives* (pp. 70–88). London: Palgrave.

Carter, P. (2003). *Managing offenders, reducing crime: A new approach*. London: Cabinet Office.

Cavadino, M., & Dignan, J. (2006). Penal policy and political economy. *Criminology and Criminal Justice*, *6*(4), 435–456.

Centre for Crime and Justice Studies (CCJS). (2014). *UK justice policy review* (Vol. 3). London: CCJS.

Clarke, J., & Newman, J. (1997). *The managerial state*. London: Sage.

Corcoran, M. S. (2011). Dilemmas of institutionalisation of the penal voluntary sector in England and Wales. *Critical Social Policy*, *31*(1), 30–52.

Corcoran, M. S., & Hucklesby, A. (2013). *The third sector in criminal justice*. ESRC End of Award Briefing paper. Retrieved from http://www.law.leeds.ac.uk/assets/files/research/ccjs/130703-thirdsec-crimjust-briefing-2013.pdf

Coyle, A., Campbell, A., & Neufeld, R. (2003). *Capital punishment: Prison privatisation and human rights*. London: Zed Books.

Dorling, D. (2011). *Injustice: Why social inequality persists*. Bristol: Policy Press.

Garland, D. (2001). *The culture of control*. Chicago, IL: University of Chicago Press.

Gottschalk, M. (2006). *The prison and the gallows: The politics of mass incarceration in America*. Cambridge: Cambridge University Press

Grayling, C. (2012). *Rehabilitation revolution – the next steps. Speech delivered by the minister for justice*. Tuesday, 20 November, 2012.

Guardian. (2012). London 2012 Olympics: G4S failures prompt further military deployment. *Guardian*, July 24, London.

Guardian. (2013). Justice Ministry outsourcing could lead to 'train crash', says watchdog. *Guardian*, June 20, London.

Guardian. (2013). Scale of overcharging for electronic tagging of offenders who were not monitored is at least three times higher than thought. London. *Guardian*, December 19, London.

Hansard. (2012). House of Commons Parliamentary Debates, 15 March 2012, col. 366W.

Hansard. (2013). House of Commons Parliamentary Debates, 20 June 2013, col. 296WH.

Harvey, D. (2007). *A brief history of neoliberalism*. Oxford: Oxford University Press.

Hayek, F. (1960/2009). *The constitution of liberty*. Oxford: Routledge.

H. M. Government. (1991). *Criminal Justice Act*. London: HMSO.

H. M. Government. (2013). *The coalition: Together in the national interest*. London: Cabinet Office.
H. M. Inspectorate of Prisons. (2012). *Report on an announced full follow-up inspection of HMP Wolds*. London: Her Majesty's Inspectorate of Prisons.
H. M. Treasury. (2013). *Spending round 2013*. London: H. M. Treasury.
Incite! Women of Color Against Violence. (2007). *The revolution will not be funded: Beyond the non-profit industrial complex*. Cambridge, MA: South End.
Independent. (2014). G4S allowed to bid for new government contracts after tagging scandal. *Independent*, 14 April, London.
Justice Committee. (2009). *Cutting crime: The case for justice reinvestment*. London: The Stationery Office.
Karstedt, S. (2007). From the crimes of the powerful to the crimes of power: An uncomfortable situation. *Monatsschrift fur Kriminologie und Strafrechtsreform, 2*(3), 78–90.
Lacey, N. (2008). *The prisoners' dilemma: Political economy and punishment in contemporary democracies*. Cambridge: Cambridge University Press.
Le Grand, J. (2007). *The other invisible hand: Delivering services through choice and competition*. Oxford: Princeton University Press.
Leys, C. (2001). *Market-driven politics: Neoliberal democracy and the public interest*. London: Verso.
Lippert, R. K., & Walby, K. (2014). Marketization, knowledge work, and visibility in 'Users Pay' policing in Canada. *British Journal of Criminology*, *54*(2), 260–280.
Ministry of Justice. (2013a). *Transforming rehabilitation: A strategy for reform (2013)*. London: Ministry of Justice.
Ministry of Justice. (2013b, September 4). *Modernisation of the prison estate* (press release). Ministry of Justice, London.
Ministry of Justice. (2013c, December 19). *Best in the business bidding to rehabilitate offenders* (press release). Ministry of Justice, London.
Ministry of Justice. (2013d, June 20). *Updated impact assessment for the offender rehabilitation bill*. Ministry of Justice, London.
National Audit Office. (2003). *The operational performance of PFI prisons*. London: National Audit Office.
Panchamia, N. (2012). *Competition in prisons*. London: Institute for Government.
Pollock, A. M. (2004). *NHS Plc: The privatisation of our healthcare*. London: Verso.
Pratt, J. (2008). Scandinavian exceptionalism in an era of penal excess. Part I: The nature and roots of Scandinavian exceptionalism. *British Journal of Criminology*, *48*(2), 119–137.
Pratt, J., & Erickson, A. (2013). *Contrasts in punishment: An explanation of Anglophone excess and Nordic exceptionalism*. Oxford: Routledge.
Pozen, D. (2003). Managing a correctional marketplace. *Journal of Law and Politics*, *19*, 253–284.
Prison Reform Trust. (2013). *Bromley briefings prison factfile – August*. London: Prison Reform Trust.
Public Accounts Committee. (2013). *Evidence: November 20, 2013*. London: The Stationery Office.
Public Accounts Committee. (2014). *Contracting out public services to the private sector*. 47th report of Session 2013–14. London: The Stationery Office.

Rynne, J., Harding, R. W., & Wortley, R. (2008). Market testing and prison riots: How public sector commercialization contributed to a prison riot. *Criminology and Public Policy*, *7*(1), 117–142.

Standing, G. (2011). *The precariat: The new dangerous class*. London: Bloomsbury.

Telegraph. (2014). G4S pays £109m in prisoner tagging settlement. *Telegraph*, March 12, London.

Telegraph online. (2013). *Ministers keep three South Yorkshire prisons in public hands as fall-out from criminal probe into Serco's tagging contracts continues.* Retrieved from http://www.telegraph.co.uk/finance/newsbysector/supportservices/10467360/Serco-loses-out-on-UK-prisons-contract.html

Wacquant, L. (2000). The new 'peculiar institution': On the prison as surrogate ghetto. *Theoretical Criminology*, *4*(3), 377–393.

Wacquant, L. (2009). *Punishing the poor: The neoliberal government of social security*. London: Duke University Press.

Walmsley, R. (2013). *World prison population list* (10th ed.). Colchester: University of Essex International Centre for Prison Studies.

Wilkinson, R., & Pickett, K. (2009). *The spirit level: Why equality is better for everyone*. Harmondsworth: Penguin.

'*CECI N'EST PAS UNE FOUILLE À CORPS*': THE DENIAL OF STRIP SEARCHES IN BELGIAN PRISONS

Tom Daems

ABSTRACT

Purpose – *This chapter reconstructs and critically examines the recent history of strip searches in Belgium. About 10 years ago the Belgian parliament adopted its first law on prisoners' rights. A major part of the Prison Act of 12 January 2005 deals with disciplinary and control measures. Article 108, in particular, has provoked quite some controversy. It introduced a clear distinction between the (more superficial) search of an inmates' clothes on the one hand, and the (substantially more intrusive) measure of strip searching on the other hand. The main difference between these two measures is that the latter involves forcing prisoners to strip naked. Because of their intrinsic intrusiveness, such strip searches were meant to be exceptional measures: they should only take place following an individual assessment and decision by the prison governor. In practice, however, the prison administration tended to interpret Article 108 somewhat differently and the line between searching an inmate's clothes on the one hand and strip searching on the other became blurred.*

Punishment and Incarceration: A Global Perspective
Sociology of Crime, Law and Deviance, Volume 19, 75–94

ISSN: 1521-6136/doi:10.1108/S1521-613620140000019003

Design/methodology/approach – *I first discuss the problem of order in prisons and explore how strip searches have been regulated in Europe. I then reconstruct the recent history of the regulation of strip searches in Belgium. In order to make sense of this history, I mobilize some of the ideas of Stanley Cohen's sociology of denial, in particular, his distinction between literal, implicatory and interpretive denial, and apply these to the history of strip searches in Belgium.*

Findings – *A consistent finding from this chapter is that the Belgian prison administration has – through creative manoeuvres of interpretive denial – been able to circumvent the new barriers that were erected by the Prison Act of 12 January 2005 and, in doing so, it has been able to continue stripping detainees naked without an individualized decision from the prison governor. The approach that I develop throughout this chapter helps us better appreciate the limits of legal reform and top-down (European) regulation of strip searches.*

Originality/value – *The chapter demonstrates that Stanley Cohen's work on denial is not only useful for scholars who do research on gross human rights violations but also for interpreting more down-to-earth aspects of criminal justice systems across the globe.*

Keywords: Punishment; prison; strip search; denial; dignity; degradation

INTRODUCTION

In popular culture, strip searches in a prison context are sometimes depicted as laughable events. In reality, however, these are often truly invasive and potentially degrading procedures. At the heart of a strip search, which makes it such a contentious part of the problem of order maintenance within a prison setting, is the question of striking a balance between dignity and security. At times, the lack of such a balance is quite obvious to the outside observer. In April 2012 the American Civil Liberties Union (ACLU) called on the Michigan Department of Corrections to abandon a degrading body cavity search. Female inmates were, so the ACLU reported in a press release, '... forced to spread open their labia using their hands, often under unsanitary conditions and in full view of other prisoners' (ACLU, 2012a). Some of the inmates postponed or avoided family visits because they did not want to be subjected to such a procedure. The routine implementation of this body search was halted but nonetheless it was still possible if there was a suspicion of concealed contraband (ACLU, 2012b). More generally, as the treatments of some high-profile foreign suspects such as the French former head of the IMF Dominique Strauss-Kahn or the Indian diplomat Devyani Khobragade indicate (Harris, 2013), and a recent US Supreme Court ruling confirms (Liptak, 2012), strip searches are an integral, routine part of the US criminal justice system.

Evidently, strip search practices vary throughout the world. It seems plausible therefore that, in line with James Whitman's (2003) comparative degradation thesis, which in broad strokes contrasts American harshness with continental European dignity and mildness, a contrast between Europe and the United States can be observed. Such a comparative exercise would require a full-scale research project which has, to our knowledge, not been undertaken thus far. Nonetheless, there are some indications that, in line with other aspects of prison and penal policy (Daems, Van Zyl Smit, & Snacken, 2013; Van Zyl Smit & Snacken, 2009), Europe has also become more strict in terms of regulating strip searches as well as more vigilant about its potentially degrading aspects than other parts of the globe (see below).

This chapter, however, aims to raise some questions about such a seemingly more benign image of European practice. Because strip searches are perceived to be a central and indispensable part of security by prison administrations and staff alike we will argue that such procedures are particularly vulnerable to what Stanley Cohen (2001) referred to as denial: they tend to return in other guises; they are given different names and surrounded by legal euphemism and bureaucratic embellishments aimed at transforming the meaning of what goes on in practice, with the practical result that prisoners themselves, at the end of the day, are still required to strip naked and have their bodies exposed to prison staff. In this chapter we will illustrate such processes of denial by reconstructing the recent history of strip searches in one European jurisdiction, that is Belgium.

The Belgian case is, indeed, particularly interesting to shed light on processes of denial. About 10 years ago, after many years of international critique and internal debate, the Belgian parliament adopted its first law on prisoners' rights. A major part of the Prison Act of 12 January 2005 deals with disciplinary and control measures in a prison setting. Article 108, in particular, has provoked quite some discussion over the past decade. It introduced a clear distinction between the (more superficial) search of an inmate's clothes on the one hand, and the (substantially more intrusive) measure of searching the inmate's body on the other hand. The main difference between these two measures is that the latter involves forcing prisoners to strip naked. Because of their intrinsic intrusiveness, such strip searches were meant to be exceptional measures: they should only take place following an individual assessment and decision by the prison governor. In practice, however, the prison administration tended to interpret Article 108 somewhat differently and the line between searching an inmate's clothes on the one hand and strip searches on the other became blurred. In the section 'Strip Searches in Belgium: A Brief History' of this chapter we will reconstruct the peculiar history of Article 108. In the section 'A History of Interpretive Denial' we will interpret these developments by using some concepts derived from Stanley Cohen's sociology of denial. But before turning to the case of Belgium we will first, in the next section, briefly discuss how strip searches form part of the problem of order within a prison setting and how this practice has come to be regulated within Europe.

ORDER IN PRISON AND THE EUROPEAN REGULATION OF STRIP SEARCHES

The problem of maintaining order has been since long a central and popular theme within the sociology of imprisonment (for useful overviews, see Crewe, 2007; Matthews, 1999; Sparks, Bottoms, & Hay, 1996). Indeed, at first sight it seems somewhat puzzling that institutions, which lock up a large number of (often young and male) inmates and where (unarmed) guards are a minority group, are most of the time relatively peaceful places. Donald Cressey wrote the following about this:

> One of the most amazing things about prisons is that they 'work' at all … Any on-going prison is made up of the coordinated actions of hundreds of people, some of whom hate and distrust each other, love each other, fight each other physically and psychologically, think of each other as stupid or mentally disturbed, 'manage' and 'control' each other, and vie with each other for favours, prestige and money. Often the personnel involved … are not sure whether they are the managers or the managed. Despite these conditions, however, the social system which is a prison does not degenerate into a chaotic mess of social relations which have no order and make no sense. (Cressey, 1961, p. 2, quoted in Sparks et al., 1996, p. 37)

But not all prisons are the same – nor do they stay the same. Recent prison research, in particular, has drawn attention to variations in the social organization of prisons as well as transformations in how order is being negotiated behind prison walls. It has been argued that contemporary prisons in the West have become 'post-disciplinary' (Chantraine, 2006) or 'post-authoritarian' (Van Zyl Smit & Snacken, 2009) where some of the more total or oppressive characteristics of closed institutions, as observed and analysed in early sociologies of imprisonment (e.g. Goffman, 1961; Sykes, 1958), have become more relaxed or replaced by new techniques of prison management. One key theme in such studies on variations in prison regimes concerns the issue of legitimacy, '... the extent to which the staff of different prisons succeed or fail in legitimating their deployment of power and authority and the techniques and strategies which they deploy in seeking to secure such legitimacy' (Sparks et al., 1996, p. 35). Relatedly, there has been a growing academic interest in the so-called 'moral performance' or 'moral climate' of prisons. This type of research aims to go one step further than the question about legitimacy because, as Liebling suggests, '... prisons are about *more* than power relations' (Liebling, 2004, pp. 473–474). Indeed, as she explains, '... what matters to those who live and work "where the action is" in prison is a set of concepts that are all about relationships, fairness, and order, and the quality of their respective treatment by those above them' (Liebling, 2004, p. 458). Prisons, then, even though they share some essential characteristics, can differ markedly in a number of features which have a lasting impact on the experience of imprisonment: '... some prison environments are more survivable than others' (Liebling, 2011, p. 535).

Such findings have been translated into policy formulations about order maintenance which aim to take into account the circumstances that are deemed to be necessary to enhance the legitimacy of decisions and procedures in a prison setting, as well as to increase the quality of life behind bars for inmates and prison staff alike. The notion of 'dynamic security' is probably the best-known of such policy formulations, that is, '... an approach to security, which combines positive staff prisoner relationships with fair treatment and purposeful activities that contribute to their future reintegration into society' (Penal Reform International, 2013, p. 4). The UN *Prison Incident Management Handbook* formulates it as follows:

> Prison staff members need to understand that interacting with prisoners in a humane and equitable way enhances the security and good order of a prison ... Irrespective of staffing ratios, each contact between staff and prisoners reinforces the relationship between the two, which should be a positive one, based on dignity and mutual respect in how people treat each other, and in compliance with international human rights principles and due process. (United Nations, 2013, pp. 21–22)

The 2006 European Prison Rules, which emanate from the Council of Europe, stipulate the following in rule 49 and rule 51.2:

> 49 Good order in prison shall be maintained by taking into account the requirements of security, safety and discipline, while also providing prisoners with living conditions which respect human dignity and offering them a full programme of activities in accordance with Rule 25.
>
> ...
>
> 51.2 The security which is provided by physical barriers and other technical means shall be complemented by the dynamic security provided by an alert staff who know the prisoners who are under their control. (Council of Europe, 2006)

Against such a background it should not come as a surprise that strip searches have become the object of debate and regulation. Strip searches are an integral yet controversial part of prison systems across the globe as they are deemed to be indispensable in order to detect prohibited or dangerous items or substances. But how can such procedures be made more fair and legitimate? Rule 54 of the European Prison Rules gives the following guidelines:

> 54.1 There shall be detailed procedures which staff have to follow when searching:
>
> a. all places where prisoners live, work and congregate;
> b. prisoners;
> c. visitors and their possessions; and
> d. staff.
>
> 54.2 The situations in which such searches are necessary and their nature shall be defined by national law.
> 54.3 Staff shall be trained to carry out these searches in such a way as to detect and prevent any attempt to escape or to hide contraband, while at the same time respecting the dignity of those being searched and their personal possessions.
> 54.4 Persons being searched shall not be humiliated by the searching process.
> 54.5 Persons shall only be searched by staff of the same gender.
> 54.6 There shall be no internal physical searches of prisoners' bodies by prison staff.
> 54.7 An intimate examination related to a search may be conducted by a medical practitioner only.
> 54.8 Prisoners shall be present when their personal property is being searched unless investigating techniques or the potential threat to staff prohibit this.
> 54.9 The obligation to protect security and safety shall be balanced against the privacy of visitors.
> 54.10 Procedures for controlling professional visitors, such as legal representatives, social workers and medical practitioners, etc., shall be the subject of consultation with their professional bodies to ensure a balance between security and safety, and the right of confidential professional access. (Council of Europe, 2006)

In its report about a recent visit to the Netherlands (10–21 October 2011) the European Committee for the Prevention of Torture, a monitoring body that visits detention centres across the 47 member states of the Council of Europe, commented as follows on the fact that it received numerous complaints concerning the frequency of strip searches in Dutch prisons:

> A strip search is a very invasive – and potentially degrading – measure. Therefore, resort to strip searches should be based on an individual risk assessment and subject to rigorous criteria and supervision. Every reasonable effort should be made to minimise embarrassment; detained persons who are searched should not normally be required to remove all their clothes at the same time, e.g. a person should be allowed to remove clothing above the waist and to get dressed before removing further clothing. In addition, more than one officer should, as a rule, be present during any strip search as a protection to detained persons and staff alike. Further, inmates should not be required to undress in the presence of custodial staff of the opposite sex. (European Committee for the Prevention of Torture, 2012, p. 23)

The European Court of Human Rights has dealt at several occasions with the question whether strip searches are acceptable under Article 3 of the European Convention of Human Rights (for a discussion of this issue, see e.g. Van Zyl Smit & Snacken, 2009, pp. 285–290). In principle, prisoners continue to enjoy all the fundamental rights and freedoms guaranteed under the European Convention. Prisoners should not forfeit their Convention rights merely because of their status as persons detained following a conviction. Restriction on those rights must be justified in each individual case (see e.g. European Court of Human Rights, 2011, para. 99). In its case law the European Court has acknowledged that strip searches may be necessary on occasions to ensure prison security or prevent disorder in prisons. Nonetheless, they must be conducted in an appropriate manner so as to show respect to the human dignity of the inmate (European Court of Human Rights, 2001, para. 59). Moreover, they should not be conducted in an arbitrary way (European Court of Human Rights, 2007, para. 47). In addition, the court has argued that strip searches should not take place in a systematic way and need to be precisely motivated with reference to the behaviour of the inmate who is subjected to such a procedure (European Court of Human Rights, 2010, para. 117).

STRIP SEARCHES IN BELGIUM: A BRIEF HISTORY

In the previous section we discussed briefly how strip searches have come to be regulated within a European context, and how such safety procedures relate to larger discussions about 'dynamic security' which, in turn, is informed by recent findings from prison studies. But how does this work out in practice? Below we will reconstruct the recent history of the regulation of strip searches in Belgium. Our objective is to illustrate how the intended effects of innovative legal reform aimed at restricting the use of strip searches and at making them more fair, humane and legitimate in the eyes of inmates have become neutralized by continuing and inventive bureaucratic manoeuvres which intend to redefine what goes on when prisoners are forced to strip naked.

Phase 1 – Legal Innovation: Towards a Restricted Use of Strip Searches (1996–2005)

It has taken a particularly long time before Belgium adopted its first prison law. In June 1996 the then Minister of Justice published a white paper on prison policy and penal policy, which announced a large-scale reform of the prison system. In this white paper it was acknowledged that Belgium lagged behind within Europe in terms of the enactment of prisoners' rights and that immediate legislative action was necessary in order to fulfil its international treaty obligations. The white paper mentioned that the Minister had requested Lieven Dupont, a professor in criminal law and penitentiary law at KU Leuven, to write a draft text for Belgium's first prison act. One year later, in September 1997, professor Dupont finalized his assignment and published the results of his research which were subsequently presented and discussed at a one-day conference in February 1998 (Dupont, 1998). In his draft proposal Dupont stated that strip searches had become routine procedures which were perceived and justified as indispensable instruments in the fight against drug smuggling and drug use inside Belgian prisons. However, so he added, strip searches were not regulated by law and were probably being used way too often. Dupont advised to substantially revise existing practices in order to restrain the use of strip searches (Dupont, 1998, p. 224).

Dupont's recommendations were subsequently forwarded to a newly created commission of experts, chaired by Dupont himself, whose task was to evaluate, elaborate, rework and translate the contents of his report into a draft legal text. In February 2000, this commission published its report and it endorsed Dupont's position to restrain the use of strip searches. To this end the commission advised to introduce an extra procedural barrier: strip searches should no longer be possible without an individualized decision of the prison governor, based on an individual case-by-case assessment.

After several years of parliamentary debate – and some wilful manoeuvres aimed at delaying the legislative process – the Prison Act of 12 January 2005 was eventually adopted (for a discussion, see Daems, Maes, & Robert, 2013; Maes, 2009, 2012; Mary, 2006, 2013; Snacken, 2007). Article 108 of the Prison Act introduced a clear distinction between a search of an inmate's clothes on the one hand, and a search of the body, that is a strip search, on the other. The searching of clothes has the objective to verify that the inmate does not have any objects or substances in his possession that are forbidden or potentially dangerous. In case such a search of a prisoner's clothes is judged to be insufficient, the prison director could by means of an individual decision, order for a search of the body. This includes, if necessary, stripping an inmate of his clothes and inspecting his naked body without touching it. It was explicitly stated that such searches of the body are particularly invasive measures of control and that they should never be executed in a routine way:

> The search of the body is … a much more intrusive measure which is in itself an encroachment of the feeling of honour. Such a search may certainly never be executed in a routine way and is only justified when given specific circumstances or suspicions a search of the prisoner's clothes is not sufficient. (House of Representatives, 2001, p. 179)

Moreover, it was emphasized that there is an important, gradual difference between the search of an inmate's clothes and the search of the body. Searching one's clothes could therefore never include the obligation to fully undress:

> The search of an inmate's clothes means that the clothes are touched and searched in order to verify that the inmate does not have any objects or substances in or underneath his clothes that are forbidden or dangerous. In this respect, one can request an inmate to take of his outer clothes, but one cannot force him to fully undress. The search of the body is a measure that goes much further. This measure not only gives prison staff the permission to force an inmate to fully undress but even to inspect the cavities of his body externally without touching the body. (House of Representatives, 2001, p. 250)

This new legal framework for strip searches was explicitly related to the concept of 'dynamic security' (see above), as formulated in Article 105 of the Prison Act.

Phase 2 – Bureaucratic Obstruction, Act I and Prisoners' Judicial Activism (2007–2013)

On 15 January 2007, Article 108 of the Prison Act came into force but it rapidly became the object of serious controversy. Indeed, notwithstanding the law's rationale to restrict the use of strip searches, prisoners were still forced to strip naked as a standard procedure. On 19 February 2007 the prison administration sent a Collective Letter (no. 86) to all Belgian prisons in order to explain and clarify the new framework for executing strip searches. This Collective Letter introduced a distinction between three different searches of an inmate's clothes: a summary search, a thorough search and a full search of the clothes. In the last case, that is, the full search of an inmate's clothes, prisoners were instructed to fully undress and to hand over their clothes to a prison officer. The prison officer, then, verified – by looking briefly at the naked body of the detainee – whether the inmate had handed over all his clothes and subsequently inspected his clothes. According to the prison administration there was no individual decision of the prison director required for such a procedure since it was, in its opinion, a search of the clothes and not a search of the body (Prison Administration, 2007).

This interpretation, however, provoked critical responses. A number of prisoners openly disagreed with these new procedures and objected that they violated Article 108. Because some prisoners were sanctioned by local prison governors for lack of cooperation with the safety procedures, they filed formal complaints with the Council of State in order to nullify such sanctions arguing that a legal basis was absent because the evidence that led to the disciplinary sanctions was obtained by means of searches that violated Article 108. Between 2007 and 2013 a substantial number of disciplinary sanctions were nullified by the Council of State. In line with the argumentation of the prisoners and their lawyers, the Council of State argued in a large number of cases that the prison administration's so-called 'full search of an inmate's clothes' was, in fact, a search of the body which required an individualized decision of the prison governor. This interpretation was also supported in a number of commentaries on judicial decisions by Belgian legal scholars (see, e.g. De Hert, 2011; Hanoulle & Verbruggen, 2009).

Phase 3 – Legal Change: Introducing Systematic Strip Searches (February–September 2013)

In April 2012 the Minister of Justice declared in the House of Representatives that she planned to revise the whole policy of strip searches. In the wake of a number of violent incidents in prisons and various strikes of prison officers throughout the country, she promised to change the Prison Act of 12 January 2005 in order to make it possible for prison officers to strip search inmates without prior order from the prison governor. In February 2013 the Council of Ministers approved a draft law that would make the necessary adaptations to Article 108. In May 2013 the House of Representatives approved the new rules. On 16 September 2013 the law of 1 July 2013, which introduced a number of important changes to the policy of searches, came into force.

The new Article 108 no longer formulated the search of the inmate's body as an exceptional control measure that was only permitted after an individualized order by the prison governor. Rather, the search of the prisoner's body became a standard procedure in three cases: upon entrance in the prison; prior to being detained in a safety or disciplinary cell; and after a visit at a table in the visiting room or after a conjugal visit. In these cases a separate order from the prison governor was no longer required. In a new Collective Letter (no. 125) of 6 September 2013 the prison administration explained that searches of the prisoner's body were permitted without order from the governor when an inmate had been in contact with persons that were not to be considered as prison staff (Prison Administration, 2013). It was hoped that this legal change would discourage inmates to challenge the strip searches before the Council of State since they were deprived of their ammunition to contest the now legalized practice of standard strip searches. Moreover, the government added an additional justification for making searches of the prisoner's body a standard procedure: it was not only necessary for security reasons but it also helps protecting vulnerable prisoners since they are often put under pressure to smuggle forbidden goods and substances into the prison.

Phase 4 – Judicial Backlash (October 2013–January 2014)

Nonetheless, this legal reform aimed at rewinding the clock proved to be quite controversial. In its advice of 14 March 2013 the Council of State had already formulated serious objections to the draft law. In particular the standardization of the search of the inmate's body, with no possibility to abstain from such a procedure when there is no threat for security, could possibly violate Article 3 of the European Convention of Human Rights, so the Council of State warned. Moreover, the Council of State was very critical about the paucity of the justification for the planned changes to the procedures: the government restricted its explanation to some vague notions about 'multiple problems' and the 'inefficiency' of existing procedures but failed to clarify clearly why the substantial changes were necessary. In addition, some Members of Parliament had objected that the new procedures would be detrimental to the philosophical foundations of the Prison Act and raised doubts about whether it would pass the test of Strasbourg (Daems, 2013). Expressions of concern about the changes were also heard in other corners of the Belgian society: in August 2013 a major Flemish newspaper published a critical article about the standardized strip searches on its cover page (Vanhecke, 2013) and, one month later, the Belgian section of the *Observatoire International des Prisons* criticized the law of 1 July 2013 and warned, again, that the new policy would violate Article 3 of the European Convention of Human Rights (Observatoire International des Prisons, 2013, pp. 56–57).

Against the background of the earlier post-2007 phase of prisoners' litigation against the rules as introduced by the prison administration (see above), it was to be expected that inmates and their lawyers would also challenge this new policy. And, indeed, on 12 September 2013, less than a week after the publication of the law of 1 July 2013 in the Belgian Official Journal, and just a couple of days before these rules came into force, a former inmate who ran the risk of being imprisoned again, filed a complaint with the Constitutional Court, arguing inter alia that the new policy violated Article 3 of the European Convention of European Rights. With its arrest of 30 October 2013 the Constitutional Court suspended the new rules relating to strip searches: it found that the automatic strip searches in the three cases mentioned in the reformulated Article 108 were not sufficiently justified on the basis of the behaviour of the detainee and, therefore, went beyond what is strictly necessary (Constitutional Court, 2013, para. B.9).

Shortly thereafter the UN Committee against Torture (CAT) also joined the debate. Under the heading 'Full body searches' the CAT adopted the following concluding observations at its 1201st meeting, held on 18 November 2013, when it considered the third periodic report of Belgium:

> The Committee is concerned about the amendments made to the Principles Act by the Act of 1 July 2013, which authorizes routine full body searches when a detainee has been in contact with the outside world. Although the Constitutional Court has ruled that the application of these measures should be suspended, the Committee is still concerned that they have not yet been repealed and could be implemented in the future ... The Committee urges the State party to repeal the provisions of the Act of 1 July 2013 which authorize systematic body searches. The State party should ensure that body searches are conducted only in exceptional cases and by the least intrusive means possible, with full respect for the dignity of the person. The State party should

> take steps to adopt precise and strict instructions to restrict the use of body searches. (Committee against Torture, 2014, p. 5)

On 29 January 2014 the Constitutional Court, which had earlier provisionally suspended the new rules related to strip searches, repealed the relevant passages of Article 108, based on its earlier reasoning, that is that systematic strip searches that are not being justified precisely with reference to an inmate's behaviour are excessive measures of control (Constitutional Court, 2014, B13).

Phase 5 – Bureaucratic Obstruction, Act II (January 2014–...)

The repeal of the relevant passages of Article 108 may, at first sight, seem like a victory for those inmates (and their lawyers) who have fought a long battle over the admissibility of strip searches in Belgian prisons. However, the story does not end here. The day after the decision of the Constitutional Court the prison administration issued a new Collective Letter (no. 126) on 30 January 2014 which intended to clarify the new rules on strip searches. In this letter the prison administration introduced a new distinction, that is between the so-called 'one-off search of the inmate's body' on the one hand, and the 'recurrent search of the inmate's body' on the other. In the latter case, the prison governor can decide that an inmate's body has to be searched systematically, over a fixed period of time, on a number of occasions, as mentioned in the decision (Prison Administration, 2014). These rules apply at the time of writing (May 2014) and it is to be expected that, once again, they will be challenged before the Belgian courts.

A HISTORY OF INTERPRETIVE DENIAL

How can we make sense of the recent history of strip searches in Belgium? And what does this history tell us about the effectiveness of (European) regulatory action in this field? Stanley Cohen's work on denial might be a useful guide here. In his last major research project Cohen was mainly preoccupied with the question: 'what do we do with our knowledge about the suffering of others, and what does this knowledge do to us?' (Cohen, 2001, p. x). Cohen focused his attention in particular on serious human rights violations, ranging from the torture and ill-treatment of Palestinian detainees by Israeli security forces during the *intifada* (Cohen & Golan, 1991) to major atrocities committed by authoritarian regimes (Cohen, 1993, 1995a, 1996, 2001). His own personal experience in the human rights movement in Israel, and, in particular, his sense of disillusionment with the fact that almost nothing happened with the information about human rights violations that was abundantly available and that circulated widely through various communication channels, sparked his interest in the question about what happens with all this information once it is out there (Cohen, 1995b; Taylor, 2005). As he wrote in the introduction to a report devoted to this theme:

> My project might be called 'After The Report'. Its aim is to place on the agenda of the human rights community some serious consideration about what happens to all the knowledge that we generate. There is a paradox in the heart of the human rights movement: we believe that if people 'only knew' what was happening they would do something, but we have learnt that just letting know is not enough. (Cohen, 1995b, p. iv)

Cohen became particularly concerned with the role of language and how certain acts, such as torture, which are often unambiguously exposed and vividly described in human rights reports become the object of 'a struggle to define reality' or 'epistemological politics':

> The event itself should be simple enough to describe … the primal scene is simple, and sickeningly identical from case to case … But the technical problems inherent in representing this scene – how the experience is memorized, conveyed to others, corroborated, translated into a public language – are only compounded by its political context. There is always a struggle to define reality, an epistemological politics. On the one side, there are the forces to whom torture is real, to be denounced, to be abolished: the victim, international prohibitions and laws, human-rights organizations. On the other, there is the organized power of the state, denying that 'it' happens, calling it something else, or justifying it as necessary, or even as something that serves a higher moral good. A history of torture is a history of talking about torture. (Cohen, 1991, p. 23)

Cohen's case of the interrogation of Palestinian detainees in the Occupied Territories illustrates this nicely. In 1987 the so-called 'Landau-Commission', which had to report on the interrogation practices of the Israeli secret services, suggested that some form of 'moderate physical pressure' might be necessary in order to interrogate efficiently. This phrase was widely criticized as it opened the door for abuse: '… the Commission ended up legitimating the use of torture under another name' (Cohen & Golan, 1991, p. 25). In their report for human rights organization B'Tselem Cohen and his colleague Daphna Golan inserted drawings about the interrogation techniques that were routinely used by the security forces in order to pierce through such talk. As Cohen explained: 'We wanted to undermine the function of political language ("moderate physical pressure") that Orwell pointed to: "Such phraseology is needed if one wants to name things without calling up mental pictures of them"' (Cohen, 1991, p. 27). History repeated itself more recently, in the war against terrorism after 9/11, when various interrogation techniques – such as waterboarding – became the object of similar 'struggles to define reality' (on this, see Cohen, 2006).

Cohen usefully distinguishes between three variations of denial: *literal* denial ('the assertion that something did not happen or is not true'), *interpretive* denial ('the raw facts or not being denied, but they are given a different meaning from what seems apparent to others') and *implicatory* denial (denial of the 'psychological or moral implications that might follow from the facts') (Cohen, 1995b, pp. 23–24). These distinctions, as well as Cohen's general observations on denial, are also instructive for understanding the recent history of strip searches in Belgium. *Literal* denial hardly happened. There have been occasions where inmates and prison authorities have disputed about the presence or absence of a decision of the prison governor but literal denial was not the dominant form of denial. *Implicatory* denial took place more often. In one case before the Council of State, for example, the government deliberately tried to minimize the implications of a strip search by arguing that under the rules as stipulated in Collective Letter no. 86 an inmate was never asked to present himself naked before the prison guards. The detainee was 'only' obliged to take off his clothes and to hand these over for inspection. In addition, inmates can undress in a cubicle or behind a screen and a prison guard 'only' checked if all clothes had been handed over (Council of State, 2011, para. 4.2). The suggestion to the judges in the court was obvious: the so-called full searches of the clothes, as executed in daily life, are significantly less intrusive than described by the litigating inmates. In another case the government argued that, since the procedure did not involve touching the body of the inmate, and the verification of whether the inmate had handed over all his clothes to the guard took place in a 'very discrete' way, one could hardly state that the detainee's feelings of dignity were violated (Council of State, 2012, para. 5.5). In such cases of implicatory denial, then, the raw facts are not denied but it is argued that the applied procedures are not that intrusive: procedures are carefully adhered to and monitored; the objective of the search is an inspection of the clothes of the detainee, not his body which implies that his naked body is only briefly and superficially watched at in order to verify that all clothes have been handed over; in the end, then, so the authorities argue, full searches of the clothes belong unmistakenly to a different category than searches of the body and these are, in any case, indispensable to guarantee security within the institution.

It is Cohen's third form of denial, however, which dominates our historical reconstruction: the history of strip searches in Belgium is above all a story of *interpretive* denial where inmates (and their lawyers) and the prison authorities (and their lawyers) have disputed the meaning of what actually happens when inmates are being searched. The Collective Letter no. 86 of 19 February 2007 clearly intended to neutralize the innovative aspects of the Prison Act of 12 January 2005 and to prevent realizing its overall objective, that is to restrict the use of strip searches. By introducing a new figure (the 'full search of an inmate's clothes'), which was neither mentioned in Article 108 nor in the Parliamentary preparatory documents, the prison administration circumvented the procedural barriers that the legislator had erected: it cleverly re-classified what it was doing and continued forcing prisoners to strip naked.

The large number of disputes that inmates brought before the Belgian courts since 2007 demonstrates how vigorously this interpretation came to be challenged – and partly with success. The government's attempt to stop prisoners' litigation by turning strip searches into a standard procedure via the law of 1 July 2013 backfired. The Constitutional Court reinstated the original wording of Article 108 and therefore endorsed the original objective of the Prison Act of 12 January 2005, that is that strip searches should not be treated lightly. Nonetheless, as we have seen, the story does not end here. One day after the decision of the Constitutional Court the prison administration conjured up yet another creative manoeuvre by introducing the so-called 'recurrent search of the inmate's body' which is, arguably, again violating the original intentions of the legislator. The prison administration, then, continues constructing a parallel system of norms, with a central objective to continue with standard strip searches, as if the Prison Act of 12 January 2005 was never voted in parliament.

CONCLUSION

In *La trahison des images*, the Belgian surrealist painter René Magritte depicted a smoking pipe and added the French words '*ceci n'est pas une pipe*' ('this is not a pipe'). When you look at the painting you see a pipe – but it is not a pipe, so Magritte argued: it is an image of a pipe. As he explained:

> The famous pipe. How people reproached me for it! And yet, could you stuff my pipe? No, it's just a representation, is it not? So if I had written on my picture 'This is a pipe', I'd have been lying! (Magritte, cited in Semrau, 1989, p. 141)

Our case of interpretive denial in a prison context – where things are not always what they seem – has some links to Magritte's 1929 canvass but the consequences are obviously much less innocent. Framing the history of strip searches with the assistance of Cohen's work on denial also helps us better appreciate the limits of legal reform and top-down (European) regulation of strip searches. Undoubtedly, some major progress has been made throughout Europe in terms of prisoners' rights. Moreover, the basic fact that rules that are written in law books can be challenged before the courts is a major step forward, in particular in an area of social life that has for too long been literally closed off from legal regulation. Nonetheless, new rules and stricter regulations are no guarantee for practices to change or disappear. A focus on processes of denial demonstrates that, notwithstanding major legal reform, the same old practices can continue happening but that they are just named differently. Moreover, as the Belgian case demonstrates, such struggles to define reality can go on for many years with various twists at the level of discourse, but with little changes in the field. We can write a history on torture about progress and abolition but also a history of the justifications of torture, so Cohen (2006) instructed his readers. The same holds for strip searches: a story of progress and stricter regulation can definitely be written but the more revealing history – and at the same time the more disturbing one – is a history of justification and denial.

REFERENCES

ACLU. (2012a). *Body cavity searches at Michigan's women's Huron valley correctional facility*. Retrieved from https://www.aclu.org/print/prisoners-rights-womens-rights/body-cavity-searches-michigans-womens-huron-valley-correctional. Accessed on April 12.

ACLU. (2012b). *Michigan women's prison halts degrading routine body cavity searches.* Retrieved from https://www.aclu.org/print/womens-rights/michigan-womens-prison-halts-degrading-routine-body-cavity-searches. Accessed on April 12.

Chantraine, G. (2006). La prison post-disciplinaire. *Déviance et Société*, *30*(3), 273–288.

Cohen, S. (1991). Talking about torture in Israel. *Tikkun*, *6*(6), 23–30, 89–90.

Cohen, S. (1993). Human rights and crimes of the state: The culture of denial. *Australian and New Zealand Journal of Criminology*, *26*(2), 97–115.

Cohen, S. (1995a). State crimes of previous regimes: Knowledge, accountability, and the policing of the past. *Law and Social Inquiry*, *20*, 7–50.

Cohen, S. (1995b). *Denial and acknowledgement: The impact of information about human rights violations*. Jerusalem: The Hebrew University of Jerusalem – Center for Human Rights.

Cohen, S. (1996). Government responses to human rights reports: Claims, denials, and counterclaims. *Human Rights Quarterly*, *18*(3), 517–543.

Cohen, S. (2001). *States of denial. Knowing about atrocities and suffering*. Cambridge: Polity.

Cohen, S. (2006). Neither honesty nor hypocrisy: The legal reconstruction of torture. In T. Newburn & P. Rock (Eds.), *The politics of crime control: Essays in honour of David Downes*. Oxford: Oxford University Press.

Cohen, S., & Golan, D. (1991). *The interrogation of Palestinians during the intifada: Ill-treatment, 'moderate physical pressure' or torture?* Jerusalem: B'Tselem, The Israeli Information Center for Human Rights in the Occupied Territories.

Committee against Torture. (2014). *Concluding observations on the third period report of Belgium*. CAT/C/BEL/CO/3. Retrieved from http://daccess-dds-ny.un.org/doc/UNDOC/GEN/G14/400/46/PDF/G1440046.pdf?OpenElement. Accessed on January 3.

Constitutional Court. (2013). Decision no. 143/2013 of 30 October 2013.

Constitutional Court. (2014). Decision no. 20/2014 of 29 January 2014.

Council of Europe. (2006). *Recommendation Rec(2006)2 of the Committee of Ministers to member states on the European Prison Rules (Adopted by the Committee of Ministers on 11 January 2006 at the 952nd meeting of the Ministers' Deputies)*. Strasbourg: Council of Europe.

Council of State. (2011). Decision no. 216.284 of 16 November 2011.

Council of State. (2012). Decision no. 218.695 of 28 March 2012.

Crewe, B. (2007). The sociology of imprisonment. In Y. Jewkes (Ed.), *Handbook on prisons*. Cullompton: Willan Publishing.

Daems, T. (2013). De geest is uit de fles: Wijzigingen titels V, VI en VII van de basiswet gevangeniswezen en rechtspositie van gedetineerden. *Panopticon*, *34*(6), 513–522.

Daems, T., Maes, E., & Robert, L. (2013). Crime, criminal justice and criminology in Belgium. *European Journal of Criminology*, *10*(2), 237–254.

Daems, T., Van Zyl Smit, D., & Snacken, S. (Eds.). (2013). *European penology?* Oxford: Hart Publishing.

De Hert, P. (2011). Onderzoek van gevangeniskledij of fouillering op het lichaam? *Tijdschrift voor Strafrecht*, *12*(1), 80–83.

Dupont, L. (Ed.). (1998). *Op weg naar een beginselenwet gevangeniswezen*. Leuven: Universitaire Pers Leuven.

European Committee for the Prevention of Torture. (2012, August 9). *Report to the Government of the Netherlands on the visit to the Netherlands carried out by the European Committee for the Prevention of Torture and Inhuman or Degrading Treatment or Punishment (CPT) from 10 to 21 October 2011*. Strasbourg: Council of Europe.

European Court of Human Rights. (2001). Iwanczuk v. Polen, Decision no. 25196/94 of 15 November 2001.

European Court of Human Rights. (2007). Frérot v. France, Decision no. 70204/01 of 12 June 2007.

European Court of Human Rights. (2010). Ciupercescu v. Roumania, Decision no 35555/03 of 15 June 2010.

European Court of Human Rights. (2011). Stummer v. Austria, Decision no. 37452/02 of 7 July 2011.

Goffman, E. (1961). *Asylums: Essays on the social situation of mental patients and other inmates*. Garden City: Doubleday.

Hanoulle, K., & Verbruggen, F. (2009). 'Fouille'-arrest? Foei, arrest! Het schaamteloos uitkleden van (de rechten van) gedetineerden. *Nullum Crimen*, *4*, 208–211.

Harris, G. (2013). Outrage in India, and retaliation. Over a female diplomat's arrest in New York. *The New York Times*, December 17.

House of Representatives. (2001). Final report of the commission 'Principles Act on the prison system and the legal position of detainees'. *Parliamentary documents of the House of Representatives*. DOC 50 1076/001, February 2.

Liebling, A. (2004). *Prisons and their moral performance. A study of values, quality, and prison life*. Oxford: Oxford University Press.

Liebling, A. (2011). Moral performance, inhuman and degrading treatment and prison pain. *Punishment and Society*, *13*(5), 530–550.

Liptak, A. (2012). Supreme Court ruling allows strip searches for any arrest. *The New York Times*, April 2.

Maes, E. (2009). *Van gevangenisstraf naar vrijheidsstraf. 200 jaar Belgisch gevangeniswezen*. Antwerp: Maklu.

Maes, E. (2012). From prison sentence to deprivation of liberty. A brief history of two centuries of legal regulation of the Belgian prison regime (1795–2006). *European Journal of Crime, Criminal Law and Criminal Justice*, *20*(1), 81–97.

Mary, P. (2006). La nouvelle loi pénitentiaire belge. Retour sur un processus de réforme (1996–2006). *Courrier hebdomadaire du CRISP*, *1916*, 5–51.

Mary, P. (2013). *Enjeux contemporains de la prison*. Brussels: FUSL.

Matthews, R. (1999). *Doing time. An introduction to the sociology of imprisonment*. Basingstoke: Palgrave.

Observatoire International des Prisons. (2013). *Notice de l'état du système carcéral belge*. Brussels: OIP – section belge.

Penal Reform International. (2013). *Balancing security and dignity in prisons: A framework for preventive monitoring*. London: Penal Reform International.

Prison Administration. (2007). *Collective letter no. 86 of 19 February 2007*. Brussels: FOD Justitie.

Prison Administration. (2013). *Collective letter no. 125 of 6 September 2013*. Brussels: FOD Justitie.

Prison Administration. (2014). *Collective letter no. 126 of 30 January 2014*. Brussels: FOD Justitie.

Semrau, J. (1989). Magritte, Godard, and Walter Abish's architectonic fiction. *Studia Anglica Posnaniensia*, *22*, 141–152.

Snacken, S. (2007). Penal policy and practice in Belgium. *Crime and Justice: A Review of Research*, *36*, 127–215.

Sparks, R., Bottoms, A., & Hay, W. (1996). *Prisons and the problem of order*. Oxford: Clarendon.

Sykes, G. M. (1958). *The society of captives. A study of a maximum security prison*. Princeton, NJ: Princeton University Press.

Taylor, L. (2005). The other side of the street. *Social Justice*, *32*(2), 82–88.
United Nations. (2013). *Prison incident management handbook*. New York, NY: United Nations.
Vanhecke, N. (2013). Harde kritiek op naaktfouilles. *De Standaard*, August 12.
Van Zyl Smit, D., & Snacken, S. (2009). *Principles of European prison law and policy: Penology and human rights*. Oxford: Oxford University Press.
Whitman, J. Q. (2003). *Harsh justice. Criminal punishment and the widening divide between America and Europe*. Oxford: Oxford University Press.

STUCK: CONDITIONS OF CANADIAN CONFINEMENT

Rose Ricciardelli, Hayley Crichton and Lisa Adams

ABSTRACT

Purpose – *In this chapter, we explicate the evolution of Canadian corrections, the political, social and judicial realities that have shaped punishment and imprisonment over history. We reveal how such factors continue to leave their mark on the current Canadian federal criminal justice system and its structures of incarceration.*

Design/methodology/approach – *A comprehensive review of accessible literatures detailing the nation's development of punishment and incarceration is presented. The history of imprisonment is traced up to the current year and the role of penal populism as theorized by Garland (2001) and, later, Pratt (2007) is presented to discern the motivations for the current punitive correctional rhetoric, as well as its impact on conditions of confinement and program implementation in penitentiaries.*

Findings – *Canada's correctional history is largely shaped by how punishment is defined and how such definitions are influenced by members of society; including victims, perpetrators, politicians and media personalities. The realities of current conditions of confinement have been impacted by social and political pressures that encourage increasingly*

Punishment and Incarceration: A Global Perspective
Sociology of Crime, Law and Deviance, Volume 19, 95–120

ISSN: 1521-6136/doi:10.1108/S1521-613620140000019004

punitive policies oriented towards 'tough on crime' initiatives. Current corrections are characterized by overcrowding, concerns about rehabilitative programming and resource allocation and mental health care.

Originality/value – *Recent legislative amendments have solidified a 'tough on crime' agenda in Canada, however the process underlying the movement towards the acceptance, even public demand, for such legislative changes remain in need of dissemination; particularly in light of the decades of decreasing crime rates in the country.*

Keywords: Prison; Canada; penal populism; correctional system; overcrowding; punishment

INTRODUCTION

Corrections in Canada function as one branch of the broader criminal justice system; they are heavily shaped by public and political pressures enacted in governmental legislation and policy decisions. Conditions of confinement in penitentiaries are then influenced by political shifts in conceptualizations of incarceration (and the objectives of imprisonment). The relatively recent return to a punitive agenda in Canadian incarceration can be understood, at least in part, as a result of shifting Canadian ideologies and from historical shifts in the United States; the increasing punitiveness first exemplified in the 1970s by American policy makers and political actors. The transition in correctional rhetoric, away from rehabilitative practices to punitive measures, in the 1970s was evident in both North America and Britain; despite emergent academic literature supporting less punitive movements (Grassian, 2006; Pratt, 2013a, 2013b).

'Penal populism', as conceptualized by Garland (2001) and later embraced by Pratt (2007), suggests that, increasingly, changes in penal policy are the result of public pressures and political actors looking to ensure votes – often through 'get-tough' initiatives focused on crime control. Although the Canadian criminal justice system differs from the American (e.g. sentence lengths, correctional structures and judicial processes), Canada has adopted many of the same practices and thought processes surrounding incarceration and conditions of confinement as evidenced by recent policy changes. For example, Bill C-10, as passed under the Harper administration in September, 2011, included amendments to previous bills that sought to increase sentence length, implement harsh mandatory minimum sentencing practices and ensure persons convicted of many offences, specifically convictions that now carry mandatory minimums, are ineligible for conditional sentences. Though such legislative amendments may be impacted by the proximity of the United States, the result of these changes inevitably change how Canadian prisoners 'do time' (Grassian, 2006; Jackson, 1983).

Over decades, even centuries, changing demographic trends, as well as social and political idiosyncrasies influenced Canadian corrections. Canada's correctional history is largely shaped by how punishment is defined as well as how such definitions are influenced by members of society; including victims, perpetrators, politicians and media personalities. The Correctional Service of Canada (CSC) is the organizing entity responsible for the care, control and custody of federally sentenced prisoners in Canada as well as policy implementation and the execution of rehabilitative programs and services. Yet, corrections have evolved out of inquiries and commissions that developed through – what may resemble – a back and forth staggering of objectives tied to punishment and/or humanist concerns that seemed to always exist in a constant state of reform. Starting around the 17th century, penal sentences imposed on *wrong doers* largely *were* to act as deterrents, as a means of maintaining public confidence in the *justice* system and as barriers to recidivism; the latent function was to promote the prisoner's potential for rehabilitation, often intended by altering his or her psychological state and personality. In the 20th century, scholars confirmed that the prison environment was shaped by its own rules, ethics and codes of conduct (Ricciardelli, 2014b; Sykes, 1958; Trammell, 2012), constituting, arguably, a total institution (Goffman, 1961). In such an environment, some have argued, the reshaping of each prisoner's identity was expected (Goffman, 1961; McGrath, 1976, p. 577). The intention of prison then, understood as behavioural reformation through punishment, was to discourage recidivism and, even more arguably, rehabilitate persons convicted of a crime.

Recently, despite the steady decline in Canadian crime rates over decades (Correctional Service of Canada [CSC], 2010) and in part as a result of the 9/11 terrorist attack on the United States, any positive evolution in attitudes towards crime and its perpetrators among the public was muted and instead attitudes again favoured tougher stances on crime and offenders. This transition was supported by political pressures (e.g. the overt operational changes emphasizing issues concerning public safety) and the establishment of Public Safety Canada in 2003 (CSC, 2010). Policy initiatives, such as those that exemplify 'tough on crime' rhetoric, demonstrate these operational changes and directly impact the increasingly overcrowded prisons. This is despite the widespread recognition that incarceration does not deter or prevent future crime or create retribution and is counterproductive to rehabilitation.

To this end, after reviewing the history of corrections more generally, we begin with a presentation of how the influence of British and French rule, combined with American influences, left the Canadian correctional system traversing many challenges; each influence contributing to its evolution. Next we highlight how, in the 20th century, many social and political changes, such as the various commissions and/or inquiries, continued to shape imprisonment. We present specific challenges facing corrections today and elaborate on how, in essence, 'prisons reflect the society which constructs them' (Gosselin, 1982, p. 14). The objective is to demonstrate the current state of corrections in Canada in light of its humanitarian and punitive ideals.

EARLY DAYS: THE START OF CORRECTIONS IN CANADA

In the 16th century, European explorers, like Jacques Cartier in 1534 and Marquis de La Roche in 1598, brought with them to North America the influence of the French government. In this political climate, prisoners underwent harsh punishment, consisting of physical pain and humiliation, or were transported and then abandoned in other countries. The 17th and 18th centuries represented a punitive movement in corrections, in an environment characterized by imported illness and cultural nuances from France (e.g. drawing from the mutilation, floggings and hangings common place in France, exemplified in the fate of those who attempted to take their King's life) and the rapidly growing fur trade. Any rule violators were executed (e.g. hung) or subjected to brutal treatment and their remains were often left for public viewing as a method of deterrence and disgrace. The prohibition movement of the mid-1600s exacerbated the use of physical punishment, banishment and execution; some fuelled by criminal activities involving alcohol consumption and distribution (Carrigan, 1991). Thus, in the 17th and 18th centuries the necessity of prison was less pronounced given the preference for corporal and capital punishment (Cellard, 2000). Prisons and holding centres, designed for the short-term incarceration of people – persons treated with little humanity – awaiting trial, execution or release, were fortress-type facilities (Kirkpatrick, 1965).

In this era, English law differed little from French law and the British or English settlers, too, made a punitive mark in the then recognized English Canada (the Maritimes). Most often men, although women were not fully excluded, were victims of corporal and/or capital punishment; punishment was viewed as the State's retribution against the 'criminal' (Carrigan, 1991, p. 299). Later, in newly found Halifax (1749), identifying criminals and what defined a crime remained haphazard; common inhabitants were given permission to arrest *suspicious* people. Pre-confederation crimes in the Maritimes were either simplistic acts (e.g. fortune telling, keeping a disorderly house, obstructing the street, fighting) or involved political bureaucracies (e.g. citizens were abducted and forced into naval and military combat without any negative judicial impact on the naval officers behind the movement) (Carrigan, 1991). The fact that crime was framed as a nuisance and was largely undefined led to English settlers building their first jail and as political bureaucracies continued to prosper in English Canada – early evidence of penal populism – prominent citizens were spared more severe punishments; their cases were even dropped after their 'disappearance' (Carrigan, p. 303). Overall, *an eye for an eye* philosophy dominated (see Carrigan, 1991) under British and French rule.

The late 1700s, however, brought about new influences (arguably an age of enlightenment) shaped by American practice. The American Quakers of Philadelphia (1789) introduced the penitentiary as an alternative to corporal punishment; they argued that 'offenders' could become 'penitent' and their behaviours could be reformed if imprisoned in segregation and offered opportunities for rehabilitation through labour and reflection. In Canada, administrators of the U.S.'s Philadelphia Quakers penitentiary in 1789 played a central role in the development of the Kingston penitentiary (opened in 1835) as an arguably more humane alternative to the harsh punishments of the time (CSC, 2007). The idea that work and training lead to a reduction in crime supported a movement towards long-term imprisonment in corrections – an idea that spread to England as an alternative to exiling 'offenders' to the colonies, which includes Canada (CSC, 2007). In the 18th century 'thinkers', like Cesare Beccaria, who opposed the death penalty and instead advocated for fair and proportional punishment in accordance to the crime committed, viewed punishment as an opportunity for the criminal to 'mend his ways' (Cellard, 2000).

The works of John Howard (a former prisoner) and Elizabeth Fry (a wealthy English mother of 11), both motivated towards reform, also moulded Canadian corrections in the 18th century. Fry, influenced by the conditions of incarceration of female prisoners, was in sync with Howard's views that the well-being of a prisoner should be prioritized. Said another way, they argued that prison should be a place for 'penitence, learning, self-discipline, meditation and repentance' (Cellard, 2000, p. 11) where prisoners can reflect on their actions, lessons learned and grow as people. Prison was to no longer represent a place of exile or punishment. Instead it was a communal work environment, segregated by gender and age (e.g. adult, youth, male, female), with periods of silence during the day to allow prisoners time to reflect and solitary confinement at night as time for prisoners to seek repentance.

MORE RECENT TIMES: THE 19TH CENTURY

Historical wars (e.g. American Revolutionary and Napoleon), riots and political turmoil in the early 19th century increased immigration to the Maritimes (Carrigan, 1991). Violence, incivility and crime escalated yet conviction rates remained low; prisons could not hold high numbers of 'criminals'. This triggered the opening of the Kingston prison in 1835, which, in the 1940s, united Upper and Lower Canada so both could use the facility to house 'criminals' (Carrigan, 1991). Many suggest that Canadian corrections as recognized today 'dates back to the building of the Kingston Penitentiary in 1835. For more than 30 years, Kingston Penitentiary was operated as a provincial jail until the passage of the *British North America Act* (1867) established federal and provincial responsibilities for justice' (CSC, 2010). This Act divided corrections between central Parliament (federal, persons sentenced to two years or more) and provincial legislatures (provincial or territorial, persons sentenced to a maximum of two years less a day) (Cellard, 2000). Moreover, it directed increased attention towards meeting the needs of individuals, across gender, age, mental and social health as well as skill development (e.g. a carpentry shop, shoemakers shops and other venues of vocational learning were included in Kingston Penitentiary), an ideal previously introduced in Canada by Howard (Cellard, 2000).

The humane values and principles that were to inform the initial objectives of the Kingston Penitentiary slowly deteriorated as the operational functioning of the prison began to contradict such ideals. The increased costs to run Kingston's prison created a great deal of disillusion as did trying to reconcile punishment (reparation) with rehabilitation. Attitudes of 'vengeance and dissuasion' among prison officials quickly prompted increased confinement – viewed as a cheaper option than running programs – a belief that has become far too entrenched in social thinking (Cellard, 2000, p. 14). In 1848, George Brown, a member of parliament, led an investigation that resulted in a 300-page document – the Brown Commission – citing 11 criminal charges and 121 counts that uncovered the abuses of Kingston Penitentiary's first warden, Henry Smith, who was suspended and later – after serving for 14 years as warden – dismissed by Governor General Lord Elgin (CSC, 2010). Indeed, 20 years after the Kingston Penitentiary opened, the Brown Commission revealed the prevalence of the inhumane treatment of prisoners including prisoners being whipped and flogged – even children as young as eight (Cellard, 2000). Other challenges, beyond sentencing principals being inconsistent, included food rations often being restricted to bread and water (*punishment diet*); prisoners being shackled; submersed in water; boxed; prohibited from speaking to; looking at or gesturing towards other prisoners; darkened, small and ill-equipped cells and formally untrained officers operating the facilities (Coyle, 2012; CSC, 2010). It was clear, the warden – in his or her position of authority – was influential and strategic in determining the treatment of prisoners, and even with the building of new facilities, prisons remain intentionally 'separate and away' from where people[1] live in communities (Coyle, 2012; Pratt, 2013a, 2013b).

In 1868, the first *Penitentiary Act* was passed, leading to existing prisons (e.g. Saint John, New Brunswick 1841 and Nova Scotia 1844) in the Maritimes coming under federal jurisdiction and later to the construction of more federal prisons in Quebec (1873), Manitoba (1877), British Colombia (1878) and New Brunswick (1880) (CSC, 2010), as well as a recognized need for the administrative responsibility of prisons and the death penalty[2] to be revisited; resulting in the 'widening of the penal net' (Cellard, 2000, p. 18). Changing understandings of crime combined with new rationales (e.g. social conditions, like poverty and industrial growth) for why people commit crimes emerged in the 19th century. These reasons led the press and government officials across Canada to voice concerns about the *purported* rise of a 'permanent criminal class'; especially in Ontario where urbanization and industrialization were most expansive (Beattie, 1977; Bellomo, 1972; Boritch, 2005, p. 139). By mid-century, crime and disorder in Ontario were *alleged* to have reached epidemic proportions. The advent of Confederation (1867) in Canada urged Prime Minister John A. MacDonald to adopt a more uniform approach to penal law; one consistently followed across the expanding country (as provinces continued to join the confederation). The first ever Criminal Code of Canada emerged in

1892, with the new philosophy of 'innocent until proven guilty', which denoted the continued abolition of the physical torture of prisoners and the right of the accused to seek legal representation to help prove his or her innocence (Cellard, 2000).

A growing and united Canada then brought increased structure to how prisons should be administrated, monitored and made accountable; yet operational costs continued to escalate alongside rates of incarceration and recidivism. This was compounded by the recognition that many prisoners had diagnosable mental illnesses; prompting the need for additional resources and facilities to meet prisoners' unique health needs – the advent of the *asylum*. Throughout Canada's correctional history 'the criminally insane were handed off between prison cells, infirmary beds, and provincial asylums until after the Second World War – confined, but not treated' (CSC, 2010). Although efforts were made towards implementing justice in a consistent manner, with fiscal responsibility and appropriate treatment, that sought to acknowledge prisoners' needs and the possible impetus for their criminal activity, prison conditions continued to deteriorate; living conditions became, in essence, the primary means of punishment – laced with physical and psychological hardship (Cellard, 2000).

A NEW ERA: OR MORE OF THE SAME?

Corrections in the early 20th century were shaped by war, prison riots and the Great Depression, although World War I had a liberating influence on societal values (a movement away from the conservative restrictions of the late 19th century) where instant gratification prospered and respect for law and authority dwindled (Boritch, 2005; CSC, 2007). Rising prison costs within an economically unstable social climate necessitated fewer persons be incarcerated to save money (Boritch, 2005). Meanwhile, the Biggar–Nickle–Draper Committee in the early 1920s, appointed through the Department of Justice, advocated for changes in penitentiary regulations including that prisoners be paid wages for their work, given more time outside their cells and that libraries and educational facilities be improved.

Later, the government sought to create a 'social safety net' (e.g. Medicare and unemployment insurance) (Carrigan, 1991; CSC, 2010), and the rise in prisoner strikes and riots suggested attention needed to be focused on penal philosophy and management style. Thus, the Archambault Royal Commission of Inquiry was formed; finding that over 70 percent of prisoners were recidivists, overcrowding was a growing concern and both reform in penal management and a centralized authority to deal with issues of parole (or remission) were needed (CSC, 2010). This Commission (1938) recommended (leading to the revision of the *Penitentiary Act*) that prison conditions be focused on rehabilitation, through programming and education. This was subsequently reinforced in the Fauteux Committee of 1956, in light of penal overcrowding, however few of its recommendations were ever implemented; somewhat a consequence of the emergent World War II (CSC, 2007). Also around this time the first Women's Prison (1934), in Kingston Ontario, opened. Indeed, a long-awaited facility given the need to separate female from male prisoners and the thoughts and philosophy of Howard and Fry persisted forwards; now joined by the Prisoners' Aid Association, the Salvation Army religion (operating in Canadian prisons since 1882) and the Elizabeth Fry Society (for female prisoners) (CSC, 2007).

The need for more infantry in World War II made correctional officers and prisoners eligible to enlist while penitentiary farms produced thousands of tonnes of vegetables to feed the armed forces; giving prisoners plenty of work and preoccupation (Harris, 2003). After this war, crime rates increased anew; furthering overcrowding, violence and rioting in prisons. The Fauteux Committee established in 1953 was then formed to investigate the prison system, but, nonetheless, the 1954 riot at the Kingston Penitentiary resulted in 200 of the 1,000 prisoners setting fire to the building. A debate followed between those who wanted prisoners to be stripped of the few liberties they had and those seeking the continued reform of the system. The Fauteux Commission, on the side of penal reform, recommended more opportunities for vocational training, pre-release and after-care programs as well as that more and better-trained (e.g. in social work, psychology, psychiatry, criminology and law) professional staff be employed in the prisons (CSC, 2007). Around this time Canada also named its first Prison Commissioner, Major-General R. B. Gibson, whose commitment to prison reform was clear in his institution of more than 100 recommendations made in the Archambault Report. For Gibson, 'the Archambault report became his bible, and he honestly tried to put it into practice. There was a perceptible lightening of the atmosphere in Canadian prisons. Rules and regulations were softened, and there was new hope for rehabilitative treatment' (CSC, 2010). Recognizing the needs of prisoners with mental illness, the first full-time psychiatrist was appointed in 1958. Programming options for prisoners with such needs also expanded and three regional psychiatric centres – Abbotsford, BC, Saskatoon, SK, and Kingston, ON – opened in the early 1970s. Specifically, it was the opening of the Regional Psychiatric Centre at the University of Saskatchewan in 1978, later accredited by the Canadian Council on Health Services Accreditation (CCHSA) in 1984, that led to some positive change in the mental health care for prisoners.

The Correctional Planning Committee came into existence in 1960; housed in the Federal Department of the Justice with the purported objective of fortifying positive attitudes towards prisoner rehabilitation. Although prison life was difficult, prisoners were to be able to take up hobbies and play select sports, listen to radio and subscribe to newspapers (CSC, 2010). The *Penitentiary Act* was amended (1961) to establish new procedures for the operation of penitentiaries and in 1963 a plan to construct 10 new penitentiaries, reflecting the Fauteux Committee's visions, across Canada was implemented (CSC, 2007). The former included the constitution of a body that could receive and investigate the complaints of prisoners (a result from the *Commission of Inquiry into Certain Disturbances at Kingston Penitentiary*), the Canadian Penitentiary Service (developed in 1965 and amalgamated with the National Parole Service in 1976 to then become the CSC in 1979) and the Department of the Solicitor General emerged in 1966 to place national police, penitentiaries and parole under the authority of one minister. It was the establishment (1973) of the Office of the Correctional Investigator (OCI), whose job is to report prisoners' problems to the Solicitor General, that first started the process of giving voice to prisoners (CSC, 2010).

The year prior to the establishment of the OCI, Jackson (2002) suggested that impartial disciplinary tribunals, consisting of independent chairpersons trained in law appointed to conduct prisoner hearings, were needed to avoid bias when dealing with prisoners' rights. In 1977, the year after the death penalty was abolished[3] – marking a significant advance in the recognition of prisoners' rights to life as enshrined in the Canadian Charter of Rights and Freedoms – the Parliamentary Sub-Committee on the Penitentiary System in Canada endorsed Jackson's idea 'as a basic demand of justice at all Penitentiary institutions in Canada' (CSC, 2010). In response, the CSC began appointing independent chairpersons on disciplinary boards at maximum-security institutions and, by 1980, in medium-security institutions (CSC, 2010). To add to the works of Howard, Fry and the Salvation Army, Citizens Advisory Committees were then made mandatory for every federal prison in Canada as a body that gives voice to prisoners; advocacy to maintain their rights and freedoms when incarcerated.

Nonetheless, abuse within the prisons continued leading to, in the late 1970s, a call for *another* new approach in correctional management based on 'the belief that many of the abuses in the system would not take place if proper public accountability existed and public involvement in correctional policy development was sought' (CSC, 2007). In response, citizen advisory committees were established (e.g. grievance committees, independent chairpersons and prisoner committees) as well as further regulations to govern the rights of prisoners and staff (CSC, 2007). Simultaneously, prisoner training programs that 'fulfilled provincial standards for certification, and work programs with adequate payment and incentives' were established that allowed prison labour to become a viable competitor on the open market (CSC, 2007). CORCAN, for example, was created to provide the opportunity for the goods manufactured by prisoners to be sold outside the prisons. Gradual release programs, starting at Collin's Bay (Kingston, ON), allowing prisoners to leave the prison to work during the day, were also implemented. Reintegration was targeted through training, employment and more humane prisoner treatment; for example the 'number system' of identifying prisoners was abandoned, they were addressed by their names, and permitted to write letters (Cellard, 2000). Other positive movements include the launch of the *Exceptional People's Olympiad*, a track-and-field day hosted by federal prisoners for developmentally challenged athletes, at Collins Bay in 1977. This event, now annual and hosted in prisons across the country, pairs each participant with a prisoner (who acts as a coach by offering encouragement and advice) and ostensibly provides prisoners with an opportunity to contribute positively to society (CSC, 2007).

In 1978, the first Commissioner of the CSC replaced the Commissioner of Penitentiaries (CSC, 2010). Then, in 1982, the government of Canada unveiled a new Charter of Rights and Freedoms that recognized, clarified and reinforced the rights of all citizens, including minority and disadvantaged groups. The CSC also redefined its mission to state: 'as part of the criminal justice system and respecting the rule of law, [the CSC] contributes to public safety by actively encouraging and assisting offenders to become law-abiding citizens, while exercising reasonable, safe, secure and humane control'(CSC, 1991). Public safety, here, included a commitment to providing prisoners with programming (e.g. violence prevention, drug treatment, aboriginal- and female-specific programs) that was to sufficiently assist with rehabilitation; assuming programming encourages individuals to refrain from criminal activity post-release. This commitment is reaffirmed in the Corrections and Conditional Release Act (CCRA, 1992) that asserts penitentiaries, operating under the CSC, are accountable for and ensure

> (a) the care and custody of inmates; (b) the provision of programs that contribute to the rehabilitation of offenders and to their successful reintegration into the community; (c) the preparation of inmates for release; (d) parole, statutory release supervision and long-term supervision of offenders; and (e) maintaining a program of public education about the operations of the Service. (c. 20, s. 5)

Included in this legislation are provisions that address health care accessibility, general living conditions and, arguably, adequate programming provisions. Thus, the focus in corrections turned more towards the rights of imprisoned minorities, specifically persons of Aboriginal decent, women and those with infectious diseases.

New approaches, such as tribunal processes, were developed for prisoners who were identified as Aboriginal which recognized the role of colonialization, history and socio-economic conditions in the disproportionate number of Aboriginal people incarcerated (Harris, 2003). In March of 1987, the newly developed *Task Force on Aboriginal Peoples in Federal Corrections* concluded that equity for Aboriginals in the correctional system depended on their increased participation and control over programs and services; the programming needed to reflect their culture and person. To this end, two healing lodges, one for Aboriginal men and another for women, were opened in the 1990s (CSC, 2010). Later, in 1998, an Aboriginal Action Plan focused on the needs of Aboriginal communities – based on the principles of mutual respect and recognition, responsibility and sharing – was announced.

The 1990s saw the replacement of the Kingston Prison for Women, which closed (see the Arbour Report of 1995 for insight into motivations for the closure), by five new regional institutions designed to better meet the 'needs' of women as put forth in the Task Force Report on Federally Sentenced Women (1990) entitled *Creating Choices*. The authors recommended creating a new correctional philosophy for female offenders (focused on empowerment; meaningful and responsible choices; respect and dignity; supportive environments; and shared responsibility) with complementary programming (CSC, 2010). Also in the 1980s and 1990s, concerns around the increasing numbers of persons diagnosed with HIV, AIDS and Tuberculosis in Canadian prisons started to take priority. For example reported cases of HIV/AIDS rose from 14 in January 1989 to 159 in March 1996 – and to a startling 217 in December 2000 (Cellard, 2000). In the 1990s, HIV/AIDS was 6–7 times more likely to be contracted in prison than in the general population; a finding that prompted prison officials to promote measures to decrease the risk of transmission (e.g. passing out condoms and educating prisoners about HIV/AIDS) and to provide some consultation for those affected by the illness. CSC reported that in 2003, more than half of all HIV-positive prisoners voluntarily sought HIV treatment. Despite the many downfalls in health care for those incarcerated, particularly in high-security institutions, at least Canadian prisoners with chronic conditions do receive some positive care. Thus, legislation increasingly acknowledged the needs of the prisoner population – needs that should be addressed in prison to better equip prisoners for community re-entry.

One possible mechanism towards this end was the formal intake process, in reception (often housed in prisons classified as maximum security), that involves the construction of an individualized correctional plan for each prisoner that should document his or her specific needs. This plan outlines the intervention measures deemed appropriate for ensuring the prisoner is able to properly adapt to penal living, as framed by institutional rules and regulations. It also includes suggestions for appropriate programming to, allegedly, assist with rehabilitation and ensures prisoners abide by court-ordered requirements, such as restitution and child-support payments (CCRA, 1992, s. 15, a. 1). The correctional plan is created and maintained to support correctional staff and individual prisoners, working together, towards the client's successful community reintegration post-incarceration. The national, regional and institutional (operational) management bodies within the CSC are to function together to support this objective, although each management level has specific responsibilities.

The national level operates out of corrections headquarters in Ottawa, led by the Canadian commissioner, and is the overarching body responsible for approving and implementing new programs, polices and legislation, operational planning (including budgetary concerns and auditing the penitentiaries) and managing the five regions (Atlantic, Quebec, Ontario, Prairie and Pacific) (Jackson, Mumford, & Jobe-Armstrong, 2009). Regional management involves organizing programs for offenders, resource allocation and overseeing and addressing concerns in all federal institutions in the jurisdiction (e.g. the Prairie region, specifically, is currently focused on prisoner overcrowding and the heightened prevalence of double-bunking (Sapers, 2012)). The institutional (operational) level (see Table 1) focuses on daily operations, including matters specific to each institution and the prisoners within (e.g. program implementation, daily operations and conditions of confinement). Prisoners are placed in institutions of different security classifications (e.g. maximum, medium or minimum) according to their security needs; each prison placement is to provide only the necessary restrictions and control measures as outlined in

Table 1. Canadian Provincial Correctional Institutions.

Region	Name	Location	Security Classification	
Atlantic region	Atlantic Institution	Renous, New Brunswick	Maximum security	Male
	Dorchester Penitentiary	Dorchester, New Brunswick	Medium security	Male
	Springhill Institution	Springhill, Nova Scotia	Medium security	Male
	Nova Institution	Truro, Nova Scotia	Multi-level	Female
	Westmorland Institution	Dorchester, New Brunswick	Minimum security	Male
	Shepody Healing Centre (Regional Treatment Centre)	Dorchester, New Brunswick	Multi-level	Male
Quebec region	Archambault Institution	Sainte-Anne-des-Plaines, Quebec	Medium security	Male
	Cowansville Institution	Cowansville, Quebec	Medium security	Male
	Donnacona Institution	Donnacona, Quebec	Maximum security	Male
	Drummond Institution	Drummondville, Quebec	Medium security	Male
	Federal Training Centre	Laval, Quebec	Minimum security	Male
	Joliette Institution	Joliette, Quebec	Multi-level	Female
	La Macaza Institution	La Macaza, Quebec	Medium security	Male
	Montée St.-François Institution	Laval, Quebec	Minimum security	Male
	Port-Cartier Institution	Port-Cartier, Quebec	Maximum security	Male
	Regional Mental Health Centre	Sainte-Anne-des-Plaines, Quebec	Multi-level	Male
	Saint-Anne-des-Plaines Institution	Sainte-Anne-des-Plaines, Quebec	Minimum security	Male
Ontario region	Bath Institution	Bath, Ontario	Medium security	Male
	Beaver Creek Institution	Gravenhurst, Ontario	Minimum security	Male
	Collins Bay Institution	Kingston, Ontario	Medium security	Male
	Fenbrook Institution	Gravenhurst, Ontario	Medium security	Male
	Frontenac Institution	Kingston, Ontario	Minimum security	Male
	Grand Valley Institution	Kitchener, Ontario	Multi-level	Female
	Joyceville Institution	Kingston, Ontario	Medium security	Male
	Millhaven Institution	Bath, Ontario	Maximum security	Male
	Pittsburgh Institution	Kingston, Ontario	Minimum security	Male
	Warkworth Institution	Campbellford, Ontario	Medium security	Male

Prairie region	Bowden Institution and Annex	Innisfail, Alberta	Multi-level	Male
	Drumheller Institution and Annex	Drumheller, Alberta	Multi-level	Male
	Edmonton Institution	Edmonton, Alberta	Maximum security	Male
	Edmonton Institution for Women	Edmonton, Alberta	Multi-level	Female
	Grande Cache Institution	Grande Cache, Alberta	Medium security	Male
	Grierson Centre	Edmonton, Alberta	Minimum security	Male
	Okimaw Ohci Healing Lodge (Aboriginal-specific)	Maple Creek, Saskatchewan	Multi-level	Female
	PêSâkâstêw Centre	Maskwacis, Alberta	Minimum security	Male
	Regional Psychiatric Centre	Saskatoon, Saskatchewan	Multi-level	Both
	Riverbend Institution	Prince Albert, Saskatchewan	Minimum security	Male
	Rockwood Institution	Stony Mountain, Manitoba	Minimum security	Male
	Saskatchewan Penitentiary	Prince Albert, Saskatchewan	Multi-level	Male
	Stony Mountain Institution	Winnipeg, Manitoba	Medium security	Male
	Willow Cree Healing Centre	Duck Lake, Saskatchewan	Minimum security	Male
Pacific region	Fraser Valley Institution for Women	Abbotsford, British Columbia	Multi-level	Female
	Ferndale Institution	Mission, British Columbia	Minimum security	Male
	Kent Institution	Agassiz, British Columbia	Maximum security	Male
	Kwìkwèxwelhp Healing Village	Harrison Mills, British Columbia	Minimum security	Male
	Matsqui Institution	Abbotsford, British Columbia	Medium security	Male
	Mission Institution	Mission, British Columbia	Medium security	Male
	Mountain Institution	Agassiz, British Columbia	Medium security	Male
	Pacific Institution (Regional Treatment Centre)	Abbotsford, British Columbia	Multi-level	Male

the prisoner's correctional plan and risk-assessment results (CCRA, 1992: c. 20, s. 30). Placement is also influenced by measures related to security (e.g. of public, prisoners and staff), accessibility (e.g. to family, culturally compatible environment and linguistic environment) (CCRA, 1992: c. 20, s. 28) and client scores on the Custody Rating Scale (e.g. drawn from scores from two rating systems). The Commissioner, however, reserves the right to classify a client to a sub-classification, such as Dangerous Offender (DO) status. In these instances, for example, those classified as DO may become subject to indeterminate (life) sentences, with no chance of parole for a minimum of seven years (Pubic Safety Canada, 2010).

CORRECTIONAL SERVICES OF CANADA MOVING INTO THE NEW MILLENNIUM: CURRENT REALITIES

The Canadian prisoner population in the 21st century continues to include many prisoners with histories of criminality, starting in their youth, influenced by negative experiences (at home, and so on), addiction, economic hardship, low levels of education, learning disabilities and employment inexperience; all factors that further thwart the possibility for 'successful' reintegration post-release. Further complicating penal realities and reintegration needs is the ageing prison population that also requires additional chronic and palliative care, both inside prison and in the community; particularly important and challenging given federal (not provincial) prisoners receive care but are excluded from the Canada Health Act (Health Canada, 2012). Nonetheless, as of 2012, the majority of federal prisoners were housed in medium security (62.3%), followed by low security (22.0%), with the fewest in maximum security (15.7%). The number of prisoners incarcerated in federal penitentiaries increased from 14,027 to 14,987 between March 2010 and March 2012 and continued to rise surpassing 15,000 in 2013 (Brosnahan, 2013). Further, between March 2010 and March 2012, the number of federally incarcerated women increased 21 percent, demonstrating that the number of women incarcerated has surpassed 600 for the first time in Canadian correctional history (Sapers, 2012). Though an increase in the size of the prisoner population may suggest an increased crime rate, Canada has experienced a steady decline in crime rates over the past 40 years; with an all-time low in 1972. The increase in the number of incarcerated persons in the United States, however, has been directly tied to policy changes (see Pizarro, Stenius, & Pratt, 2006) and the same may be said in the case of Canadian corrections.

Recent policy changes and commissions impacting corrections in the new millennium include the Independent Review (2007) by the Honourable Stockwell Day, the Transformative Agenda (2008) and the legislative amendments tied to Bill C-10 (2012). Stockwell Day's review (2007) sought to assess the 'operational priorities, strategies and business plans as part of the Government's commitment to tackling crime' (CSC, 2010). It concluded with recommendations for 'offender accountability, eliminating drugs from prison, offender employability to enhance reintegration, improving physical infrastructure, and moving to earned parole' (CSC, 2010) and a commitment of $122 million over two years to implement such recommendations. Indeed, even with declining crime rates, recidivism remains problematic; often tied to former prisoners being barred from successful reintegration and, in consequence, desistance (CSC, 2007). The federal government's Transformation Agenda, adopted in 2008, also focused on 'public safety and on ensuing consistency, integration and accountability throughout Canada's corrections system' (CSC, 2010). In light of the CSC's positive international reputation, this agenda was adopted by many other countries (e.g. Kosovo, Afghanistan, Iraq and Haiti) (CSC, 2007).

The greatest impact on corrections through policy changes is tied to Bill C-10, legislation passed in September of 2011 with implementation beginning in 2012. This legislation represents the amalgamation of a number of previous bills that failed to pass in parliament, directly (e.g. new criminal offences) and indirectly (e.g. subsequent changes in conditions of confinement) affecting the Canadian justice system; specifically corrections. This 'Omnibus' crime bill, C-10, amended the Criminal Code, the Controlled Drugs and Substances Act, the 1992 CCRA (1992), the Youth Criminal Justice Act, as well as other policy legislation – with a lesser impact on corrections – such as the Justice for Victims of Terrorism Act (Parliamentary Information and Research Service, 2011). Included in these revisions was the creation of new criminal offences related to sexual and drug offences and the implementation of new and/or increased mandatory sentencing. Amendments, further, involved the selective elimination of conditional sentences, increased pre-trial detention and new, harsher sentencing principles for young offenders (Canadian Civil Liberties Association, 2014). The impact of such policy change has been and will continue to change the 'profile' of imprisoned Canadians as people will be incarcerated for longer periods of time and more frequently.

Concerns in Corrections: Overcrowding

In Canada, like in many other countries, prisons are constructed away from urban centres or heavily populated districts, thus, conditions of confinement tend to remain unnoticed by community members. Punitive policy change further fuels a lack of support for improving prison conditions, particularly when discussion includes the per person costs of federal incarceration in the country. In 2010–2011, the annual average per person cost of incarceration was, in Canadian currency, $114,364, an increase of over $20,000 since 2006–2007 (annual per prisoner costs were $93,030 in 2006–2007). Costs also vary by the prisoner's gender, with female prisoners costing substantially more to incarcerate in comparison to male prisoners. For example, in 2010–2011, the annual average cost for a male prisoner was $111,042, over $100,000 less than the annual average cost ($214,614) for imprisoning a female (Public Safety Canada, 2010). Interestingly, the fact that mandatory minimums will increase, and currently are increasing, the number of persons incarcerated will further strain an already strained correctional system (where the government has cut funding), despite the fact that it costs much less to supervise a client in the community ($31,148). Instead, overcrowding is becoming an increasingly unmanageable reality in the country.

All five regions of federal corrections are experiencing overcrowding to varying degrees; the most affected regions are the Prairie and Ontario (Sapers, 2013). The Prairie region, in particular, is struggling to accommodate the growing numbers of prisoners and many institutions have resorted to extreme measures like involuntary transfers to other institutions (e.g. further removing prisoners from their family) and increasing rates of double-bunking (e.g. eliminating privacy and a known correlate of penal violence) (Sapers, 2013). Despite the problematic nature of overcrowding, the Canadian Commissioner (2010) approved an increase in the number of prisoners permitted to be double-bunked in all federal prisons to 20 percent. As of March 31, 2013, however, the national rate of double-bunking was 20.98 percent and, most alarmingly, the proportion of prisoners housed in double-bunking conditions in the Prairie region exceeded 25 percent (an increase of 264 percent between March 2010 and March 2013) (Sapers, 2013). Such conditions inherently affect the safety and security of prisoners and correctional staff, as noted by the OCI; 'Prison crowding is linked to increased levels of institutional violence and unrest, and may be a contributing factor to higher instances of disease transmission and infection rates in federal penitentiaries' (Sapers, 2011, p. 38). Correctional reports from the Prairie region confirm the OCI's statement, as the region experienced a 60 percent increase in assaults and a 48 percent increase in use of force incidences over the last five years (Sapers, 2013). Although CSC continues to assert that the increases in double-bunking are a temporary strategy for dealing with overcrowding, comprehensive efforts to reduce overcrowding and, therefore, the usage of double-bunking remains negligible.

Concerns in Corrections: Mental Health and Programs

Growth in the penal population, combined with funding cuts for corrections, has negatively impacted prisoner access to rehabilitative programming and therapeutic resources (The John Howard Society of Alberta, 1998). Correctional programs, as understood by the CSC, constitute controlled interventions focused on the factors that motivate criminal behaviours and result in convictions (Commissioner's Directive, 2013). These programs are offered to support 'the rehabilitation of offenders and their reintegration into the community as law-abiding citizens through the provision of programs in penitentiaries and in the community' (CCRA, 1992, s. 3) – making correctional programming an imperative feature of incarceration as long as the end goal is rehabilitative. Indeed, the need for programming is evidenced by the fact that four of five clients arrive in federal prison with histories of substance abuse and 50 percent of clients directly tie their substance abuse issues to their criminal history. Prisoners, not surprisingly, are encouraged to participate in available programs, as recommended in their correctional plans, although participation is always with consent and voluntary (Commissioner's Directive, 2013).

The range of substance abuse programs offered by the CSC are differentiated by intensity level (e.g. high to low), risk (e.g. of recidivism) and target population (e.g. gender and Aboriginal status). Programming completion rates are highest for male prisoners and decrease with program intensity (e.g. 76 percent of those in high-intensity programming, 84 percent for men in moderate-intensity and 94 percent for those in maintenance – low-intensity). Female and Aboriginal prisoners, however, have a lower (56 percent for female, 56 percent for Aboriginal males at the high-intensity level) completion rate, and the CSC refrains from reporting rates based on program intensity for women (CSC, 2013). Such trends in completion rates are also evidenced in completion rates of Violence Prevention (e.g. also ranging in intensity) and Maintenance programming. These programs are based on the social learning model that frames violent crime as 'learned patterns of behaviour' that can be altered to encourage desistance from crime post-incarceration (Pubic Safety Canada, 2010). Given the convictions of approximately 67 percent of federal prisoners are tied to violence (Public Safety Canada, 2010), successful and effective violence prevention programming is beneficial. In 2009, however, completion rates for such programs could be improved (e.g. 80 percent for male, 73 percent for Aboriginal and unknown for female prisoners) (CSC, 2013). Aboriginal persons represent 22 percent of the prison population and 33.6 percent of all federally incarcerated women claim Aboriginal ancestry (Sapers, 2013) – leaving the lower completion rate for Aboriginal prisoners most distressing.

Completion rates for all programs are of concern and suggest a number of inadequacies in the operations of these programs. First, population-specific programs (e.g. female-specific and Aboriginal-specific) may not sufficiently address the needs of the targeted populations; evidenced in the comparatively lower completion rates of female and/or Aboriginal in comparison to non-Aboriginal male clients. Incarcerated women also have distinctive needs that influence their lived experiences in prison; for example in terms of needs for substance abuse programming, 50 percent of incarcerated women report histories of self-injurious behaviours, 68 percent report experiencing sexual abuse and 85 percent histories of substance abuse at intake (Sapers, 2012). Moreover, difference exists in how such self-injury and substance abuse are used between men and women – men report instrumental use of self-injurious behaviour (to make a point) and women use self-harm to cope with emotional distress related to penal living (Sapers, 2012). Programming designed for male prisoners may be insufficient for addressing the needs of female and Aboriginal prisoners.

Also impacting corrections in Canada is the high prevalence of mental health problems and disorders. Recent figures indicate that nearly 35 percent of the 13,300 prisoners in federal penitentiaries have a mental health need that requires treatment; numbers tripling the estimated amount of prisoners with mental health concerns since 2004 and far higher than the incidence of mental illness in the general population (Makin, 2011; Service, 2009). The proportion of clients with mental health needs, as identified at intake, doubled between 1997 and 2008. Female prisoners are also more likely than male to acquire a mental health related diagnosis upon admission to federal custody; as 2008 statistics indicate that 13% of all male and 29% of all female prisoners were identified as having mental health concerns by the Computerized Mental Health Intake Screening System (CoMHISS) (Sapers, 2012; Service, 2009).[4] The tool, found effective in a study conducted by Martin et al. (2013), assists in identifying prisoners requiring mental health resources, who invariably may 'do time' differently. Indeed, symptoms of such disorders (e.g. anxiety, depression) can be intensified by the often stressful prison environment. Aggravated mental health symptoms can also manifest in disruptive behaviour, too often misunderstood by correctional staff as disciplinary problems, which may subsequently be managed by more punitive measures (e.g. involuntary separation or segregation, transfer to observation cells or higher security institutions and/or disciplinary sanctions) that further exasperate the problem (Sapers, 2012). The Sapers (2013) reports that CSC has experienced continued difficulties managing the higher proportion of the federal prisoner population with mental health needs (Sapers, 2013). Budgetary restrictions, compacted by the strain of the growing prisoner population, are all factors further influencing all types of available programming and resources – including for the mental health needs of prisoners.

Recalling that corrections in Canada are under the influence of the recent political turn towards increasingly punitive measures and crime control, the CSC, although purportedly working to address concerns related to rehabilitation, continues to adopt and implement punitive changes in policy. As such, correctional officers too play an integral role in the implementation (or lack of implementation) of programming and the construction of an environment conducive to rehabilitation. Prisoners' most direct line of communication, correctional officers, is vital to the implementation or rejection of rehabilitative initiatives (Ricciardelli, 2014a; Robinson et al., 1993). Their attitudes towards their occupational role, the prisoners and the objectives of incarceration, more generally, are often reflected in their support for rehabilitative programming. The push for punitiveness in Canadian incarceration (e.g. support for 'tough on crime' agendas) seems to contradict the mandate of 'care, custody and control' in the CSC (CSC, 2010). Recognizing that correctional officers are more likely to hold punitive attitudes towards prisoners, in comparison to other staff (Kifer et al., 2003; Ricciardelli, 2014a; Robinson et al., 1993; Tewksbury & Mustaine, 2008; Young & Antonio, 2009), the increasingly strained contact between officers and prisoners – in part a result of overcrowding – may intensify negative attitudes and fuel a control, rather than rehabilitative, orientation among officers.

The most comprehensive study on officer attitudes in Canada was conducted in 1991 by Plecas and Maxim, who followed a group of correctional officers through their training and first six years of employment. They found that officers' attitudes towards prisoners became increasingly negative and punitive as their careers progressed (Plecas & Maxim, 2001). This furthers concern, as the successful implementation of rehabilitative programming is in part dependent on the attitudes of the officers who ensure program accessibility and effectiveness for prisoners; imperative supports for successful reintegration.

CONCLUSION

Corrections have evolved in Canada, shaped throughout history by the countries that first appropriated the lands, the French and British colonial settlements, and later the United States, as well as the various Aboriginal populations who first occupied the 'country'. Over the last 150 years, commissions, inquiries and reports have repeatedly drawn attention to the need for an increasingly humanitarian approach to corrections, striving towards greater and more effective rehabilitative conditions, positive treatment and accessible resources for prisoners. This is most evident in the abolition of the death penalty as well as corporal punishment. However, these attempts to emphasize and implement more positive aspects of incarceration, such as rehabilitation through programming, have been largely hindered by political and social movements towards increasingly punitive conceptualizations of the objectives of incarceration. Indeed, the concept of penal populism as discussed by Garland (2001) and Pratt (2007) may be applied to the Canadian criminal justice system to suggest that social pressures on political actors have affected incarceration. These affects include the push for, and subsequent creation of, punitive policies reflecting the popular 'tough on crime' rhetoric that has negatively impacted conditions of confinement (e.g. tied to overcrowding and inadequate rehabilitative resources).

All five correctional regions currently experience levels of overcrowding and some, like the Prairie region, have adopted extreme strategies to 'manage' the surge of prisoners. Such measures likely have a negative influence on experiences of incarceration, derailing attempts to rehabilitate prisoners, rather than working towards the successful future reintegration. Low program completion rates for imprisoned populations (e.g. most tryingly Aboriginals and female prisoners) further suggest that resources are not being used effectively to address the specific rehabilitative needs of this group of people. Moreover, it must be recognized that prison, in its past or present form, has not been deemed successful for the rehabilitation of prisoners, the deterrence or prevention of future criminal behaviours and providing retribution – serving justice to those who were victimized by crime.

The future of corrections in Canada, punishment and imprisonment more specifically, will be shaped by funding cuts and political directives; as new prisons continue to be built and others renovated. The oldest penitentiary in Canada, Kingston Penitentiary, closed its doors in 2013, after 178 years in operation. A prison, built with ostensibly largely positive intentions, that was renovated after riots and later modernized, and 'famously' home to many men classified to maximum security penal living, is no longer in operation – despite being used as an educational facility for Queen's University in Kingston, ON, and dedicated as a heritage site in 1990. Past employees, volunteers and even former prisoners reminisced as it closed – a bitter sweet emotional reality that marks the end of an era.

NOTES

1. Kingston Penitentiary (KP), then and now, has been somewhat of a tourist attraction. Then, admission to see the prison was actually a charged service (e.g. the infamous author Charles Dickens was one such tourist) and now, recently after its closure in 2013, citizens again paid to tour the establishment. KP, despite having been designed with the best intentions, the penitentiary was a place of violence and oppression (Cellard, 2000; CSC, 2010).

2. Hanging was once the only method of execution; crimes punishable by death ranged from, in 1859, mistreatment of a girl under 10 to intentional murder. By 1869, only three offences were punishable by death: murder, rape and treason. It was not until 1976, after many years of debate, that the death penalty was struck from the *Criminal Code* of Canada. This decision was made by parliament, who argued that the State could *not* decide to put an end to a person's life, the risk of convicting an innocent person was too high, and that there was no certainty that the death penalty presents an effective deterrent. The death penalty was replaced by parliament with a mandatory life sentence with no eligibility for parole for 25 years in the case of first-degree murder, and for 10–25 years in cases of second-degree murder (The John Howard Society of Alberta, 1998).

3. Prior to the death penalty being abolished, in 1976, over 1,500 persons had been sentenced to death (Cellard, 2000; CSC, 2010).

4. The effectiveness of this tool in screening male prisoners was accessed by Martin et al. (2013), who found it increased the accuracy of mental health screening by decreasing false positives (e.g. when a prisoner is inaccurately labelled as 'needing mental health treatment') and thus also increased the accuracy of resources-need assessments.

REFERENCES

Beattie, J. M. (1977). *Attitudes toward crime and punishment in Upper Canada 1830–1850: A documentary study*. Toronto, ON: University of Toronto Centre of Criminology.

Bellomo, J. J. (1972). Upper Canadian attitudes towards crime and punishment (1832–1851). *Ontario History*, *64*, 11–26.

Boritch, H. (2005). The criminal class revisited, recidivism and punishment in Ontario, 1871–1920. *Social Science History*, *29*(1), 137–170.

Brosnahan, M. (2013). *Canada's prison population at an all-time high. CBC News*. Retrieved from http://www.cbc.ca/news/canada-s-prison-population-at-all-time-high-1.2440039. Accessed on November 25, 2013.

Canadian Civil Liberties Association. (2014). *Bill C-10: The omnibus crime bill unwise, unjust, unconstitutional*. Retrieved from http://ccla.org/omnibus-crime-bill-c-10/

Carrigan, D. (1991). *Crime and punishment in Canada: A history*. Toronto, ON: McClelland & Stewart.

Cellard, A. (2000). *Punishment, imprisonment and reform in Canada, from New France to the present*. Ottawa, ON: Canadian Historical Association.

Commissioner's Directive. (2013). *Mission, values and ethics framework of the correctional service of Canada*. Ottawa, ON: Correctional Service of Canada. Retrieved from http://www.csc-scc.gc.ca/politiques-et-lois/001-cd-eng.shtml

Correctional Service of Canada (CSC). (1991). Jim Vantour, "Foreword". In J. Vantour (Ed.), *Our story: Organizational renewal in federal corrections*. Ottawa, ON: Correctional Service of Canada.

Correctional Service of Canada (CSC). (2007). *Penitentiaries in Canada*. Retrieved from http://www.csc-scc.gc.ca/about-us/006-1006-eng.shtml

Correctional Service of Canada (CSC). (2010). *Corrections in Canada: An interactive timeline*. Retrieved from http://www.csc-scc.gc.ca/hist/1900/index-eng.shtml

Corrections and Conditional Release Act (CCRA). (1992). Retrieved from http://laws-lois.justice.gc.ca/eng/acts/C-44.6/FullText.html

Coyle, J. (2012). *Kingston penitentiary, a piece of Canadian history with a long record of brutality*. Retrieved from http://www.thestar.com/news/canada/2012/04/19/kingston_penitentiary_a_piece_of_canadian_history_with_a_long_record_of_brutality.html

Garland, D. (2001). Introduction. In D. Garland (Ed.), *Mass imprisonment: Social causes and consequences*. Thousand Oaks, CA: Sage.

Goffman, E. (1961). *Asylums: Essays on the social situation of mental patients and other inmates*. New York, NY: Penguin.

Gosselin, L. (1982). *Prisons in Canada*. Montreal, QC: Black Rose Books.

Grassian, S. (2006). Psychiatric effects of solitary confinement. *Washington University Journal of Law and Policy*, *22*(1), 327–380.

Harris, M. (2003). *Corrections in Canada*. Toronto, ON: McClelland and Stewart.

Health Canada. (2012). Canada Health Act Annual Report 2010–2011. Retrieved from http://www.hc-sc.gc.ca/hcs-sss/pubs/cha-lcs/2011-cha-lcs-ar-ra/index-eng.php

Jackson, M. (1983). *Prisoners of isolation: Solitary confinement in Canada*. Toronto, ON: University of Toronto Press.

Jackson, M. (2002). *Justice behind the walls: Human rights in Canadian prisons*. Toronto, ON: Douglas & McIntyre. Retrieved from www.justicebehindthewalls.net

Jackson, M., Mumford, S., & Jobe-Armstrong, M. (2009). *Management challenges in Canadian federal corrections*. Burnaby, BC: Simon Fraser University Publications.

John Howard Society of Alberta. (1998). *History of the John Howard society of Alberta*. Retrieved from http://www.johnhoward.ab.ca/pub/C2.htm

Kifer, M., Hemmens, C., & Stohr, M. (2003). The goals of corrections: Perspectives from the line. *Criminal Justice Review*, *28*, 47–98.

Kirkpatrick, A. M. (1965). Penal reform and corrections. In W. T. McGrath (Ed.), *Crime and its treatment in Canada* (pp. 469). Toronto, ON: Macmillan of Canada.

Makin, K. (2011). *Why Canada's prisons can't cope with flood of mentally ill inmates*. Retrieved from http://www.theglobeandmail.com/news/national/why-canadas-prisons-cant-cope-with-flood-of-mentally-ill-inmates/article563604/?page=all

Martin, M., Wamboldt, A., O'Connor, S., Fortier, J., & Simpson, A. (2013). A comparison of scoring models for computerised mental health screening for federal prison inmates. *Criminal Behaviour and Mental Health*, *23*(1), 6–17.

McGrath, W. T. (1976). *Crime and its treatment in Canada* (2nd ed.). Toronto, ON: Macmillan of Canada.

Parliamentary Information and Research Service. (2011). *Legislative summary of Bill C-10*. Publication number 41-1-C10-E.

Pizarro, J., Stenius, V., & Pratt, T. (2006). Supermax prisons: Myths, realities, and politics of punishment in American society. *Criminal Justice Policy Review*, *17*(6), 6–21.

Pratt, J. (2007). *Penal populism*. New York, NY: Taylor & Francis.

Pratt, J. (2013a). *A punitive society: Falling crime and rising imprisonment in New Zealand*. Wellington, New Zealand: Bridget Williams Books.

Pratt, J. (2013b). Punishment and the civilizing process. In J. Simon & R. Sparks (Eds.). *The Sage handbook of punishment and society*. London: Sage.

Public Safety Canada. (2010). *Corrections and conditional release in Canada – A general primer (2010)*. Publication number 978-1-100-14788-8.

Ricciardelli, R. (2014a). The inmate code: Looking at men in Canadian penitentiaries. *Journal of Crime and Justice*, *37*(2), 234–255. Available online December 3, 2012. doi:10.1080/0735648X.2012.746012

Ricciardelli, R. (2014b). *Surviving incarceration: Inside Canadian penitentiaries* (p. 312). Waterloo: Wilfrid Laurier University Press.

Robinson, D., Porpino, F., & Simourd, L. (1993). The influence of career orientation on support for rehabilitation of correctional staff. *The Prison Journal*, *73*(2), 162–177.

Sapers, H. (2012). *Annual report of the office of the correctional investigator of Canada 2011–2012*. Ottawa, ON: Office of the Correctional Investigator, Public Works and Government Services Canada.

Sapers, H. (2013). *Annual report of the office of the correctional investigator of Canada 2012–2013*. Ottawa, ON: Office of the Correctional Investigator, Public Works and Government Services Canada.

Service, J. (2009). *Under warrant: A review of the implementation of the correctional service of Canada's 'Mental Health Strategy'*. Prepared for the Office of the Correctional Investigator of Canada by John Service Consulting.

Sykes, G. (1958). *Society of captives: A study of a maximum security prison*. Princeton, NJ: Princeton University Press.

Tewksbury, R., & Mustaine, E. (2008). Correctional orientations of prison staff. *The Prison Journal*, *88*, 207–233.

Trammell, R. (2012). *Enforcing the convict code: Violence and prison culture*. Boulder, CO: Lynne Rienner.

Young, J., & Antonio, M. (2009). Correctional staff attitudes after one year of employment: Perceptions of leniency and support for rehabilitation. *Corrections Compendium*, *34*(3), 9–17.

WOMEN PRISONERS: THEORY AND REALITY IN MEXICO

Elena Azaola

ABSTRACT

Purpose – *This chapter discusses the confinement conditions that women doing time for federal offenses in Mexico nowadays face. This discussion focuses on two conditions: the evolution of theories about feminine criminal behavior; and the effects that policies against drugs, prevailing in Latin America and other world regions, have on this population.*

Design/methodology/approach – *Some 149 out of 300 women doing time in an Island prison in Mexico were interviewed by the author, who tried to understand the conditions that women faced before committing the crime and once they were in prison.*

Findings – *The study shows that policies against drugs have caused severe damage and brought about few, if any, benefits. A cost-benefit approach and more rational policies are suggested.*

Originality/value – *The chapter will describe relevant punishment conditions, including involuntary or trickery transfer of women to the Island prison; difficulties to communicate with their families and ill-treatments, humiliation, and abuses from personnel and will hear several of their stories.*

Keywords: Women; prisons; Mexico; stories; drug policies

Punishment and Incarceration: A Global Perspective
Sociology of Crime, Law and Deviance, Volume 19, 121–138

ISSN: 1521-6136/doi:10.1108/S1521-613620140000019005

INTRODUCTION

Although the late inclusion of women as subjects of interest for empirical studies and criminological theories is a common place and has been extensively documented (Heidensohn, 1995), it is still surprising and still has an impact, even now when there is abundant literature trying to fill the empty space that prevailed for so long. In Zaffaroni's words (1993), women have been excluded from the dominant criminological and law discourse as well as from those related to punishment.

Rosa Del Olmo (1998) distinguishes between three stages in the development of theories regarding the delinquent woman. She calls the first one "traditional theories" which were imbued with the well-known precepts of positivist criminology attributed to biology and the supposed inherent nature of women as the cause of their criminal behavior. Representative of this stage is the text from Lombroso and Ferrero, *La donna deliquente*, containing the vast majority of stereotypes that for so long prevailed in descriptions of women indulging in criminal behavior.

Del Olmo calls the second stage "modern theories" as they came out at the same time as the women liberation movement from the seventies and as a reaction to biological positivism. These theories predicted a supposed increment in feminine criminal behavior (that did not happen) as a consequence of women emancipation and their increasing participation in public life. Characteristic of this stage are texts on the role of women in crime from Freda Adler and Rita Simons, both published in 1975. The third and last stage is that of "feminist theories" which have incorporated a gender perspective to the study of criminal behavior, one of the most significant changes and of the greatest importance in the criminological thought of all times (Del Olmo, 1998, pp. 19–34; Heidensohn, 1995; Azaola, 2001; Azaola & José, 1996).

Another recent study (Franklin, 2008) carries out an ample review on specialized literature and finds three subjects systematically treated when analyzing answers different justice systems have given in regard to the criminal woman: her invisibility, concern for her body and sexuality, and the imposition of a traditional gender role in the punishments. According to the author, after going through all this literature, it seems clear that women, their lives, and their criminal conducts have been virtually ignored when constructing theories trying to explain criminal behavior. It seems also clear that when justice institutions and their actors have paid attention to the lives of women, they have consistently showed concern for their bodies and sexuality. Finally, it is also clear that those institutions adopted as a mission to impose in women the traditional gender role, and those women not adjusting to that role were treated in a different way and more severely punished (Franklin, 2008, pp. 342–343).

The author quotes several studies showing that while justice systems simultaneously ignored criminal female patterns and their involvement in criminal behavior, they were consistently interested in their sexuality using the legal apparatus as a vehicle to impose moral sanctions. These women were in fact judged for threatening the existing social order when questioning a structure based on male superiority and putting themselves, in this way, out of the gender roles socially prescribed.

In this way, women labeled as "problematic" or those who had conducts considered out of the traditional feminine role have been treated by justice more severely or have been subdued to treatment models to adjust their behavior to those patterns. Similarly, women who showed in their behavior an "excess of masculinity" were punished more severely than those found guilty with deviation forms considered "more feminine" (Franklin, 2008, pp. 344–345).

The same study points out that nowadays even policies that have taken into account findings contributed by the gender perspective have had negative consequences on women. Among those policies, she highlights the war against drugs and mentions several studies that consistently have shown the close relationship existing among physical and/or sexual abuse suffered by women and the greater propensity they have of using drugs as an escape method, or in order to feel some "relief" in front of such abuses. For example, a study by Chesney-Lind and Sheldon, from 2004 (cited by Franklin), states that justice systems are responsible for criminalizing survival strategies that these women use in an attempt to escape from those abuses, being more often that these measures have had the consequence of enrooting them in the criminal career.

In the same way, the war against drugs has brought as one of its nondesired consequences the marked increase of the feminine population in prisons, especially of poor women, single mothers, migrants, and women belonging to ethnic minorities, who get involved in these crimes for lack of alternatives to support their children. Legal reforms have aggravated this situation by increasing in a disproportionate way punishments for any drug-related crimes. This has affected street distributers, and consumers of small quantities, many of whom happen to be women (Franklin, 2008, p. 352).

Following the copious literature on the subject, this study has managed to document one of the more surprising topics; worth pointing out is the great amount of similitudes that can be found when describing not only the problematic situations women deprived from their freedom find in different countries but also the great coincidences in the circumstances that encourage those women to get involved in criminal conducts. These coincidences which are particularly striking when happening in regions with very different standards of living, like, for instance, Europe and Latin America, allow us to support the relevance of the gender perspective that points out the role men and women play, the differences in the way they are socialized, and the different positions that they have in society. All this manifests in the criminal behaviors they incur, beyond and independently of national or regional borders.

Although the extension of this work does not allow us to talk in detail about the numerous coincidences found in the studies documenting the situation of criminal women in different countries and regions, in the following paragraphs we will talk about some of them in order to illustrate, particularly, the coincidences among women deprived of their freedom due to drug-related crimes.

WOMEN DOING TIME IN THE EUROPEAN UNION

The European Union recently conducted a study in six countries: France, Germany, England, Spain, and Hungry (European Union, 2005). The objective of the study was to measure the efficacy of social and prison policies in order to promote labor and social integration of women, particularly once they have ended their stay in prison. As a departing point, the study states that in the European Union countries, the feminine population in prisons has increased in proportions much higher than that of males. The study explains this phenomenon as a result of a series of factors in the penalizing processes affecting women more than men. Among them are: higher rates of unemployment; the massive strike affecting especially young people, women, and less-integrated sectors; labor shortage; lack of institutional supports; scarce education; housing problems; lack of income; absence of family structure; single-parent families; lack of social networks; migration processes; drug trafficking; prostitution; belonging to a ethnic minority; as well as personal factors such as the critical variables of age and gender, illnesses, drug dependency, violence, and ill-treatment (European Union, 2005).

The basic premise of this study is that prison is regularly and disproportionally imposed on those who are already excluded; a premise that is not only valid in the European Union but in other regions also, particularly in

Latin America. It also points out that gender is a vital factor in the production of exclusion forms, so the study had the purpose to improve the understanding of primary factors for women exclusion, the patterns this exclusion conforms, as well as factors determining secondary exclusion, from inside the prison preventing an adequate reinsertion in society. Another purpose of the study was to understand the way in which prison has an impact on women depending on the level and type of primary exclusion they have suffered.

Reports from each European country studied mention one and again the most common factors among women doing time: poverty, unemployment, and being a single mother. In Germany, for instance, the links between starting drug consumption at a very young age with poverty, violence, self-aggression, and lack of resources were clear. The study states that those who have the greatest risk of starting using drugs when young are those with addict parents, abandoned, or those who have suffered sexual abuse. It is relevant to say that the average number of women in prison using drugs in the European countries studied varies between 60% and 80% (European Union, 2005).

Another factor found often is domestic violence previously suffered by inmate women. Reports from England state that, for instance, more than half of the inmates report having suffered domestic violence, and one of each three, sexual abuse. Reports from France, Spain, and Hungry also point out that severe violence has marked in a decisive way the lives of these women. Many times their criminal career starts when they leave home after having suffered physical or sexual violence. In the same way, another characteristic of these women is the dependency bonds that they establish with their partners, in spite of having been objects of their abuse. This dependency takes them to the criminal career in which they participate to cover their partners, or as more or less voluntary conspirators.

The study finds that prisons exclusively for women have advantages over those units that are in male prisons, as the first ones allow focalization, in a more adequate way, to address specific women needs.

Regarding children, only a few European prisons are equipped to accommodate children with their mothers, except in France where 25 prisons have these services. In Germany, women are allowed to go to their homes over the weekend to be with their families. In other countries women with young children can have house arrest or can participate in early release programs. The discussion now revolves around not only mothers having these benefices but that other women with specific needs can also have access to them (European Union, 2005).

In the European countries studied, there are different programs to prepare women who are to recover their freedom after being sentenced for a long or not so long time; although sentences for women tend to be much shorter than in Latin America. In fact, the prison legislation in Europe is clearly oriented and has established a mission: to contribute to reintegrate inmates, specifically through educating programs, training, work, preparing for reintegration, and personal development.

What follows is the situation of women doing time for federal offences in Mexico.

WOMEN DOING TIME IN MEXICO

In Mexico, just as in other countries, the population of women in prison has increased at a rate much faster than that of men. Nevertheless, the proportion of women doing time has remained stable, representing a little less than 5% of the total population in prison. That is, according to data from Secretaría de Seguridad Pública (2010), while the male population has incremented almost 40%, during the last decade, going from 136,000 inmates in 1999 to 225,000 in 2010, the female population practically doubled in the same period, going from a little less than 6,000 to 11,000 inmates. It is necessary to add that at the beginning of 2014, the male population in prison was 238,000 while that of females was 12,000. Rate of inmates per habitant is 210 per 100,000. This growing rate of the population in prison has to do, as several studies have pointed out (Patiño, 2009), with the hardening of punishments, increment in crimes qualified as grave, length of judicial processes, abuse of preventive prison, and lack of alternative measures. This situation has contributed to the 25% overpopulation in Mexican prisons.

Another element characteristic of Mexico and other countries is the greater proportion of women doing time for federal offence, especially for drug-related crimes. While in 2010, 23% of the male population was doing time for federal jurisdiction crimes, 35% of the women were in that situation, the great majority due to drug-related crimes. Nevertheless an element worth pointing out is that women doing time in federal prisons in Mexico have been convicted in its great majority due to drug-related crimes, but not violent crimes. These are women with no criminal records, 99% have never been convicted before; 88% committed a drug-related crime but not combined with any other crimes, and 92% did not use weapons to commit the drug-related crime (Pérez Correa & Azaola, 2012).

Worth pointing out also is that when comparing male and female populations convicted for federal offence, it is interesting to see that regarding the socio-family environment they grew up in, all indicators point out that women have faced more adverse life conditions than men; their educational level is lower, the level of vulnerability and violence that they suffered in their family is higher, and the employments they had access to were almost always informal and poorly reattributed. Also, they got a partner and had more children at a younger age than men. Proportionally there are ten times more women (2% of men vs. 22% of women) who have their partners in prison, compared with inmate men who find themselves in the same situation. Similarly, their children are more exposed to be abandoned.

WOMEN DOING TIME IN ISLAS MARÍAS

Mexico currently has 423 prisons; 406 are state and municipal prisons and 17 are federal centers. Until 2007, Mexico had only six federal prisons but in the last years it has been constructing 11 more centers at a dramatic rate. This can be explained considering that private companies have been participating seeing prisons as a juicy business, not only building the premises but also providing several services, except for security which stays in the hands of the State. In this way, in only three years more than 25,000 inmates doing time in state prisons have been moved to federal centers.

This has been the case of women doing time for federal crimes in state prisons who were transferred to new federal centers that are always far from where their family lives. Now we will talk about women doing time in a prison complex built very fast during the last three years in one of the Islas Marías, situated in the Pacific Ocean at 112 kilometers from the coast of the State of Nayarit. This prison complex has five federal centers, one of which accommodates 300 women while the other four have a total population of a little more than 5,000 inmate men.

In 2011 and 2012 I had the opportunity to visit Islas Marías three times in order to see the population characteristics of women doing time there and listen personally to their concerns and the circumstances they face. In one of these visits I was able to stay for a week in the island and managed to interview 149 women, a little more than half the inmates. What follows is a description of the results I found from the study I made.

The characteristics of the female population doing time in Islas Marías are the following:

There are 289 inmate women. Regarding age: 25% are between 21 and 30 years of age; 40%, between 31 and 40; 26%, between 41 and 50 years; 7% are between 51 and 60 years, and 1% is older than 61 years of age.

Regarding marriage status: 40% are single, 35% live in common-law marriage, 3% are divorced, and 3% are widow. The average number of children is 2.5.

Education level: 26% are illiterate; 19% completed or attended some elementary school; 39% attended some junior high school; 13% some high school, and 3% started college.

The crimes they committed are: 85% drug-related crimes, 7% aggravated robbery, 3% homicide, 2% carry or gathering weapons, and 1% counterfeit currency.[1]

The length of their sentence is: 21% up to 5 years; 55%, 5.1 to 10 years; 19%, 10.1 to 15 years, and 5%, 15.1 years or more.

Regarding their health conditions: 28% of them have a chronic illness. Among the most frequent ones stated are: hypertension, diabetes, lower back pain, and asthma.

Now I will describe the main problems faced by these women doing time in Islas Marías related to the disciplinary regime characteristics they are subject to. It is worth to keep in mind that having interviewed a clearly representative population from the totality of inmates and having found the same problems repeatedly stated, I do not have any doubt that these are the problems affecting the totality of women doing time in this female center.

IMPRISONMENT CONDITIONS

1. *Involuntary transfer*

The great majority of inmates talk about having been transferred against their will and using measures to intimidate or subdue them. They pointed out that their transfer was not notified with anticipation but that they were asked at night to go to the authorities who came to look for them by their name and ordered them to sign and put their fingerprint in a document by which supposedly they were "voluntarily" accepting to be transferred. All that happened in spite of them resisting doing it or pointing out that they have not been notified and they did not want to be transferred. In the great majority of cases, they were not allowed to take with them their clothing or personal belongings which they have managed to acquire with a great deal of effort; many of them were not able even to take the information to communicate with their relatives to tell them of their transfer. For many the way they were transferred was specially denigrating as they were taken out in their sleeping clothes with no underwear, they were handcuffed and asked to keep their heads down during the transfer. When they arrived their clothes were taken off and they were inspected in front of the group who was being transferred with them. For some the insult still lasted longer as they did not receive underwear for a while, for others, more insulting was the fact that they were given male underwear.

2. *Transferred with trickery*
A small number of inmates said to have asked or accepted to be transferred, because their partners have been previously transferred and they have the expectation to reunite with them, or because they were shown a video where the life regime seemed different from what they found; a regime in which they could basically circulate with certain freedom through the island, where even dancing and a boutique were shown. Besides, being said that they will have a job and an income, they were told that they could "pay" their sentence "two for one," that is, that their sentence could be reduced in half. Evidently, these women were hurt because they were deceived and they felt defeated by the authorities who had convinced them in this way to accept the transfer.

   Additionally, the inmates said that they were having problems with their relatives as the same video had been shown to some of them, and they had now a very different idea of the circumstances in which they are living, and in some instances they had stopped supporting them because they think that the inmates do not need help anymore.

3. *Difficulties to communicate with their families*
Undoubtedly, communication with their families is the main concern of the inmate women and it is also what, according to a great deal of specialized studies, can assure a successful reincorporation to society. In fact, the main reason why these inmates were opposed to their transfer was fear to live further away from their families and lose contact with them, through telephone calls and through visits. Most women complained that in the prison where they were, they were able to communicate daily with their families, through a public telephone, while in

the island they can only make one 10-minute phone call every 15 days. Besides, they can register only three phone numbers they can call; if they do not find their relatives in these numbers or the social worker communicating them makes a mistake while dialing, they lose their turn and should wait another 15 days in order to try to contact their families. To this regime that allows them very little contact with their families, inmates added the very little understanding and even pejorative attitude social workers have; with any pretext they end up their turn to call their families, without taking into consideration that this means one month without any news from them.

4. *Difficulty to receive visits from their relatives*
   In spite of the regime of the Island allowing them to have a visit from their relatives every three months for one week, almost no one has been able to receive them, nor do they think they will ever be able to do so, due to the high cost that it represents for their relatives to get to the Port of Mazatlán and from there take the official boat that will carry them to the Island at no cost. For most of the inmates this means that during their time in prison, they will not be able to see their relatives, a fact that is experienced by them as an additional pain, added to having lost their freedom, and as a right that in fact has been denied to them.
5. *Contact with their partners is forbidden*
   Inmates who accepted to be transferred to the Island with the expectation of keeping contact with their partners, as well as those who have male relatives in the Island or who would like to relate with a male inmate, have seen that all their requests have failed as male and female inmates have determinately forbidden to have any kind of contact. Some inmates see this regime as excessive and with no justification as they are not allowed to have a conjugal visit, something they consider contrary to human nature, having as one of their fundamental needs to link with others and to create affectionate bonds that are especially important for those who find themselves deprived of their freedom. The female inmates talked about the fact that their space is getting more and more constrained and that they are not allowed to abandon the area where the female center is located, with particular pain and worry. In the same way, they talked about sanctions as severe as isolation for two or three weeks that have been imposed on some inmates because they tried to have contact through greetings or letters with any of the male inmates who are in one of the four male centers in the Island.

6. *Lack of work, activity, and income*
Another topic that women inmates in the Island refer to is to have lost their jobs and the possibility of obtaining an income as they use to have in the state prison where they were, that not only allowed them to take care of their most basic needs, but also permitted them to send a small amount to pay for their children. Not being able to pay for their basic needs and having to ask their relatives, who are taking care of their children, to do so, affects them in a particular way. Only a few inmates receive payment for washing the clothes of some guardians, or for making *tortillas*, but the rest of them do not have a job or any income, nor do they have any type of activities that can give meaning to their lives. Some are required to work in the kitchen or to do other tasks (what they call "melga") but do not get any payment for that.
Many women were used to be active and working but now feel intense pain for not being able to do so; they try to mitigate it by sleeping excessively. Educational activities are also scarce; some go to basic literacy lessons, others to English lessons taught by one of the inmates.
As the great majority does not have any income and depends on the support received from their families, they resent even more that packages sent by mail are not given to them timely and that they do not always receive the goods that their relatives claim to have sent to them.
7. *Unworthy life conditions*
Women inmates complained that food is insufficient, that it has little variety, quality, and nutritional value, which explains why many of them have often suffered intestinal infections that have lasted for two weeks in some instances. In the same way, inmates who suffer from chronic illnesses like hypertension or diabetes do not get the special diet they need.
The institution provides them with basic articles for their personal care, like toilet paper, sanitary towels, soap, and dental paste, but inmates complain that the quantity is not sufficient and the quality could be largely improved, and resent even more the fact that they do not have a personal income which would allow them to acquire this or other products which they consider indispensable for their image and self-esteem, such as cream, shampoo, or a hair brush.
8. *Deficient medical care*
Inmates complained that medical care is deficient, especially for those who have had intestinal infections for up to 15 days without receiving

any medication, as well as for those having chronic ailments that are not adequately treated due to lack of necessary medications. In the same way, the Island does not have a gynecologist although when I was visiting six inmates were pregnant.

9. *Legal uncertainty*

   A topic particularly sensitive for inmates, which is understandable, is the need of having a clear understanding regarding their legal situation and the length of the punishment they have to serve out. They say that the Island does not have personnel willing to review their cases and resolve their doubts regarding the possibility that they have, or not, of reducing their sentences through obtaining freedom benefits.

   To this uncertainty we should add the lack of regulations to normal life in the female center, giving clear parameters and certainties regarding limits for inmate behavior as well as that of the responsible authorities. With no regulations inmates fear to find themselves at the discretion of the authorities and the possible arbitraries on their part prevail.

10. *Ill-treatments, humiliation, and abuses from personnel*

    Another matter of special relevance which I personally was able to witness was an attitude of rejection, disdain, and constant ill-treatment from the great majority of the authorities. Even when this ill-treatment could, at least in some part, be originated in their own discomfort – personnel complain that they feel under a similar regimen as the one applied to inmates – it cannot be justified. We are talking about a regimen that could be characterized by an intention of excessive and overpowering control over people, inmates, and personnel, which imposes unjustified restrictions, lacking all legal basis and that do not seem to be oriented by rationality, proportionality, or a sense of humanity. We should keep in mind that this last one is one of the sources feeding philosophy, law, regulations and, national and international treaties, regarding principles that should orient and characterize the application of punishments.

The fact that during the few months previous to the visit, five inmates tried to take away their own lives talks about an uncommon situation which authorities should listen to in a careful way in order to make the required changes to eliminate the profound causes that have established a regimen feeding despair and a lack of sense.

What follows is a transcription of fragments of the life stories of some inmate women in Islas Marías which illustrate with clarity the features that we have found so often in women deprived of freedom.

STORIES OF FEMALE INMATES IN ISLAS MARÍAS

"My name is Elisa, I've been here for seven months and I come from the State of Aguascalientes. Since I can remember, when I was 6 years old, I haven't lived with my mother who was an alcoholic. I was the oldest of 10 children and I was an undesired daughter. My grandmother took care of me. My mother ill-treated me, she used to beat me and I couldn't understand why. It was not until I arrived here that I realized that she was beaten by my father; she was also a victim. I got together with my partner when I was 15 and at 16 I had my first child. I left home so I didn't have to take care of my siblings and cook for them. Then my partner was unfaithful to me, and hatred and resentment filled me. When I had already three children, I started to use drugs. The time came when I needed to do it daily. My mother got sick and I wouldn't go to see her, I was not interested; what interested me was the drug so I can drowned the pain I was feeling. I didn't use to cry, nor did I want people to see me crying, I didn't want people to be pleased by watching me crying. Later on, my children came to be irrelevant to me; I was not taking care of them not of myself. I was living just for living and I started to sell drug. I wanted to stop using it but I couldn't. I wanted to do rehabilitation but my family did not support me. I was taking drug day and night until I ended up here with my partner for selling it. The worst part of being here is that our five children were left alone and there is no support here to send someone who could go and see our families. They can't come here either because they do not have the money. Besides, we are not allowed to be with our partners here."

Another inmate says: "My name is Juana and I come from Mexico City. Since I was a child my family was poor and disintegrated. My father was a dead beat dad, he was never with us; I used to see him only once in a while. My mother was frustrated; my father would arrive to the house and beat her and she started to vent her anger on me. She didn't let me talk with any man or go anywhere. I was fed up with the situation and left home with a girlfriend. I got a boyfriend and ended up being pregnant. I had a beautiful baby and came back home but I still didn't get along with my mother. I worked selling roses and then I had a little stand to sell trinkets. I was accused of stealing 100 pesos. My mother had cancer and died the month I was in prison. I came out but I had lost everything and was selling whatever I could. My son had left home and then came back, and I was supporting him but in the streets there are a lot of vices and I fail again because I liked alcohol. A policeman arrested me and started beating me and I was given four years because I broke a window from a police car. I came out and then was detained again for robbing a cell phone. I was given eight years then for being a re-offender. I accepted coming here because I was told that probably here I could get a husband, but things are not as they told us. We all came here deceived … ."

Another one says: "My name is Lucia and I come from Mexico City. Since I was a little girl, my parents taught me to work, they used to take me to sell artificial flowers; we were a very poor family. My father had to go to jail and we did not have anyone to support us. I used to look for food for my siblings. My mother was very sick and we couldn't take care of her. My siblings and I were left alone and I was the one in charge. My sister left and the others became beggars; we use to go to garbage dumps in order to eat. My father was put in jail because he was accused of stealing in a charcuterie. My mother died and we went to Puebla. My father came out of jail and made us a plastic house; we were squatters and suffer because of cold and rain. At 15 I left home to live with the father of my children. He used to humiliate me and beat me, and did many ugly things to me. My father became an invalid and I was taking care of him. I was working as a maid. I asked the lady of the house to lend me some money but she did not do it. I took it as my father needed very expensive medicines and we couldn't afford them. I took the money and was accused of aggravated robbery."

Gloria says: "I come from Mazatlán, from a very poor family. My parents maltreated me; my life has been like the one of a little animal: I have been defending myself as good as I have been able to. I fell here because I went in a bus to help a lady who was carrying a suit case. The soldiers got me and as I don't know anything about law, I was put in prison for two years. Suddenly I was brought here; they didn't let me bring with me even a telephone number. My family doesn't know how to reach me. I got sick because I don't know anything about my children and my family. I don't do anything here, I only try to endure the anguish I feel and read the bible. I was given ten years for carrying a kilo of marihuana; they give me more years because I don't know about law, and as there is no money, the lawyers don't move our cases."

Another one tells: "I am Beatriz and come from a dysfunctional family. My father was from Oaxaca and my mother from Guadalajara. Both of them were orphans. We were 11 siblings. My father was an alcoholic and my mother a shopkeeper. There used to be beating and shouting; they did not beat us, but beat and insulted each other, my mother also beat my father. My father was a loader in the market La Merced, and my mother use to sell in a market. Due to their work they did not take good care of their children, I don't judge them. Due to being one of the last ones in the sibling order, the absence of my mother lead me to have an absent personality; I did not have a fatherly or motherly image. I married a violent man who used to beat me and my children. My mother use to say that that was my burden but I was full of hatred and wanted to take revenge on that man who treated us like prisoners. I was offered a job to introduce drug in the prisons and I accepted because I hated my husband. I have been seven years and a half in jail and have learned through courses that this is a vicious circle in which you change from being a victim to being the perpetrator. Now I feel responsible and I don't blame my parents or my husband. I have become Christian and that has given me a lot of peace. Nevertheless I don't understand who took the decision to bring us here taking us apart from our children. I don't know when I will see them again … ."

Another inmate who was transferred from the State of Morelos and had been accused of drug-related crimes, stated: "I'm paying a mistake that I incurred in because of hunger, because I wanted to take money to my home to take care of my father and my children. My father is already dead and I'm still here paying my mistake … ."

We could go on telling stories but that is not necessary in order to realize the elements repeated in these stories again and again: misery, violence, abandonment, lack of opportunities. In some cases, these women tried to mitigate the pain that their circumstances caused to them by using drugs. The answers the State had to have offered to these women never arrived, except for the final answer, clear and blunt of punishment and imprisonment. This answer has been encouraged, as we will see, by the policies against drugs, ruling in Mexico and Latin America, with equal costs and unfortunate results.

Effects of Policies against Drugs in Latin America

A recent study carried out in eight countries by the civil organization, Washington Office on Latin America, had the aim to analyze the policy against drugs and its impact on the overpopulation and detriment of prisons. The countries included in the study were Argentina, Bolivia, Brazil, Colombia, Ecuador, Mexico, Peru, and Uruguay. Among the conclusions that this study reached stands out the fact that in all countries, emphasis on the penal sanctions imposed has encouraged a major increment in numbers of people incarcerated for drug-related crimes. Nevertheless, to apply severe laws has not only been ineffective in stopping production, trafficking, and consumption of illicit substances, but has also generated negative circumstances, such as the overloading of courts and prisons, and the suffering of tens of thousands of people who are in prison due to drug-related crimes of insignificant amounts. To this circumstance, it is necessary to add that the weight of these laws has fallen in a disproportionate way on the more vulnerable sectors of the population (Washington Office on Latin America [WOLA], 2010, p. 5).

In the analysis they made regarding the legislations in the region, they point out that in spite of some differences, in general the laws do not distinguish among the levels of involvement in the business, treating small vendors, and "drug mules" or couriers in the same way as big drug traffickers; and not distinguishing either between violent and nonviolent crimes, resulting in many people getting big penalties, and many others, without having committed a serious or violent crime ending up in maximum security prisons. They also point out that the severity of the current law against drugs has contributed in a significant way to increase imprisoning rates, to the overcrowding of prisons, and to the deplorable conditions in which prisoners in the region live. In fact, between 1992 and 2007, the imprisoning rate raised more than 100% on average in all countries included in the study; at the same time, rates for drug-related crimes continue to rise in all cases.

In the same way, the study points out the abuse in preventive detention for those suspicious of drug-related crimes, a situation that often lasts for several years. In five of the eight countries studied – Mexico among them – preventive detention is inexcusable for drug-related crimes, being this grave or not. The fact that for this type of accused, the option of alternative punishments is denied, and the fact that the great majority of convicts for drug-related crimes are in prison for a minor offence, nevertheless, serving sentences disproportionally long, should also be considered (WOLA, 2010, p. 6).

The author shows concern for the increment of the feminine population accused of drug-related crimes and points out that the phenomenon of "mules" has been generalized and currently has become part of the drug-trafficking dynamics, especially in big cities.

The study concludes that legislations in the region have not only shown their inefficacy to reduce drug commercialization, but also that the manner they are currently applied has turned out to be terribly unfair as they have raised the incarceration rate and contributed to overcrowding and deterioration of life conditions for inmates, who in their greatest majority belong to the weakest sectors of society. For this reason, it formulates a series of recommendations to modify the law with the purpose in mind of protecting human rights, and at the same time promote security. These recommendations are as follows:

- Incorporate to the legislation alternative punishments to prison for those accused of minor drug-related crimes, including abolishment of punitive sanctions for owning substances for personal consumption;
- Make sure of the proportionality of punishments distinguishing between: drug trafficking and other drug-related crimes; drug-related crimes of minor, major, or medium scale; rank occupied by the person in the drug-trafficking nets; violent and nonviolent crimes, and types of drug;
- Suppress minor obligatory punishments;
- Avoid preventive detention in case of minor crimes committed by non-violent offenders;
- Increase government funds to improve the prison infrastructure and life conditions of inmates;
- Establish equality of access to law benefits and opportunities of alternative punishments offered to people involved in other types of crimes to suspects of drug-related crimes;
- Reorient efforts to apply the law, directing it to the great drug-trafficking nets and not against consumers, small farmers, or "mules";
- Consider applying special amnesties, like pardons, to people convicted for drug-related crimes who had received disproportionally large punishments (WOLA, 2010, pp. 7–8).

CONCLUSIONS

The purpose of this study has been to show that, far from what used to happen a few decades ago, currently we have enough elements; there is ample literature allowing us to know which are the factors behind criminal conducts in the case of women.

In the same way, we have been trying to show that policies against drugs, the effects of which have been studied in several countries, have caused severe damage and little benefits, if any. A cost-benefit approach and more rational policies should take us to evaluate our norms and recommend changes as the ones proposed above.

It is urgent for the State to take into consideration what so many studies have been documenting again and again, like the issue of what takes women to commit crimes, and to consider the task to establish policies and programs that effectively deal with violence against women and promote their equity. The costs of not solving this situation not only have a direct impact on women but also have multiple effects, severely damaging their families, their environment, and the whole society.

In the same way, it is necessary to reinforce programs directed to prevention, care, and rehabilitation of drugs consumers, stressing the need to design programs specific for women, due to the fact that using drugs has different characteristics and motivations in men and women which should be taken into consideration, otherwise they will not be effective.

NOTE

1. We should remember that the reason for the high percentage of women doing time for drug-related crimes is that these women are in prison for crimes of federal jurisdiction. That is, 85% of these women in prison for drug-related crimes do not represent a percentage of the totality of women in prison in Mexico but of women in prison for crimes of federal jurisdiction, which are close to 4,000.

REFERENCES

Azaola, E. (2001). *El delito de ser mujer*. Mexico D. F.: Plaza y Valdés, 2ª. Edición.

Azaola, E., & José C. (1996). *Las mujeres olvidadas. Un estudio sobre la situación actual de las cárceles de mujeres en la República Mexicana*. Mexico D. F.: El Colegio de México.

Del Olmo, R. (Ed.). (1998). *Criminalidad y criminalización de la mujer en la región andina*. Caracas: PNUD.

European Union. (2005). *Women, integration after prison: Analysis of the processes of socio-labor integration of women prisoners in Europe*. Retrieved from www.surt.org/mip

Franklin, C. A. (2008). Women offenders, disparate treatment, and criminal justice: A theoretical, historical, and contemporary overview. *Criminal Justice Studies*, *21*(4), 341–360.

Heidensohn, F. (1995). *Women and crime*. New York, NY: New York University Press.

Patiño, P. (2009). Fundamentos históricos, situación actual y bases para un nuevo modelo de administración penitenciaria, Mexico D. F.

Pérez Correa, C., & Azaola, E. (2012). *Resultados de la primera encuesta realizada a población interna en Centros Federales de Readaptación Social*. Mexico, D. F.: Centro de Investigación y Docencia Económicas.

Washington Office on Latin America. (2010). *Sistemas sobrecargados. Leyes de drogas y cárceles en América Latina*. Washington, DC: WOLA.

Zaffaroni, R. (1993). La mujer y el poder punitivo. en: *Sobre patriarcas, jerarcas, patrones y otros varones*, ILANUD, Instituto Latinoamericano de las Naciones Unidas para la Prevención del Delito y el Tratamiento del Delincuente, San José, Costa Rica.

THREE WAVES OF AMERICAN PRISON DEVELOPMENT, 1790–1920

Ashley T. Rubin

ABSTRACT

Purpose – *This chapter calls attention to penal regime shifts, emphasizing the importance of comparing different periods of prison development. In particular, it examines different instantiations of prison across time.*

Design/methodology/approach – *I discuss three periods of prison development (1790–1810s, 1820–1860, and 1865–1920), focusing on the nature of prison diffusion across the United States. Specifically, I discuss the homogeneity and diversity of prison forms in each period.*

Findings – *I demonstrate that the first two periods were particularly homogenous, as most states that adopted prisons followed a single model, the Walnut Street Jail model (1790–1810s) and the Auburn System (1820–1860), respectively. By contrast, the post—Civil War period experienced the emergence of women's prisons, adult reformatories, and distinctively Southern approaches to confinement. Using neo-institutional theory, I suggest this post-war proliferation of prison forms was only possible because the prison had become institutionalized in the penal landscape.*

Punishment and Incarceration: A Global Perspective
Sociology of Crime, Law and Deviance, Volume 19, 139–158

ISSN: 1521-6136/doi:10.1108/S1521-613620140000019006

Originality/value – *Scholars rarely examine multiple shifts in penal regime together, reducing their ability to make comparative insights. This chapter juxtaposes three historical periods of prison development, thereby illustrating the diversity of the third period and improving extant understandings of prison evolution.*

Keywords: Prison; penal change; penal reform; neo-institutional theory

INTRODUCTION

Different periods throughout American history are associated with different styles of incarceration. Most recently, American confinement is defined by the "warehouse" model of prison (Irwin, 2005). (Commentators have half seriously, half tongue-in-cheek used the coterminous rise of the "Big Box Store" as a metaphor for contemporary prisons.) Styles of incarceration often entail both distinctive architectures and purposes. The blandly geometric warehouse prison encapsulates the contemporary (since the 1970s) emphasis on long prison sentences intended to incapacitate allegedly dangerous criminals (and deter other would-be offenders). The modern "supermax" prison is the most extreme example of prisons that are little more than boxes intended to hold people for storage until their sentence is over. Before this, however, the "correctional institutions" model characterized American prisons. Names of prisons constructed between the 1940s and 1970 often included "correctional," "institution," or some related word, while many existing prisons were renamed. Prison guards were increasingly called "correctional officers." Rather than a storage model of prison, prisons sought to "correct" their "inmates" (instead of "prisoners") through individual and group psychotherapy, bibliotherapy (therapeutic reading and writing), and educational and vocational training.

This shift from a correctional institution to a warehouse is the most recent and perhaps represents the strongest reversal of penal ideology in American history (Allen, 1981). Its (not unrelated) coincidence with the emergence of mass incarceration and a variety of punitive laws aimed at lengthening sentences (e.g., "three strikes" laws), sending more people to prison (e.g., criminal penalties for drug possession), and restricting early release from prison (e.g., truth-in-sentencing laws) has made this an especially interesting development to penologists and other observers. However, seismic shifts like this have occurred throughout American penal history. Unfortunately, scholars do not often examine these shifts together, except in extensive histories of American punishment (Blomberg & Lucken, 2000; McKelvey, 1977) or in the survey of introductory chapters to works on contemporary punishment (Irwin, 1980, 2005).

To be sure, scholars have examined these shifts. Scholars have been most interested in the emergence of carceral punishments in general, beginning with prisons modeled on Philadelphia's Walnut Street Jail (1790–1810s) and a second generation of prisons modeled on the Auburn State Prison (1820–1860) (e.g., Hindus, 1980; Hirsch, 1992; Meranze, 1996; Rothman, 1971). Others have examined the emergence of Big House prisons in the 1920s (Bright, 1996; Jacobs, 1977). Each of these prisons characterized distinctive periods in American penal history. Others have explored the emergence of women's prisons (Dodge, 2006; Rafter, 1985), federal prisons (Keve, 1991), adult reformatories (Pisciotta, 1994), convict leasing and chain gangs (Ayers, 1984; Lichtenstein, 1996; Oshinsky, 1997), and southern plantation-style prisons (Oshinsky, 1997), each developing primarily between prisons on the Auburn model and the Big House model. However, these developments have not been analyzed together. Indeed, many commentators often skip over the period between the Auburn-style and the Big House prisons (e.g., Irwin, 2005, chapter 2; Simon, 2007, pp. 145–146). In some cases, scholars describe the Big House as an extension and a larger version of Auburn, connecting the emphasis on hard labor in the design of prisons from both eras. To some extent, this description is correct; however, it overlooks a substantial period of prison development after the early prisons. The uneven attention on some periods of innovation or incomplete examinations of the prison's trajectory has precluded certain insights that this chapter seems to illustrate.

This chapter describes the three major eras of prison development between 1785 and 1920. The first period (approximately 1785 to the 1810s) represents America's first sustained experiments with long-term confinement as punishment for serious offenders. This period observes the diffusion of penitentiary houses, or what I call, "proto-prisons," on Philadelphia's Walnut Street Jail model. The second period (approximately 1820–1860) represents the emergence of the first modern cellular prisons. Scholars have disagreed over which of these two periods represents the "birth" of the prison, but both represent significant watershed moments in American prison history. The third period (approximately 1865 to the 1910s) represents a different watershed moment in which multiple models of prisons proliferated across the United States. The period between 1865 and the 1910s experienced the rise of female-only prisons, juvenile facilities, federal prisons, adult reformatories, and a distinctive southern-style prison. These models persisted for varying lengths of time, and some did not survive long into the twentieth century. But unlike the earlier periods, this third phase represents a period of previously unmatched diversity in prison development.

Indeed, by not exploring prison regime shifts together, scholars have overlooked the growing diversity in prison development. While the first two periods were primarily homogenous in their reliance on prison, the third represents a period of increasing diversity in prison models. What explains the initial homogeneity of the first two periods and the growing diversity by the final period? This chapter first describes each period and its respective prisons, illustrating this distinctive trajectory of prison development, and then offers some insights into why prison history unfolded in this manner.

EARLY REPUBLIC: REVOLUTIONARY OFFSPRING

Following the American Revolution, Americans' (and Europeans') attitudes towards punishment changed. Capital punishment that had been, if not the primary form of punishment, a significant pivot around which criminal justice revolved appeared increasingly problematic (Banner, 2002). Those offenders whose crime did not merit execution often received some form of corporal punishment like whipping, branding, or time in the pillory or stocks. Confinement in dingy, local jails was mostly an administrative strategy: those awaiting execution, witnesses waiting to testify, debtors, and others were often confined together in large rooms for relatively brief periods, but not for punishment. But the Enlightenment, changes in religious doctrine, and the experience of war rendered existing penal strategies problematic. Following the Revolution, groups of middle- and upper-class citizens gathered in reform societies, wrote pamphlets and public letters philosophizing over what punishment should look like. As states wrote new constitutions after Independence, several built in dictates to revise their penal laws such that capital punishment would be restricted to only the most serious offenses (murder). Alternatives to death were necessary, but existing strategies were themselves problematic. During the search for an alternative, states increasingly relied on their ancient jails, which quickly became overcrowded. For a short period (1785–1789), Massachusetts sent its serious offenders to a military fortress on Castle Island (in Boston Harbor) (Hirsch, 1992). In 1786, Pennsylvania combined public works during the day with confinement at night for its serious offenders. After several failed experiments, however, Pennsylvania authorized long-term confinement as an alternative to capital and corporal punishments. Following a substantial renovation, Philadelphia's Walnut Street Jail received that state's serious offenders.

Several features of Walnut Street distinguished it from traditional colonial jails. First, inmates were classified by gender, age, and criminality and then separated into different rooms accordingly. Reformers believed that colonial jails were problematic because old and young, hardened criminal and new recruit, debtors and criminals were held together; crime, they believed, spread like a disease from one infected inmate to another. Indeed, most prisoners were still held together in congregate confinement, but reformers believed segregating offenders by their overall criminality would prevent the spread of vice. Second, those inmates who broke the prison rules would spend time in solitary confinement. This was one of the first sustained uses of solitary confinement, but there were only 16 solitary cells available. Third, confinement was intended to reform prisoners and deter future offenders. Inmates were given work, intended to support the prison and discipline prisoners by teaching them obedience and the importance of regular work. Solitary confinement would allow inmates time to reflect on their misdeeds and truly experience the pangs of conscience, while the threat of solitary would be a powerful deterrent (Meranze 1996).

While several states experimented with a variety of alternatives to capital and corporal punishment, Walnut Street Jail proved an incredibly popular choice. New York was the first to follow, modeling its new Newgate Prison after Walnut Street in 1796. It was followed shortly by New Jersey, Kentucky, Virginia, Maryland, and Massachusetts. By 1810, nine of the 17 states had built a penitentiary house (Rothman, 1971, p. 61), and more states continued to adopt Walnut Street-style prisons into the late 1810s. States that did not adopt a new state prison continued their reliance on capital and corporal punishment, but a shift towards incarceration was palpable throughout the country.

While the Walnut Street model was tremendously popular, these early experiments with long-term confinement quickly proved problematic. As states continued and increased their reliance on these facilities, the aging prisons grew overcrowded. In this climate, disease spread more quickly and many prisons erupted in violence, riot, and fire. In the public mind, the new Walnut Street-style prisons were associated with perceived crime waves and other signs of social disorder (McLennan, 2008; Meranze, 1996). Dissatisfied with their solution, reformers looked for new solutions.

JACKSONIAN/ANTEBELLUM PERIOD: FROM CRISIS TO INNOVATION

Reformers in the late 1810s and early 1820s revised earlier understandings of the prison to create a wholly new facility. If the congregation of prisoners was the root cause of disorder in existing prisons and the continued criminality of their graduates, separation would be the key. Moving to the opposite extreme, some advocated for solitary confinement. Walnut Street, with its small number of solitary cells, they believed, had been on the right track. Earlier reformers' efforts had failed because they let most prisoners interact with one another. Thus, as riots repeatedly struck Newgate (McLennan, 2008, p. 44), New York legislators revised a statute authorizing the construction of a new prison extending the Newgate model to include solitary confinement as well. Accordingly, a portion of prisoners at the new Auburn State Prison would be held in solitary confinement cells. Importantly, these cells were small and dark, and inmates lacked all distractions except a Bible. Many of the inmates unfortunate enough to receive these sentences to solitary confinement became physically or mentally ill, in some cases attempting (and achieving) mutilation or suicide. The experiment continued from Christmas Day 1821 to late 1823, but it left a lasting impression in the minds of reformers, legislators, and citizens about the dangers of solitary confinement (Lewis, 1922, pp. 80–82).

In the wake of the Auburn disaster, the legislature authorized a new system of confinement that came to dominate the American penal landscape. Under the Auburn System (also called the Congregate System or Silent System), inmates remained in the same small solitary cells of their predecessors at nighttime only. During the day, inmates marched in lockstep to factory-like rooms inside the prison to work before retreating once more to their cells at night. Under threat of lash, inmates were not allowed to look at one another, let alone talk to one another. Inmates would work in close physical proximity with others, thereby preventing the dangerous consequences of solitary confinement, but their contaminating influence would be prevented by the enforced silence. After the innovation at Auburn State Prison, other states quickly remodeled their existing Walnut Street-style prisons or built new prisons on the Auburn Model, including Maine (1823), Kentucky (1825), Connecticut (1827), Massachusetts (1829), Maryland (1829), Ohio (1834), and Michigan (1839).

Pennsylvania, however, remained committed to the idea of solitary confinement. It had been the early basis of Walnut Street in theory, though not in practice, and the problems with congregation, including riot, were apparent to Pennsylvanian reformers (Meranze, 1996). However, when Pennsylvania tried to impose long-term solitary confinement at its new Western State Penitentiary in the early 1820s, architectural and other problems made implementation impossible. Cognizant of the failure at Auburn with pure solitary confinement, the legislature revised its initial directive and allowed inmates to work at hard labor for the duration of their solitary sentences. This new Pennsylvania System began at the Eastern State Penitentiary in Philadelphia in 1829 (it would soon absorb the inmates from Walnut Street as well). Under the Pennsylvania System, inmates spent the duration of their sentence in comparatively large solitary cells with access to workshop-style labor, reading materials, and a small attached garden. This total physical separation of prisoners would prevent the cross-contamination reformers believed likely when prisoners were congregated, silently or otherwise. To further prevent mental illness and aid their reformation, inmates were visited by prison personnel and select penal reformers who sought to counsel and teach the inmates necessary skills like reading and writing. The perception that this model of prison was expensive to construct and less profitable than Auburn, as well as the association for many between the Pennsylvania System and Auburn's earlier version of solitary confinement, rendered the Pennsylvania System much less popular (Rubin, 2014). Outside of Pennsylvania, it was only adopted in New Jersey (1833–1858) and Rhode Island (1838–1844).

In this period, then, two models of prisons emerged. However, over the four decades between the experimentation at Auburn and the outbreak of Civil War, most states adopted a prison based on the Auburn System (Rubin, 2014). By 1860, Pennsylvania was the only state relying on its unique model of confinement. Moreover, almost every state had adopted a prison on either model. Only four states had failed to adopt a new prison: Delaware and Florida both had small populations making a prison largely unnecessary, while the Carolinas experienced intense debates over the prison question (Ayers, 1984, p. 35). Like the carceral field of the late 1810s, the carceral field of the late 1850s was incredibly homogenous: the vast majority of states had a prison, and almost all of these prisons ran on the same model.

Indeed, there were some variations. First, in most prisons, there was a wide gulf between theory and practice. The silence of the Auburn System quickly broke down, just as the full separation of prisoners under the Pennsylvania System was tenuous. Despite these discrepancies, reformers and prison administrators remained committed to the underlying logic of their chosen prison regime. Second, prison management varied by state.

In most states, prison management was contracted out to an entrepreneur who would lease the inmates from the state, in some cases supervising their labor and behavior in the prison itself. The exact nature of the arrangement, including how much control and responsibility over the prison the contractor had, varied by state. However, the basic daily routines of prisoners, and the rules to which they were subjected, were markedly similar across states. Indeed, there was little regional variation in prisons at all in this period: New frontier states like Illinois, Indiana, and Michigan adopted prisons quickly. Southern prisons were smaller and largely confined white prisoners (in contrast to northern prisons' disproportionate representation of immigrants and African-Americans), but they followed the Auburn System as enthusiastically as other states. (Support for prisons, however, came more from political and social elites than from the common man; Ayers, 1984.) Prisons in the antebellum period were incredibly homogenous in a way that prisons after the Civil War were not.

GILDED AGE AND PROGRESSIVE ERA: PROLIFERATION

The period between the Civil War and the early twentieth century witnessed the proliferation of variations on the meaning of prison. For about 10 years after the Civil War, change occurred gradually, with no major innovations. Innovation then came in two waves: first in the 1870s, during the Gilded Age, and again in the 1900s, at the peak of the Progressive Era. When innovations did occur, they spread slowly and were much less universally accepted than previously. Additionally, there was no one single innovation that characterized this period, as Walnut Street Jail and Auburn State Prison had previously characterized the Early Republic and Antebellum periods.

Indeed, this period experienced the proliferation of different prison forms and varying understandings of what a prison was. Existing prisons became places for hardened (or genetically predestined) criminals, while new reformatories emerged to reform younger and first-time criminals, similarly to the initial goals of Auburn and Eastern. Meanwhile, as women became a large enough portion of the prison population, states began creating female-only facilities. In this period, as well, a gulf emerges between prisons in the North and South as southern penitentiaries were increasingly modeled on the now-illegal slave plantations of the antebellum era. Each of these developments rendered the post-bellum carceral field more diverse than its predecessor carceral fields. This section describes each of these developments in greater detail.

The Fate of Auburn-Style Prisons

Auburn-style prisons did not disappear after the Civil War. Indeed, as more states joined the Union, Auburn-style prisons continued to diffuse across the country. However, many reformers still interested in punishment did not look at prisons as optimistically as they had previously. Like many antebellum reform movements (Walters, 1978), penal reform had lost steam by the middle decades. Slavery, and preserving the union, had become more pressing issues. Some reformers also lost faith in the promise they initially believed prisons held. Year after year, prisons returned statistics showing increasing numbers of admits, many of whom had been incarcerated before. The obvious conclusion was that prisons were not reforming, but might even have deleterious effects. Additionally, many prisons faced overcrowding. This had been a problem before the Civil War, but overcrowding reached new heights as soldiers disbanded, a downtrodden economy rendered jobs scarce, and crime rates increased. Many prison administrators and reformers had already lost hope in reformation, but overcrowding made any semblance of reformation impractical as silence, separation, labor, and discipline became more difficult to enforce. Finally, a changing orientation towards the causes of crime made many believe crime was endemic to families and some were simply born criminals. These earlier generation prisons, designed to reform prisoners, were now understood to be places for hardened criminals.

Reformatories

Reformers still wanted reformation to play a role in criminal justice. They still believed some criminals could be redeemed, but prison was the wrong place for them. Incarcerating young or new offenders in these facilities would ensure they would remain on their criminal trajectory. To prevent such outcomes, New York again embarked on a bold experiment, this time at its new Elmira Reformatory. Authorized in 1876, but fully operational in the early 1880s, the reformatory would house only young or first-time offenders. Armed with a new "penal science," prison administrators would first interview offenders to diagnose their problems, then treat them through a combination of religion, coursework, and training. Finally, offenders would be released on parole, or community supervision, to continue their reformation in a noninstitutional setting. As with the earlier prisons, there were large gaps between theory and practice; in reality, "Elmira was, quite simply, a brutal prison" (Pisciotta, 1994, p. 34). However, it was an influential model for other states and helped to bring reformation back into America's prisons, at least rhetorically (see also Rothman, 1980).

For Pisciotta (1994, p. 151), the development and spread of adult reformatories represented "America's third penal system." However, the reformatory movement had three significant differences from the diffusion of prisons on the Walnut Street and the Auburn Models. First, diffusion was somewhat slow. While Michigan adopted a reformatory the year after Elmira (1877), the next wave of diffusion took almost a full decade, beginning with Massachusetts (1884), followed by "Pennsylvania (1889), Minnesota (1889), Colorado (1890), Illinois (1891), Kansas (1895), Ohio (1896), Indiana (1897), and Wisconsin (1898)" (Pisciotta, 1994, p. 87). Eight more states adopted reformatories between 1901 and 1916 (Pisciotta, 1994, p. 127). Second, the reformatory was not universally adopted. Only 20 states had adopted reformatories by 1920. Progressive reformers supporting the reformatory had been in many ways more optimistic than their Jacksonian counterparts (Rothman, 1980), but the reformatory was far less successful than earlier models of prison. Finally, in contrast to earlier iterations of prison development, the reformatory had distinct models that coexisted. As Pisciotta (1994, p. 82) explained, states did not blindly copy the Elmira model, but modified the system to fit their local needs while pursuing the same penological goals. "By the late 1880s, three approaches to controlling criminals emerged: the 'treatment-oriented' Elmira system, the 'punishment and profit' Michigan approach, and an eclectic version introduced in Massachusetts." While the Auburn model dominated the antebellum carceral field, Elmira was only one of several versions of a reformatory.

Women's Prisons

Another area of prison innovation affected female prisoners. Historically, women were confined in the same prisons as men. Their numbers were exceptionally small, and cost-conscious prison administrators found ignoring the women a workable strategy. In some cases, women were simply held in a crowded room or attic together (the emphases on separation and silence obviously ignored); in other cases, women's cells existed in a separate wing of the prison or a building on the prison grounds. Particularly as female criminals were viewed as the roughest version of their sex, many reformers and prison administrators saw female prisoners as beyond redemption, further justifying the lack of reformative attention (Rafter, 1985, p. 13). After the Civil War, however, new prisons were erected specifically for women and designed to reflect their unique (gendered) needs. Female reformatories were inspired by similar beliefs as male reformatories, but reflected a general concern for women whose not-quite-criminal activities rendered them immoral and in need of reform. Consequently, their inmates included many petty offenders who previously would not have been incarcerated in a state prison (Rafter, 1985, p. xxii).

Like their male-focused counterparts, female reformatories spread slowly, with only 4 erected before 1900 and 17 more before diffusion halted in 1935 (Rafter, 1985, p. xxiii). By the 1930s, the characteristics that made female reformatories distinct from traditional custodial facilities melted away. Also like adult reformatories, separate facilities for women were not universal. Instead, their development displays regional variation in a way that earlier prison development did not. As Rafter (1985, pp. 9–10) explained, "The evolution of separate quarters for women tended to be most rapid in the Northeast, a bit slower in the Midwest, slower still in the South, and most laggardly of all in the West."

Southern Justice

Indeed, following the Civil War, the carceral trajectory split into decidedly regional tracks. Prisons in the South had previously experienced very few differences from prisons in the North; almost every southern state maintained a prison, each on the Auburn System. The significant differences were the size and composition of the prison population. The less populated South, with its heavier reliance on capital and corporal punishments, sentenced comparatively few people to prison. The largest source of the size discrepancy, however, was that African-Americans accused of crimes were punished at the hands of white slave masters, privately, often on a plantation. Consequently, pre–Civil War prisons were almost entirely filled with white prisoners. After the Civil War, Southern criminal justice evolved to absorb the social control of former slaves and other African-Americans. Following the Civil War, and again in the 1870s as Reconstruction came to an end, Southern states rewrote their criminal codes to heavily penalize African-Americans who committed crimes or to heavily penalize crimes typically committed by African-Americans, like various kinds of petty thefts redefined as grand larceny. Those convicted by the courts and sentenced to prison or hard labor were overwhelmingly black after the Civil War. However, most black convicts did not serve time in prisons or experience the Auburn System as it existed in the later twentieth century. Supplementing traditional Auburn-style prisons, Southern states turned to distinctively Southern forms of incarceration: convict leasing, work camps and iron cages, chain gangs, and plantation-style prisons.

Convict Leasing

In the first years following the Civil War, Southern states adopted a policy of convict leasing. Southern prisons were damaged or destroyed during the Civil War. Overcrowded county jails absorbed some of the influx. In the late 1860s, convict leasing became an informal, temporary measure to compensate for the diminished prison capacity and account for the influx of black convicts. However, the practice was formalized in the 1870s, as legislators and entrepreneurs recognized the potential for profit. Beginning with Mississippi in 1876, states virtually simultaneously rendered petty offenses punishable with multiple-year prison sentences and authorized the leasing of those same individuals (Ayers, 1984; Oshinsky, 1997).

Rather than serving their sentences in prison, prisoners were contracted out to entrepreneurs who became responsible for their care and control. These entrepreneurs then used their unfree labor to do the traditional work of slaves (e.g., plant cotton) as well as construct railroads, drain swamps, mine coal, work in saw mills or turpentine camps, and generally perform the "jobs that free labor did not like to do, in places where free labor sometimes feared to go" (Oshinsky, 1997, p. 44). Unlike the slaves they replaced, leased convicts had no economic value, and entrepreneurs lacked any incentive to keep them alive, well-fed, and healthy; mortality rates were extremely high (Oshinsky, 1997, p. 46). Entrepreneurs who won the contract, in some cases an exclusive right to lease the state's inmates, also subleased the unfree labor to other businessmen, who had even less incentives to keep the convicts alive.

Traditional prisons generally played a small role for these prisoners. Prisoner camps dotted the wilderness; many leased convicts were kept in overcrowded mobile cages at night. The prisons themselves maintained mostly white prisoners; only the very old and very sick were returned to the prison, and they were expected to die soon after. To avoid leasing white convicts, states only leased convicts sentenced to a relatively small number of years; white criminals were not sent to prison unless the crime was particularly egregious, crimes punished by sentences of 10 years or more (Oshinsky, 1997, p. 41). Some whites, however, were leased and worked in chain gangs; their experiences were the most motivating for reformers seeking to abolish the practice (Lichtenstein, 1996). Indeed, the system persisted into the 1900s, despite persistent opposition from the free labor and smaller businessmen whose interests were hurt by convict labor (Lichtenstein, 1996; Oshinsky, 1997).

Plantation-Style Prisons

However, between 1890 and 1930, states increasingly discontinued their convict leasing practices, again creating a need for alternatives. In many ways, convict leasing continued the supposedly more progressive form of chain gangs in which prisoners helped to construct the nascent system of highways crisscrossing the south (Lichtenstein, 1996). However, in the early 1900s, many southern states constructed new prisons to absorb the large and growing criminal population that they could no longer lease to the highest bidder. Because this population was primarily African-American, southern officials saw the plantation as "a humane and sensible response" (Oshinsky, 1997, p. 110). The prisons of this period were in fact sprawling, many-thousand-acre farms in which black prisoners worked in the fields during the day and slept in barracks at night. (Reminiscent of slavery, some black prisoners worked as servants in the warden's quarters.) Indeed, prison life for African-Americans reflected in many ways the semi-free, semi-feudal work of sharecropping, and slavery before it, that some whites could view prison "as a smooth and simple extension of normal black life" (Oshinsky, 1997, p. 136). This system continued in many Southern states until the 1960s (Feeley & Rubin, 2000).

Decentering Prison

At the same time as reformers, legislators, and prison administrators refined prison spaces for different populations of offenders, the prison itself also became decentered. Progressive reformers increasingly looked to noninstitutional forms of punishment: parole and probation (Rothman, 1980; Simon, 1993). Probation provided an alternative to incarceration that would keep marginal cases out of prison. In combination with indeterminate sentences, parole provided a means of letting reformed prisoners out of prison earlier so they could continue to be corrected in the community. There, dedicated parole and probation agents could cater to the unique needs of individuals and give them the treatment appropriate to their particular case. In reality, reliance on incarceration increased despite intentions to the contrary. Importantly for our purposes, however, these innovations represent another alternative to the traditional Auburn-style prison in this period.

UNDERSTANDING THE TREND

What explains this curious trend? Why do the first two significant periods of prison development emerge fairly homogeneously with states following the dominant examples of Walnut Street Jail and Auburn State Prison, while the later period lacks a central model? What was different about the post—Civil War period that led to diversity instead of homogeneity, as occurred with the two previous periods?

Dominant understandings of penality have often located penal regime change in structural or ideological changes in society. Drawing on Marxist social theory, several scholars have emphasized the role of economic changes, especially labor needs, in shaping penal trends (McLennan, 2008; Melossi & Pavarini, 1981; Rusche & Kirchheimer, 1939; Simon, 1993). For Foucault (1977), the emergence of the prison as a penal technology reflected a larger change in society towards disciplinary labor, in which the factory, and its requisite form of power, became a model for everything from education to medicine. The mid-nineteenth-century decline of penal reformism can also be traced to a general disappointment American reformers experienced when their high hopes were not met (Walters, 1978). While each of these are promising explanations, they do not centrally address the proliferation of forms in the period examined.

For Rothman (1980), the variety of new facilities, programs, and practices intended to corral and correct society's deviants reflected new ideas of the Progressive Era. The unique and diverse characteristics of deviants required individual assessments and treatments. All deviants could not be treated alike, but instead needed different technologies of reform customized to their particular problem. Thus, juveniles had to be treated separately from adults, first-time offenders must be sent elsewhere from hardened offenders, and parole and probation must be available to those for whom institutionalization is too severe. For Rothman, this new mentality underlies a proliferation of different medical, psychological, and criminological treatments. However, like his earlier examination of the Jacksonian Era developments (Rothman 1971, Rubin, 2014), this explanation helps explain proliferation in the urbanized northeastern and (increasingly) midwestern states where Progressive reformers were most concentrated. Yet, the proliferation of prison forms specifically occurred nationwide and not exclusively at the behest of Progressive reformers. Another explanation is required.

Specifically, I turn to neo-institutional theory to understand how the dynamics within the carceral field – the complex of penal organizations, prisons, reformers, legislators – shaped this diversification. As for Foucault, the technology of the prison itself is central to this analysis. However, while external forces beyond the field play a role, they are not the central focus. If the emergence of prison was, for Foucault, the result of a larger shift in power relations in society, here I argue the proliferation of prison forms was the result of the prison's maturation. I will discuss other factors, such as the role of the Civil War, but these would not have had the same effects had the prison been less institutionalized.

Neo-Institutional Theory

Neo-institutional scholars locate organizational behaviors in collective understandings of legitimate behavior. Specifically, neo-institutional scholars argue that organizations visibly behave according to the normative demands or cognitive frameworks or expectations of their field (the aggregate of all similar organizations and their affiliates, e.g., regulators, resource-granting agencies, client organizations). Conformity with these norms or expectations conveys legitimacy; consequently, the norms, cognitive expectations, and legal regulations prevalent in the field determine what constitutes legitimate organizational forms or behaviors. These beliefs, rules, or cultural scripts can emerge organically and contingently in the field, or interested actors may manipulate them (DiMaggio & Powell, 1983; Meyer & Rowan, 1977). A primary consequence of this need for conformity to gain legitimacy is the overt similarity of organizational forms. Schools, factories, businesses, and prisons frequently adopt the same policies, technologies, and formal practices as others in their respective fields. This "startling homogeneity" of forms within a field is called "institutional isomorphism" (DiMaggio & Powell, 1983, p. 148).

However, scholars have pointed out that there is a vast amount of diversity nested within otherwise isomorphic fields. While most states have adopted new laws increasing penalties for sex offenders, their "type, intensity, and design" vary across states (Mancini, Barnes, & Mears, 2013). Similarly, while a majority of states had instituted hate crime statutes in the last decades of the twentieth century, groups that were given a protected status, the type of behaviors deemed criminal, and the penalty enhancement likewise varied by state (Grattet, Jenness, & Curry, 1998). Institutional isomorphism can exist on one level, but other levels may have profound diversity. In some cases, fields can simply become heterogeneous over time (Beckert, 2010; Hambrick, Finkelstein, Cho, & Jackson, 2005; Kraatz & Zajac, 1996). Understanding the conditions of this diversity enmeshed in homogeneity has thus become an important focus for neo-institutional theorists.

One explanation for this outcome is grounded in the maturation or institutionalization of a particular form. A form is institutionalized when it is taken-for-granted, accepted as legitimate, and part of basic routines. Institutionalization is both sustained and evidenced by widespread adoption. Indeed, once a form is institutionalized, the reticent organizations adopt it more rapidly (Tolbert & Zucker, 1983). However, institutionalization has other effects as well. Specifically, Grattet et al. (1998) suggest the "differentiation" in the content of a particular form "occurs only when the general construct is institutionalized." That is, some organizations simply copy an existing form, adopt it without variation (Willis, Mastrofski, & Weisburd, 2007). However, organizations that have already adopted the form begin to experiment with their existing form, tweaking it to address new challenges. As Grattet et al. (1998, p. 303) explain, "differentiation of content in the later part of the process signifies that the general construct is so taken-for-granted that states feel free to expand its domain."

Explaining the Prison's Post-War Differentiation

By the Civil War, the prison was clearly institutionalized in the United States. Nearly every state had adopted a prison, most on the same form. Failure to adopt a prison was a liability (Rubin, 2014). Even in the South, "the institution had established a tradition in the region, had developed its own inertia" (Ayers, 1984, p. 188). I argue that the extent to which the prison had become a taken-for-granted feature of the penal landscape at this point gave states license to experiment with new forms of prison, to push the existing model in new directions.

Indeed, we primarily see this variation begin in states that already had prisons. The first reformatories were in New York, Michigan, Massachusetts, and Pennsylvania, not Kansas or Nebraska, which had only adopted prisons in the 1860s. The first female reformatories for women were in New York, New Jersey, and Ohio, each of which had a prison at least since the 1830s. The first experiments with convict leasing and chain gangs were in Mississippi, not South Carolina, which had waited to adopt a prison. It was not the new frontier states entering the union, or states that had waited to adopt prisons, that experimented with prison design to fit their needs. Instead, it was states for which prison was a familiar response to crime and that no longer needed to demonstrate conformity to a field in which they had long been a member.

Maturation of the prison, however, also creates other incentives to diversify prison forms. In particular, reliance on prisons increased over time as they became more widely accepted and the default punishment for serious (and some not so serious) offenders. States constructed female prisons in large part because women were finally a large enough portion of the population to merit their own facilities. As their sheer number increased, housing women in a small attic or separate wing of the prison was no longer an option. Additionally, their increased number helped to call attention to the abuses and neglect they suffered (Rafter, 1985). Likewise, with greater numbers of prisoners in general, prison officials could increasingly distinguish between different types of prisoners. Again, the number of apparently hardened offenders and salvageable offenders increased sufficiently for administrators to perceive a need to send different populations to specialized prisons. As traditional prisons lost their reformative ethos, prisons seemed the wrong place for the growing number (particularly following the Civil War) of young offenders.

Finally, historical contingency is not irrelevant. Indeed, the timing of this proliferation of forms is not accidental. I argue that the Civil War acted as an exogenous shock on the carceral field in several ways. First, the Civil War put tremendous pressure on the capacity of existing prisons. Overcrowding had long been a problem in northern (and some southern) prisons. However, following the Civil War, prisons experienced extremely severe overcrowding. In the year after the Civil War, Eastern State Penitentiary officials were forced to double-cell their prisoners, systematically violating their rule of separate confinement (Rubin, 2013). Overcrowding led many prison administrators to ask their legislators to construct new prisons to relieve the overcrowding. The opportunity to build new prisons supplementing existing prisons provided the first opportunity for large-scale specialization.

Second, the Civil War had two significant effects in the South. First, many states had to rebuild prisons in the wake of the war. Union soldiers burned down some southern prisons (which, under the Auburn System, resembled factories; Ayers, 1984, p. 186). As with the need to compensate for overcrowding, prison building provided opportunities to experiment and create alternative models. Second, race relations in the post—Civil War South had a direct bearing on that region's distinctive prison developments. The Civil War profoundly shifted social relations in the South. Ultimately, convict leasing, chain gangs, and plantation-style prisons represent southern experiments to replace slavery as the major form of social control over African-Americans (see also Wacquant, 2001).

IMPLICATIONS

Importantly, this variation in the available models of prison did not stop in the Progressive Era. Over the course of the twentieth century, prisons continued to experience proliferation, not only in their numbers but also in their varieties. While we most often think of the Big House, Correctional Institution, and Warehouse Prison, the prison continued to experience variety. States continued to build separate women's prisons and juvenile facilities. Different prisons of each type were created for different security levels. While the rest of the country moved on to big houses and correctional institutions, the South continued its reliance on plantation-style prisons until the middle of the twentieth century (Feeley & Rubin, 2000). The super-maximum security prison (supermax) or secure housing unit (SHU) represents the most recent subvariety of warehouse prison.

Recognizing the late-nineteenth-century developments helps to historicize this last development as well. This is not the first time that a separate kind of prison has been developed for prisoners' unique levels of criminality. Many point to the Alcatraz Federal Penitentiary (1936–1963) as the supermax's predecessor. However, we can look earlier. The emergence of adult reformatories for novice criminals and young offenders occurred as traditional Auburn-style prisons were reserved for hardened, biologically determined criminals. This was the first major split in which facilities states would send types of prisoners based on their level of criminality.

REFERENCES

Allen, F. (1981). *The decline of the rehabilitative ideal: Penal policy and social purpose.* New Haven, CT: Yale University Press.

Ayers. (1984). *Vengeance and justice: Crime and punishment in the 19th-century American South.* New York, NY: Oxford University Press.

Banner, S. (2002). *The death penalty: An American history.* Cambridge, MA: Harvard University Press.

Beckert, J. (2010). Institutional isomorphism revisited: Convergence and divergence in institutional change. *Sociological Theory*, *28*(2), 150–166.

Blomberg, & Lucken (2000). *American penology: A history of control.* New York, NY: Aldine de Gruyter.

Bright, C. (1996). *The powers that punish: Prison and politics in the era of the "Big House," 1920–1955.* Ann Arbor: University of Michigan Press.

DiMaggio, P. J., & Powell, W. W. (1983). The iron cage revisited: Institutional isomorphism and collective rationality in organizational fields. *American Sociological Review*, *48*(2), 147–160.

Dodge, L. M. (2006). *Whores and thieves of the worst kind: A study of women, crime and prisons 1835–2000.* DeKalb, IL: Northern Illinois University Press.

Feeley, M., & Rubin, E. (2000). *Judicial policy making and the modern state: How the courts reformed America's prisons.* Cambridge, MA: Cambridge University Press.

Foucault, M. (1977). *Discipline and punish: The birth of the prison.* New York, NY: Vintage Books.

Grattet, R., Jenness, V., & Curry, T. R. (1998). The homogenization and differentiation of hate crime law in the United States, 1978 to 1995: Innovation and diffusion in the criminalization of bigotry. *American Sociological Review*, *63*(2), 286–307.

Hambrick, D. C., Finkelstein, S., Cho, T. S., & Jackson, E. M. (2005). Rethinking social control. *Research in Organizational Behavior*, *26*, 307–350.

Hindus, M. (1980). *Prison and plantation: Crime, justice, and authority in Massachusetts and South Carolina, 1767–1878.* Chapel Hill, NC: University of North Carolina Press.

Hirsch, A. J. (1992). *The rise of the penitentiary: Prisons and punishment in Early America.* New Haven, CT: Yale University Press.

Irwin, J. (1980). *Prisons in turmoil.* Boston, MA: Little, Brown.

Irwin, J. (2005). *The warehouse prison: Disposal of the new dangerous class.* Los Angeles, CA: Roxbury.

Jacobs, J. B. (1977). *Stateville: The penitentiary in mass society.* Chicago, IL: University Of Chicago Press.

Keve, P. W. (1991). *Prisons and the American conscience: A history of U.S. federal corrections.* Carbondale, IL: Southern Illinois University Press.

Kraatz, M. S., & Zajac, E. J. (1996). Exploring the limits of the new institutionalism: The causes and consequences of illegitimate organizational change. *American Sociological Review*, *61*(5), 812–836.

Lewis, O. F. (1922). *The development of American prisons and prison customs, 1776–1845: With special reference to early institutions in the state of New York*. Albany, NY: Prison Association of New York.

Lichtenstein, A. (1996). *Twice the work of free labor: The political economy of convict labor in the New South*. London: Verso.

Mancini, C., Barnes, J. C., & Mears, D. P. (2013). It varies from state to state: An examination of sex crime laws nationally. *Criminal Justice Policy Review*, *24*(2), 166–198.

McKelvey, B. (1977). *American prisons: A history of good intentions*. Montclair, NJ: Patterson Smith.

McLennan, R. M. (2008). *The crisis of imprisonment: Protest, politics, and the making of the American penal state, 1776–1941*. New York, NY: Cambridge University Press.

Melossi, D., & Pavarini, M. (1981). *The prison and the factory: Origins of the penitentiary system*. Totowa, NJ: Barnes and Noble Books.

Meranze, M. (1996). *Laboratories of virtue: Punishment, revolution, and authority in Philadelphia, 1760–1835*. Chapel Hill, NC: University of North Carolina Press.

Meyer, J. W., & Rowan, B. (1977). Institutionalized organizations: Formal structure as myth and ceremony. *American Journal of Sociology*, *83*(2), 340–363.

Oshinsky, D. (1997). *Worse than slavery: Parchman Farm and the ordeal of Jim Crow justice*. New York, NY: Free Press.

Pisciotta, A. (1994). *Benevolent repression: Social control and the American reformatory-prison movement*. New York, NY: New York University Press.

Rafter, N. (1985). *Partial justice: Women in state prisons, 1800–1935*. Boston, MA: Northeastern University Press.

Rothman, D. J. (1971). *The discovery of the asylum: Social order and disorder in the new republic*. Boston, MA: Little, Brown.

Rothman, D. J. (1980). *Conscience and convenience: The asylum and its alternatives in progressive America*. Hawthorne, NY: Aldine de Gruyter.

Rubin, A. T. (2013). *Maintaining organizational exceptionalism: Administrative support of the Pennsylvania System at Eastern State Penitentiary, 1829–1875*. PhD thesis, U.C. Berkeley.

Rubin, A. T. (2014). *College of criminology and criminal justice*. Tallahassee, FL: Florida State University.

Rusche, G., & Kirchheimer, O. (1939). *Punishment and social structure*. New York, NY: Columbia University Press.

Simon, J. (1993). *Poor discipline: Parole and the social control of the urban underclass, 1890–1990*. Chicago, IL: University of Chicago Press.

Simon, J. (2007). *Governing through crime: How the war on crime transformed American democracy and created a culture of fear*. New York, NY: Oxford University Press.

Tolbert, P. S., & Zucker, L. G. (1983). Institutional sources of change in the formal structure of organizations: The diffusion of civil service reform, 1880–1935. *Administrative Science Quarterly*, *28*(1), 22–39.

Wacquant, L. (2001). Deadly symbiosis: When ghetto and prison meet and mesh. *Punishment & Society*, *3*(1), 95–133.

Walters, R. G. (1978). *American reformers, 1815–1860*. New York, NY: Hill and Wang.

Willis, J. J., Mastrofski, S. D., & Weisburd, D. (2007). Making sense of COMPSTAT: A theory-based analysis of organizational change in three police departments. *Law and Society Review*, *41*(1), 147–188.

NATIVE AMERICAN INCARCERATION: A NEGLECTED PROBLEM?

Roy F. Janisch

ABSTRACT

Purpose – *In this chapter, the author outlines the historical, legal, and jurisdiction regarding incarceration rates of Native Americans. It examines reports and data in areas where problems of racial disparity continue to endure. As the smallest minority population in the United States, it raises questions as to the disparity of Native Americans. Native Americans are unique in their relationship with the federal government, and should be critically examined to distinguish what makes their involvement in the criminal justice system inimical.*

Design/methodology/approach – *The author examines the law enforcement, courts, and corrections data, through various reports; concerning causes of Native American criminality, incarceration rates, health disparities, jurisdictional schemes, human rights, and race. It is argued that federal governmental laws and various bureaucracies exacerbate conditions through overreaching policies which invalidates many of the positive aspects Native People bring to themselves.*

Punishment and Incarceration: A Global Perspective
Sociology of Crime, Law and Deviance, Volume 19, 159–177

ISSN: 1521-6136/doi:10.1108/S1521-613620140000019007

Findings – *Native Americans are overrepresented in the criminal justice system. As the smallest segment of the population, they have a higher incarceration rate per capita. It is without question that chronic underfunding of law enforcement, courts, and corrections in reservation communities continues. In light of Congressional claiming to want to alleviate problems in Indian country, little impact has been realized.*

Originality/value – *Native American societies are often considered a silent minority. Information pertaining to the many social issues enveloping Native communities often falls on deaf ears and political party leaders who are more interested in a larger constituency fail to lend their assistance in a manner deemed appropriate to truly grasp the larger problems.*

Keywords: Native American; incarceration; history; Supreme Court; prison; jail

INTRODUCTION

Problems of racial disparity in the United States continue to endure. Specifically, the incarceration rates of minorities in prisons are alarmingly high with a myriad of explanations why our country continues to incarcerate the disproportionately high numbers of minorities in the penal system. The current disparity of incarcerated persons raises questions regarding the incarceration of Native Americans in the United States. Native Americans are unique in their relationship with the federal government, and, as such, the group should be critically examined to distinguish what makes their involvement in the criminal justice system inimical.

Native American populations are subject to multiple layers of criminal jurisdiction; including federal, tribal, state, and local authorities. Furthermore, each level of governmental bureaucracy exacerbates conditions through overbearing policies that invalidate many of the positive aspects Native People bring to both themselves and society as a whole. Despite their small population numbers relative to the entire US population, Native Americans have a higher prison incarceration rate per capita when compared to either the US population as a whole or the prison population. The research examines through US Census Bureau, Department of Justice (DOJ), National Institute of Justice (NIJ), Bureau of Indian Affairs (BIA), and other not-for-profit organizational reports and statistical analyses, and seeks to understand what the fundamental criteria are in causing this disparity.

Following a discussion of the statistical analysis of the data, the research explores public policy and jurisdictional issues that may assist in determining the causes of the increases in incarceration rates of American Indians in the US prison system.

A LEGAL HISTORY OF AMERICAN INDIANS

The United States and its original Native (Indian) inhabitants have struggled with one another since the arrival of European settlers to the continent. Indian tribes have consistently been recognized, first by European nations, then by the United States as, distinct, political societies separated from others (*Cherokee Nation v. Georgia* 30 U.S. (5 Pet.) (1831)). This recognition is not through a formal delegation of authority but by reason of their original tribal sovereignty. The formulation and implementation of laws and rules applicable to Indians are grounded in the Constitution of the United States. Regarding the President, it states, "He shall have Power, by and with the Advice and Consent of the Senate, to make Treaties" (U.S. Const. art. II, § 2). It, further, lends him the power "to regulate Commerce with foreign Nations, and among the several States, and with the Indian Tribes" (U.S. Const. art. I, § 8).

In addition to constitutional oversight integration, as stated in the supremacy clause, treaties "are superior to any conflicting state laws and constitutional provisions" (Art. VI, Clause 2). Finally, there are any number of congressional authorities that govern Indian Country in the forms of executive orders, Congressional statutes, and administrative rules and regulations. These purported federal oversights, couched in claims of expertise in specific areas of Indian-run programs, are too controlling for Indian communities. As Deloria (1985) notes:

> The Indian is never alone. The life he leads is not his to control. This is not permitted. Every aspect of his being is affected and defined by his relationship to the Federal Government – primarily, to one agency of the Federal Government: the Bureau of Indian Affairs (BIA). Even when exercised illegally, the total power of the BIA is virtually unchallengeable and unreviewable. Where the normal citizen has three avenues of redress; political, judicial, administrative – the Indian has none. Through the pervasiveness of that bureau's role, the exercise of power and administration of programs by the BIA have come to ensure that every effort by the Indian to achieve self-realization is frustrated and penalized; that the Indian is kept in a state of permanent dependency

> as his price of survival; and that alienation from his people and past is rewarded and encouraged for the Indian. (p. 179)

The Constitution recognizes Indian treaties made before its adoption, an issue supported by the United States Supreme Court in *Worcester v. Georgia*, 31 U.S. 515 (1832). The verdict also held that the political existence of the tribes continued after their relations with both the states and the federal government. Because of the tribes' relationship with the federal government, federal statutes limit tribal powers of self-government, both by the terms and conditions of treaties with the federal government and by restraints implicit in the protectorate relationship itself.

In all other respects the tribes remain independent and self-governing political entities. This is an area of Indian policy where many Indian people hold the government in disregard because it administers programs that Indians believe to be theirs. Furthermore, treaties negotiated by tribes in the early days, in the area of Indian affairs, contained some very basic notion of fairness or justice. Indian people believe that if they must abide by the treaties, then the federal government must also hold steadfast in their stated obligations to the tribes.

Treaties frequently called for the delivery of goods and services to the Indian tribes by the United States, in exchange for the vast quantities of land ceded to the government. These goods and services took the form of monetary payments, annuities, or other monies that were negotiated. Other provisions were (a) health care, (b) education, (c) welfare, (d) irrigation, (e) farming implements, (f) crop seed, (g) training, and (h) land management, to name just a few. Frequently, the United States committed itself more deeply to Indian tribes because it had extended treaty rights with *special* rights, to soften the blow of land cessions. Treaties are the vehicles that legally bind the federal government to Indian governments and create their unique political relationship, most often referred to as the government-to-government relationship that exists between the federal and tribal governments of the United States. One of the major issues with which treaties dealt concerned the political and jurisdictional problems created by offenses of Indians against non-Indians or by non-Indians against Indians. This intergroup conflict only preceded what would soon become the inevitable.

In a series of cases known as the *Marshall Trilogy*, Chief Justice John Marshall delivered the opinions of the Court which are the focal points in Indian jurisprudence. The case of *Johnson v. McIntosh* concerned the validity of a grant of land made by tribal chiefs to private individuals, before passage of the Trade and Intercourse Acts, which would not have allowed the land trade. The Court held the trade of land between the parties to the suit invalid. In what is now called the "discovery doctrine," the Court ruled that the discovering European sovereign held title to the land and along with it, the sole right of acquiring the soil from the natives. Therefore, the Court concluded that the Indians' right to title of land was impaired and they traded a property right for a political right (Johnson v. McIntosh, 1823).

The other two primary cases, upon which the foundations of modern Indian law are built, stem from attempts by the state of Georgia to acquire lands from the Cherokee Indians. The Cherokee Cases highlighted the political doctrine of Manifest Destiny and the era of westward expansion, proving the Court would be the battleground where state and Indian governments would engage in additional conflicts, an adage used today. Chief Justice Marshall's opinion in *Cherokee Nation v. Georgia*, regarding the sovereign nature of the Cherokees stated that the Indian tribes were domestic dependent nations, although not foreign nations, and they did comprise themselves as possessing legitimate legal and political status, that they could manage their own affairs, govern themselves internally, and engage in relations with the federal government and its subdivisions. Additionally, Marshall remarked on the status of the Cherokees:

> Though the Indians are acknowledged to have an unquestionable, and, heretofore unquestioned, right to the lands they occupy, until that right shall be extinguished by a voluntary cession to our government; yet it may well be doubted, whether those tribes which reside within the acknowledged boundaries of the United States can, with strict accuracy, be denominated foreign nations. They may, more correctly, perhaps, be denominated domestic dependent nations. They occupy a territory to which we assert a title independent of their will, which must take effect in point of possession, when their right of possession ceases. Meanwhile, they are in a state of pupilage; their relation to the United States resembles that of a ward to his guardian. (30 U.S. (5 Pet.), 1831)

The following year in *Worcester v. Georgia*, the Supreme Court ruled against the wishes of President Andrew Jackson, who advocated the opening up of lands to White settlers for continued expansions and growth of the country. The Court also ruled that Indian tribes enjoyed limited sovereignty and states were without jurisdiction to enforce state law on Indian land. In his opinion, Marshall places the tribes in a historical context as they related to the federal and state governments. He examined the treaties, and the Trade and Intercourse Act of 1802, which provides for no land cessions by Indian tribes, except by treaty. He stated that these essential elements, manifestly, consider the several Indian nations as "distinct political communities, having territorial boundaries, within which their [State] authority is exclusive" (31 U.S. (6 Pet.) 557, 1832).

Marshall's summary concludes: "The Cherokee nation, then, is a distinct community, occupying its own territory, with boundaries accurately described, in which the laws of Georgia can have no force" (31 U.S. (6 Pet.) 561, 1832). The ruling, however, did not dissuade the President from advocating Indian removal. The increasing limitations on Indian sovereignty through treaty-making, relocation, and reservation eras decimated Indian cultures. The following evinces the struggles between Indians and Whites in American history, as Prucha (1962) laments:

> Protection of the rights and persons of the Indians remained more an ideal than a reality. Weaknesses and inadequacies are easy to catalog. Harder to judge is the over-all effect of the intercourse acts in these early years. That they prevented much open conflict between the races and allowed the inevitable westward advance of White settlement to proceed with a certain orderliness is perhaps judgment enough. (pp. 275–277)

One of the main issues with which the treaties dealt concerned the political and jurisdictional problems created by offenses of Indians against non-Indians or by non-Indians against Indians. This area of Indian law is particularly unique, in that jurisdiction can take circuitous routes. Some of the relevant variables are (a) the land status, (b) racial class, (c) tribal membership, (d) nonmember, (e) tribal member of a different tribe other than where the actionable offense occurred, and (f) type of offense.

Some of the earlier treaties adopted a principle commonly found in international treaties between equals: non-Indians who settled and committed crimes within Indian Country were subject to punishment by the Indian tribe, just as Indians committing offenses against state or federal laws outside Indian Country were subject to punishment by state or federal courts. Several treaties provided for federal jurisdiction over crimes committed by its own citizens in Indian Country, requiring the tribes to deliver such offenders to agents of the federal government. For example, "any person introducing intoxicating liquors among the Indians shall be punished according to the laws of the United States" (U.S.C. 1154, 1995, p. 619).

After the end of treaty-making in 1871, the federal government – once again, through a Supreme Court action – would erode even more sovereignty from its Indian tribes. The facts of the case are: Chief Crow Dog, a Brule Sioux was engaged in an altercation with Spotted Tail, also a Brule Sioux Indian of the same band and nation. During the ensuing altercation Crow Dog killed Spotted Tail and was sentenced to death for the offense. Crow Dog brought suit for release under a writ of habeas corpus for release on the grounds that the federal courts did not have jurisdiction over crimes committed in Indian Country by one Indian against another. The Supreme Court upheld his petition and released him. It is worth noting the scope of the differences in culture and perspective in the Court's opinion:

> It is a case involving the judgment of a court of special and limited jurisdiction, not to be assumed without clear warrant of law. It is a case of life and death. It is a case where, against an express exception in the law itself, that law, by argument and inference only, is sought to be extended over aliens and strangers; over the members of a community separated by race, by tradition, by the instincts of a free though savage life, from the authority and power which seeks to impose upon them the restraints of an external and unknown code, and to subject them to the responsibilities of civil conduct, according to rules and penalties of which they could have no previous warning; which judges them by a standard made by others and not for them, which takes no account of the conditions which should except them from its exactions, and makes no allowance for their inability to understand it.
>
> It tries them, not by their peers, nor by the customs of their people, nor the law of their land, but by superiors of a different race, according to the law of a social state of which they have an imperfect conception, and which is opposed to the traditions of their history, to the habits of their lives, to the strongest prejudices of their savage nature; one which measures the Red man's revenge by maxims of the White man's morality. It is a case too, of first impression, so far as we are advised, for, if the question has been mooted heretofore in any courts in the United States, the jurisdiction has never before been practically asserted as in the present instance. (Ex Parte Crow Dog, 109 U.S. 556, 1883)

There was such an outcry over the unfair outcome in the Crow Dog case that Congress was led to pass the *Major Crimes Act of 1885* (18 U.S.C.A. 1153), calling for Federal jurisdiction over seven major crimes. The consequential granting of Federal jurisdiction proved to place even more constraints on the tribes by limiting their ability to effectively utilize their internal sovereignty and control criminal conduct within their territories. The Major Crimes Act was, subsequently, challenged and upheld in *United States v. Kagama*, 118 U.S. 375 (1886) with the theory of guardianship established, simultaneously. The Court held that the federal government has the duty of protection against individual and state interference in Indian affairs because the federal government usurped tribal authority when it exerted its own authority over the tribes.

The issue of land has shaped a large segment of Indian law and terminology, as it relates to the federal government's allotment policy toward Indians. It has also been the single most important issue facing Indians – both historically and in contemporary times. With the passage of the General Allotment Act of 1887 (Dawes Act, 24 Stat. 388, codified as amended by 25 U.S.C. 331-334, 339, 341, 342, 348, 349, 354 and 381), the federal government theorized that Indians would become more quickly assimilated if they were to become owners of parcels of land and encouraged to pursue civilizing agricultural pursuits and cast away their traditional means of existence. Indian allotments were provided to individuals, with each head of household receiving an 80-acre parcel of agricultural land or 160 acres of grazing land (Act of February 28, 1891, 26 Stat. 794, 25 U.S.C. 331). These allotments were held in trust for individuals by the federal government. That is, the *legal* title was held by the United States and the allottee, the individual Indian, was given the *beneficial* title – the right to live on, use, and profit from the allotment. Each allottee was given a "trust patent" reflecting his or her "ownership" of the property. So long as the title was held in trust by the United States, it was not to be subject to state or local taxation or regulation.

Upon the completion of the allotment process it was common for the United States to seek agreements with the tribe for the identification of lands to be held in common by the tribe and for the cession of the remaining lands as "surplus" lands (24 Stat. 388, 389-90, 25 U.S.C. 348). This process resulted in the loss of millions of acres of tribal land between 1887 and 1934, because of the sale of "surplus" lands and alienation of allotments.

The preceding discussion on sovereignty has established the road of sovereignty for Indian tribal governments in the United States. Chief Justice John Marshall, in his trilogy cases, has told us that Indian governments are "distinct, independent, political communities, retaining their original natural rights in matters of local self-government" (*Worcester v. Georgia*, 31 U.S. 515, 559, 1832). Although no longer "possessed of the full attributes of sovereignty, [tribes remain a] separate people, with the power of regulating their internal and social relations" (*United States v. Kagama*, 118 U.S. 375, 381-82, 1886). In short, Indians possess "the right ... to make their own laws and be ruled by them" (*Williams v. Lee*, 358 U.S. 217, 220, 1959).

Indian tribes have seen their sovereignty diminished, over time, by both federal and state governments.

Criminal Jurisdiction in Indian Country

As outlined above, the Federal and Tribal governments maintain a unique government-to-government relationship steeped in the United States

Constitution. A major controlling aspect of jurisdiction resides in the definition of "Indian Country" defined by 18 U.S.C. § 1151 as:

> ... (a) all land within the limits of any Indian reservation under the jurisdiction of the United States Government, notwithstanding the issuance of any patent, and including the rights-of-way through the reservation, (b) all dependent Indian communities within the borders of the United States whether within the original or subsequently acquired territory thereof, and whether within or without the limits of a state, and (c) all Indian allotments, the titles to which have not been extinguished, including rights-of-way running through the same.

Additionally controlling statutes governing Federal criminal jurisdiction in Indian country are 18 U.S.C. § 1152 and § 1153. Section 1153, also called the Major Crimes Act, gives the Federal Government jurisdiction to prosecute certain enumerated offenses, such as murder, manslaughter, rape, aggravated assault, and child sexual abuse, when they are committed by Indians in Indian country. Section 1152, known as the General Crimes Act, gives the Federal Government exclusive jurisdiction to prosecute all crimes committed by non-Indians against Indian victims in Indian country. Section 1152 also grants the Federal Government jurisdiction to prosecute minor crimes by Indians against non-Indians, although that jurisdiction is shared with tribes, and provides that the Federal Government may not prosecute an Indian who has been punished by the local tribe. Section 1152 specifically excludes minor crimes between Indians, which fall under exclusive tribal jurisdiction. The Federal Government also has jurisdiction to prosecute Federal crimes of general application, such as drug and financial crimes, when they occur in Indian country unless a specific treaty or statutory provision provides otherwise. On a limited number of reservations, the Federal criminal responsibilities under Sections 1152 and 1153 have been ceded to the States under "Public Law 280" or other Federal laws. Federal jurisdiction was ceded under Public Law 83-280, 18 U.S.C. § 1162, which required six states to assume jurisdiction over Indian country crimes and divested the Federal Government of jurisdiction to prosecute under the Major and General Crimes Acts, while giving other states the option to assume that jurisdiction. Congress has also passed a variety of tribe-specific statutes providing for a similar framework of state jurisdiction over crimes in those locations.

The most recent legislation impacting Indian Country is The Indian Law Enforcement Reform Act, 25 U.S.C. § 2801 establishing the Office of Justice Services (OJS) within BIA, which is responsible for the overall management of (BIA) law enforcement program. The OJS has seven areas of activity: Criminal Investigation and Police Services, Detention/

Corrections, Inspection/Internal Affairs, Tribal law Enforcement and Special Initiatives, the Indian Police Academy, Tribal Justice Support, and Program Management. The OJS also provides oversight and technical assistance to tribal law enforcement. The following is a summary of the jurisdictional interplay between sovereigns pertaining to prosecution of American Indians in courts today. Crimes occurring outside Indian Country shall, regardless of whether the offender or victim is Indian, be conducted exclusively under state criminal jurisdiction. Crimes occurring in Public Law 280 states: all crimes, regardless of whether the crime occurs in Indian country, or whether the offender or victim is Indian, are under state criminal jurisdiction, and crimes occurring in Indian Country in Non-Public Law 280 states: the intersection of federal, state, and tribal jurisdiction is set forth in Table 1.

Table 1.

Offender	Victim	Jurisdiction
A. Where jurisdiction has not been conferred on the state		
Non-Indian	Non-Indian	State
Non-Indian	Indian	Federal
Indian	Non-Indian	Federal
Indian	Indian	Federal 18 U.S.C. §1153
Non-Indian	Victimless	State
Indian	Victimless	Federal/Tribal – IGRA
B. Where jurisdiction has been conferred by Public Law 280, 18 U.S.C. § 1162 (1953)		
Non-Indian	Non-Indian	State
Non-Indian	Indian	State
Indian	Non-Indian	State
Indian	Indian	State/Federal if "Option"
Non-Indian	Victimless	State
Indian	Victimless	State & Tribal – Fed. Option
C. Where jurisdiction has been conferred by another statute		
Non-Indian	Non-Indian	State
Non-Indian	Indian	Concurrent Fed/State
Indian	Non-Indian	State concurrent Fed/Tribal
Indian	Indian	State concurrent with Tribal
Non-Indian	Victimless	State
Indian	Victimless	Concurrent state/Fed/Tribal

Source: Adapted from US Attorneys Resource Manual.

American Indian Socioeconomic Status

Approximately 2.5 million individuals in the United States identify themselves as American Indian or Alaska Native (0.9 percent of the population); another 1.6 million identify as part American Indian or Alaska Native as per the U.S. Census Bureau (The American Indian and Alaska Native Population: 2000 (2002b) hereafter: Census Bureau, AI/AN Population: 2000, p. 3.). Native Americans are more geographically clustered than other populations, with 62 percent residing in 11 states (Census Bureau, AI/AN Population: 2000, p. 4.). More Native Americans live in the West than any of the other three regions of the country (48 percent) (Census Bureau, AI/AN Population: 2000, p. 8.). Among all Native Americans, 79.3 percent report being enrolled in or affiliated with a tribe (compared with 66.9 percent of those reporting themselves as Native American and another race) (Census Bureau, AI/AN Population: 2000; p. 8).

The socioeconomic condition of the Native American population in the United States reveals a dire need for increased national attention. Native Americans rank at or near the bottom of nearly every social, health, and economic indicator. For example, the national poverty rate in the Unites States for the period between 1999 and 2001 was 11.6 percent. For Native Americans nationally, the average annual poverty rate was 24.5 percent. That is, nearly a quarter of Native Americans – more than twice the national average – live in poverty (U.S. Census Bureau, *Poverty in the United States: 2001, Current Population Reports*, 2002a). Nearly one in three (31.2 percent) of those residing on reservations live in poverty. The unemployment rate in the Native American population nationwide is 12.4 percent, more than twice the general unemployment rate (U.S. Census Bureau, *Sex by Employment Status for the Population 16 Years and Over*, 2000b). On reservations, unemployment averages 13.6 percent, but varies widely across the nation. Unemployment among the Navajo, for example, is 25 percent; on the Pine Ridge and Rosebud reservations in South Dakota, unemployment exceeds 33 percent; and on the Kickapoo reservation in Texas, unemployment is nearly 70 percent (U.S. Census Bureau, *Employment Status and Commuting to Work*, 2000a). Of Native Americans aged 18–24, only 63.2 percent have graduated from high school (compared with 76.5 percent of the US population) and of those 25 years and older, only 9.4 percent have completed four or more years of college (compared with 20.3 percent nationally) (U.S. Census Bureau, *Selected Social and Economic Characteristics for the 25 Largest American Indian Tribes*, 1995).

According to the U.S. DOJ, the lack of federal resources and efforts to address these issues may explain why Native Americans are the victims of crime at more than twice the rate of all U.S. residents (*American Indians and Crime*, 1999), thus accounting for increased involvement with the criminal justice system at various levels.

American Indian Health

Throughout the development of a new national government, armed conflict, the creation of a relocation and reservation system and the accompanying cultural transplantation of traditional Native societies, American Indians have come to realize a disparity in their health when compared to the average American citizen. For example, a report by the Indian Health Service states, "... perhaps because of inadequate education, disproportionate poverty, discrimination in the delivery of health services, and cultural differences" (IHS Fact Sheet, 2000). AI/AN communities face many health challenges including higher mortality rates from tuberculosis, chronic liver disease and cirrhosis, accidents, diabetes, pneumonia, suicide, and homicide compared with other racial and ethnic groups (Anderson, R. N. & Smith, B. L., 2003). Furthermore, in the AI/AN population, chronic liver disease and cirrhosis was the sixth leading cause of death, but was not ranked in the top 10 for the White, Black, or Asian or Pacific Islander populations in 2005. Additionally, during that same year, accidents accounted for more than twice the percentage of deaths (11.7 percent) of the AI/AN population compared with other population groups combined, and their age-adjusted suicide rates were 1.73 times as high as the corresponding rates for all persons combined (National Center for Health Statistics, Health, United States, 2008, p. 1). Finally, a summary of the report finding concluded the following: "..., in general compared with other groups, AI/AN adults are more likely to have poorer health, unmet medical needs due to cost, diabetes, trouble hearing, activity limitations, and to have experienced feelings of psychological distress in the past 30 days" (National Center for Health Statistics, Health, United States, 2008, p. 6). Additional researchers indicate that the dysfunctional aspects of both urban and reservation Native Americans is a contributing variable which increases the likelihood of alcohol use and abuse by the population.

NATIVE AMERICANS IN JAIL OR PRISON

> In the last two centuries, Congress has passed more Federal laws affecting American Indians than any other group of people in the United States. The Snyder Act, the Indian Reorganization Act of 1934, the Indian Self-Determination and Education Assistance Act, the Indian Education Amendments of 1978, and the No Child Left Behind Act of 2001, which includes the Native American Education Improvement Act of 2001, are just a few of the laws that have defined the Federal authority and obligation to provide various programs and services to Indian country. (U.S. Department of Interior, Indian Affairs, Fiscal Year, 2010)

Native Americans are often looked upon as historical relics or sports caricatures in the development of the United States. The beginnings of American Indian's problems of today are deeply rooted in the federal government laws and policies of forced relocation and the reservation system. This initial closed reservation system created communities forced into Western cultural values and beliefs which were incongruous to many Native American life ways. Many of these communities have developed into historical and perpetual adverse cultures of pathology; that is, those problems associated with generations of diminished sovereignty and civil rights, forced assimilation, lost autonomy, state interference, stagnant or no economic development opportunity, poverty, unemployment, alcoholism, drug abuse, domestic violence, and crime generally.

According to the Bureau of Justice Statistics (BJS), American Indians experienced violence at a rate (101 violent crimes per 1,000 American Indians) more than twice the rate for the nation (41 per 1,000 persons) (1992–2001). Recent data suggest similar characteristics even though there have been political and funding shifts aimed to alleviate this scenario. Note the general nature of the problem as suggested by the NIJ:

"Studies suggest that crime rates are much higher for American Indians compared with the national average. According to the Bureau of Justice Statistics, (BJS) American Indians (AI) and Alaska Natives (AN) experience violent crimes at rates far greater than the general population" (BJS, 2014). Furthermore, frequently cited statistics from national surveys, such as the National Crime Victimization Survey (NCVS), Uniform Crime Reports (UCRs), come from studies completed outside Indian Country – reservations, tribal communities, and trust land – and Alaska Native villages thus transferring "crime counting" to somebody. This issue is largely structural or systemic and originates from the case *Santa Clara Pueblo v. Martinez* 436 U.S. 49 (1978); a case allowing for each of the Federally Recognized Indian

Tribes in the United States to delineate the rules associated with membership in their community, creating access to citizenship, enrollment, identity, and access to any number of other social service benefits.

Most governmental studies are unable to locate the exact status of an individual's tribal membership, or enrollment status; which is largely relied upon as the basis for claiming "Indian" membership, which of course can be different depending on the legal rules of the individual Indian tribe and those rules which it has promulgated to determine the Indian status.

There exists no one rule for being "Indian" because different definitions are accepted in cases involving health care, social services, governmental, and academic contexts. The very definition of Indian Country as geography and "Indian-ness" as personal identity creates suspicions of unjust laws that center on racial classification. This perception is thus translated into reality when an Indian is sentenced by the court system. In 2002, the United States Sentencing Commission created an Ad Hoc Advisory Group on Native American Sentencing Issues in response to concerns that Federal Sentencing Guidelines had a discriminatory impact on Indian offenders in Indian country. For example, the Advisory Group found that for sex offenders prosecuted in New Mexico state courts the average sentence is 43 months, compared to 86 months in federal court. For crimes of assault, the average sentence in New Mexico state court is 6 months, compared to 54 months in the federal court (US Sentencing Commission, *Report of the Native American Advisory Group*, 2003, p. 17).

Data on Native Americans

Access to data is paramount to professional projects and data in Indian Country is difficult to obtain. Indian country case statistics can be drawn from three different jurisdictions: federal, state, and/or tribal jurisdictions. The Federal Bureau of Investigation's UCR contains offense data from all three sources, but counts only crimes reported to law enforcement for those agencies that volunteer to submit. Furthermore, UCR does not collect the specific information on declinations and administrative closing required by the Tribal Law and Order Act (TLOA). A more complete understanding of crime rates in Indian country would require that all reported criminal offenses, whether reported to and/or filed with the tribal, state, or Federal government, be collectively assembled and analyzed. Regrettably, no single system exists that would permit collection and analysis of aggregate Indian country crime and prosecution data across sovereigns. And even if such a system existed, unreported crime would remain outstanding and uncounted.

These difficulties are due largely to the protracted timeframe of underfunding or inconsistent funding for decades; inadequate resources, personnel, training, and with no single system existing to provide those data makes the study of Native issues extremely complex. In addition to being the victims of crime more often, Native Americans are also overrepresented in jails and prisons. American Indians are incarcerated at a rate 38 percent higher than the national per capita rate (Hensen & Taylor, 2002, p. 132).

Alaska Natives are incarcerated at nearly twice the rate of their representation in the state population (Alaska Advisory Committee, *Racism's Frontier*, p. 43). The number of Native American youth in the federal prison system has increased 50 percent since 1994 (Andrews, 2000, p. 3.). Many Native Americans attribute disproportionate incarceration rates to unfair treatment by the criminal justice system, including racial profiling, disparities in prosecution, and lack of access to legal representation. Because of burgeoning crime and the lack of culturally appropriate treatment, prevention, and other programs, jails in Indian Country regularly operate beyond capacity. In 2001, the 10 largest jails were at 142 percent capacity, and nearly a third of all tribal facilities were operating above 150 percent capacity (U.S. DOJ, "Jails in Indian Country," p. 3).

As stated above, data on American Indians is difficult to amass. Couched in legal justification and a historical misnomer in the trust doctrine, the myriad of government entities entrusted with maintaining a policy of self-determination has met with little to no success. The clashing of cultures for over 200 years has seen a continual contradiction over what to do about instances of criminality in terms of legal/cultural avenues for two different world views. In a report by the U.S. DOJ, Office of Justice Programs, "[a]bout 5,881 violent offenders entered Federal prison during fiscal year 2001. American Indians were 16% (913) of all offenders entering Federal prison for violent crimes. The American Indian proportion of all violent offenders entering Federal prison has remained stable since 1996 – about 15%" (*American Indians and Crime*, 2004).

As stated earlier and to reiterate here, a major difficulty in counting crime in Indian Country stems from the fact that there exists no single system for classification in terms of race across states. National incarceration numbers approximate national census numbers, however, the number of states with a higher Indian population are disproportionally higher. For example, in Montana, according to the 2000 U.S. Census, Native Americans, the state's largest non-White group, comprise just 6.2 percent of Montana's population but 20 percent of those in correctional institutions. Nineteen percent of the 3,704 Montana men and boys being held in correctional institutions are Native American. Nearly one-third of the 429 women in correctional institutions are Native American (*Prison Working Group*, 2007).

SUMMARY

The various levels of criminal jurisdiction for example, federal, tribal, state, over American Indians place them at a disadvantage for higher rates of punishment (increased rates of incarceration) through a jurisdictional matrix over non-Indian citizens compared to non-Indian incarcerated populations. A stark example of the impact of the overreaching laws and policies over Native Americans was articulated in *United States v. Jerry Paul* (D. N. M., 1996), where the court stated:

> Due to the criminal jurisdictional scheme in Indian country, Indian offenders of major crimes are prosecuted in federal court, under the Major Crimes Act, and subject to the Federal Sentencing Guidelines. If non-Indian offenders commit the same crime they are typically subject to prosecution and sentencing by the state authorities in state court. This differing sentencing scheme for Indians versus non-Indians has a disparate impact on Native American defendants, as state criminal sentences are typically lower than federal criminal sentences. (*United States v. Jerry Paul*, 929 F. Supp. 1406, 1407-1408 (D. N. M., 1996))

According to the DOJ, the TLOA requires the BJS to establish and implement a tribal data collection system and to support tribal participation in national records and information systems (2010). This newest system is designed to work in concert with the FBI's Uniform Crime Reporting system by working with tribal criminal justice system components to improve the collection of data used in the administration of justice throughout Indian country. According to the most recent report from the BJS, the following activities occurred in Indian country law enforcement:

> The (BJS) consulted with tribal leaders through a variety of forums in 2010 and for the first time, the Bureau of Indian Affairs' (BIA) submissions to the Uniform Crime Reporting Program (UCR) were disaggregated by tribe and reported in *Crime in the U.S., 2009*. The number of tribes eligible for Byrne/JAG funding increased from 5 to 22 while in 2008, 140 tribal law enforcement staff received UCR training. BJS provided competitive funding opportunities for jurisdictions to improve criminal records keeping and developed a multifaceted data collection system that both established new collections and enhanced current programs. Furthermore, tribally operated law enforcement

> agencies employed nearly 4,600 full-time personnel, including about 3,000 sworn officers with the largest tribal agency, the Navajo Police Department, employing 393 full-time sworn personnel in Arizona, New Mexico, and Utah. Eleven of the 25 largest tribal law enforcement agencies served jurisdictions covering more than 1,000 square miles. Overall, tribal police departments cost about $257 per resident to operate during fiscal year 2008. In addition to law enforcement functions, nearly all tribal police departments performed court-related functions, such as court security and serving process. More than half of tribal police departments used community policing officers, and more than a third used school resource officers. About 4 in 5 tribal police departments participated in one or more multiagency task forces. (DOJ, Office of Justice Programs, *Compendium of Tribal Crime Data*, 2011)

The National Native American Bar Association reports Congress found that "[t]ribal justice systems are an essential part of tribal governments and serve as important forums for ensuring public health, safety and the political integrity of tribal governments" (25 U.S.C. § 3601(5)) and that "tribal justice systems are inadequately funded, and the lack of adequate funding impairs their operation" (25 U.S.C. § 3601(8)). In order to remedy this lack of funding, "the Act authorized appropriation base funding support for tribal justice systems in the amount of $50,000,000 for each of the fiscal years 1994 through 2000" (25 U.S.C. § 3621(b)). To carry out the provisions of the Indian Tribal Justice Act, Congress authorized annual appropriations of over $58 million annually for each of the fiscal years 1994–1999 with $50 million annually for base support funding for tribal justice systems. Unfortunately, however, a total of only $5 million of the more than $58 million per year appropriated was actually appropriated through 1999 (United States Commission on Civil Rights, 2003). "Since the passage of the Act in 1993, the needs of tribal court systems have continued to increase, but there has been no corresponding increase in funding for tribal court systems" (Pub. L. No. 106-559 § 202, 199, 2000). In a frank assessment of the underfunding of Indian country justice systems, *A Quiet Crisis: Federal Funding and Unmet Needs in Indian Country* stated: "As long as tribal courts are underfunded and unable to deal with tribal jurisprudence, the burden for criminal justice will continue to fall on the federal court system, where sentences are typically harsher, perpetuating a system of dual justice for Native Americans on reservations" (United States Commission on Civil Rights).

In their recent text, *The Punishment Imperative*, Clear and Frost (2014) impeach the *entire* punitive system when they say:

> … from the expansion of the prison system are broken families, weakened parental relationships with children, loss of earnings, economic damage to communities, reduced personal health, shorter life expectancies for youth, and teenage births. To top it off,

> there is growing evidence that the concentrated growth of incarceration has contributed to higher crime rates in the neighborhoods that send so many people to prison, only to receive them back a short time later. It is entirely plausible that none of the policies of the Punishment Imperative was designed to produce these results. But the concentration of the grand penal experiment among poor males, especially minority-group members, means that the collateral consequences they suffer from the expanded justice system are a main product of the generation-long changes in that system. The bottom line is that this group, the country's most vulnerable citizens suffer the consequences of both crime itself and the social responses to crime.

American Indian governments are in an appropriate position to possess, create, implement, and maintain systems of justice for their citizens. In order to control its citizenry it must continue to adhere to those institutions of cultural relevancy which contributes most to the maintenance and development of their societies. In order for this to occur, the federal government must adhere to those principles of sovereignty, self-determination, and trust utilizing their utmost capacities. Tribes must be empowered to take control over their destinies lest they remain relegated to the proverbial "third world countries" that many people still hold them out to be.

REFERENCES

25 U.S.C. § 3601(5). Findings.

25 U.S.C. § 3601(8). Findings.

25 U.S.C. § 3621(b). Findings.

Ad Hoc Advisory Group on Native American Sentencing Issues, US Sentencing Commission. (2003). *Report of the Native American Advisory Group*, p. 17.

Alaska Advisory Committee. (2002). Racism's Frontier, p. 43.

American Bar Association, Section of Individual Rights and Responsibilities, Coalition for Justice, National Native American Bar Association. (2008). *Report to the House of Delegates*.

Anderson, R. N., & Smith, B. L. (2003). *National Vital Statistics report*. U.S. Department of Health and Human Services, National Center for Health Statistics. Vol. 52, No. 9.

Andrews, C. (December 2000). OJJDP Tribal Youth Program. *Juvenile Justice Journal*, *7*(2), 3. Retrieved from http://www.ncjrs.org/html/ojjdp/jjnl_2000_12/contents.html

Bureau of Justice Statistics. (2014). *Tribal crime and justice (1992–2001)*. Retrieved on February 28, National Institute of Justice.

Cherokee Nation v. Georgia 30 U.S. (5 Pet.). (1831).

Clear, T. R., & Frost, N. A. (2014). *The punishment imperative: The rise and failure of mass incarceration in America*. New York, NY: New York University Press.

Deloria, V., Jr. (1985). *American Indian policy in the twentieth century*. New York, NY: University of Oklahoma Press.

Ex Parte Crow Dog, 109 U.S. 556. (1883).

General Allotment Act of 1887. (1887). (Dawes Act, 24 Stat. 388, codified as amended by 25 U.S.C. 331-334, 339, 341, 342, 348, 349, 354 and 381).
Hensen, E., &Taylor, J. B. (2002). *Native America at the new millennium* (p. 132). Cambridge, MA: Harvard University, John F. Kennedy School of Government, Project on American Indian Economic Development.
Indian Tribal Justice Technical and Legal Assistance Act of 2000. (2000). Pub. L. No. 106-559 § 202, 199.
Johnson v. McIntosh 21 U.S. (8 Wheat.) 543. (1823).
Major Crimes Act of 1885. (1885). 18 U.S.C.A. 115.
National Center for Health Statistics, Health, United States, (2008). With special feature on the health of young adults, Hyattsville, MD, 2009.
Prucha, F. P. (1962). *American Indian policy in the formative years: The Indian trade and intercourse acts, 1790–1834*. Cambridge, MA: Harvard University Press.
Public Law 83-280, 18 U.S.C. § 1162. (1953).
Santa Clara Pueblo v. Martinez 436 U.S. 49. (1978).
The Indian Law Enforcement Reform Act, 25 U.S.C. § 2801. (2010).
Title 18 U.S.C.A. § 1154. (1995). p. 619.
Trade and Intercourse Act of 1802, 31 U.S. (6 Pet.) 557. (1832).
Trade and Intercourse Act of 1802, 31 U.S. (6 Pet.) 561. (1832).
Tribal Law & Order Act (TLOA; Pub. L. No. 111-211, 124 Stat. 2258 § 251(b)). (2010).
United States Commission on Civil Rights. (2003). *A quiet crisis: Federal funding and unmet needs in Indian Country* 79.
United States v. Jerry Paul, 929 F. Supp. 1406, 1407-1408. (D. N. M. 1996).
United States v. Kagama, 118 U.S. 375. (1886).
U.S. Census Bureau. (1995). *Selected social and economic characteristics for the 25 largest American Indian tribes*.
U.S. Census Bureau. (2000a). *Employment status and commuting to work*.
U.S. Census Bureau. (2000b). *Sex by employment status for the population 16 years and over*.
U.S. Census Bureau. (2002a). *Poverty in the United States: 2001, current population reports*. p. 7.
U.S. Census Bureau. (2002b). *The American Indian and Alaska native population:* 2000.
U.S. Census. (2007). *Prison Working Group, Violations of Articles 1, 2 and 5 of the international convention on the elimination of all forms of racial discrimination in U.S. prisons: A response to the periodic report of the United States of America*. April 2007.
U.S. Const. art. I, § 8.
U.S. Const. art. II, § 2.
U.S. Const. art. VI, Clause 2.
U.S. Department of Interior, Indian Affairs, Fiscal Year. (2010).
U.S. Department of Justice. (2001). Jails in Indian Country, p. 3.
U.S. Department of Justice, American Indians and Crime. (1999).
U.S. Department of Justice, Office of Justice Programs. (2004). *American Indians and crime*, Steven W. Perry, BJS statistician.
U.S. Department of Justice, Office of Justice Programs. (2011). *Compendium of tribal crime data*.
U.S. Indian Health Service, Indian Health Disparities. (2000). *Fact sheet*. Retrieved from http://www.ihs.gov/newsroom/factsheets/disparities/
Williams v. Lee, 358 U.S. 217, 220. (1959).
Worcester v. Georgia, 31 U.S. 515. (1832).

CONTINUED IMPRISONMENT OF TERMINALLY ILL PRISONERS IN THE UNITED STATES: AN INTERNATIONAL HUMAN RIGHTS PERSPECTIVE

Aleksandr Khechumyan

ABSTRACT

Purpose – *This chapter aims to demonstrate that the fundamental human rights principle that no one should be subjected to (grossly) disproportionate punishment should be interpreted to take into account terminal illness of the offender. It should be applied both during imposition of the sentences and also during execution of already imposed sentences.*

Design/methodology/approach – *In order to reveal whether this principle takes into account serious medical conditions, including terminal illness of the offender in the calculus of the proportionality of punishment and whether it is applicable at the execution stage of sentences, this chapter examined the roots of the fundamental human rights principle of proportionality of punishment by briefly surveying the penal theory,*

Punishment and Incarceration: A Global Perspective
Sociology of Crime, Law and Deviance, Volume 19, 179–201

ISSN: 1521-6136/doi:10.1108/S1521-613620140000019008

jurisprudence, court cases, laws, and legislative history from the U.S. federal and state jurisdictions and from Europe.

Findings – *There is a consensus among surveyed theories that terminal illness of the offender is an element of the principle of proportionality of punishment. Thus the fundamental human rights principle must be interpreted to take it into account. The principle should be observed not only at the imposition stage, but also at the execution stage of already imposed sentences.*

Originality/value – *This chapter re-examines the roots of the fundamental human right to not being subjected to (grossly) disproportionate punishment. It does so in order to demonstrate that the right should be interpreted to take into account terminal illness of the offender and that it should be observed not only at the imposition stage, but also at the execution stage of already imposed sentences.*

Keywords: Terminally ill prisoners; principle of proportionality; human rights; penal theory; equal impact; execution of sanctions

INTRODUCTION

Over the past 30 years, the United States has experienced an unprecedented rise in the prison population, both in state and federal jurisdictions. This rise is more troubling among the elderly prisoner's group which increased more than threefold in the last 20 years (Carson & Golinelli, 2013). There are both more people who are aging behind bars and who are sent to prisons at old age (Human Rights Watch, 2012). Many elderly prisoners are terminally ill. Although terminal illness can affect also nonelderly prisoners, many of the elderly inmates will eventually fall into this category if not released early.

As of December 31, 2012, some 131,489 of the 1,511,480 sentenced state and federal prisoners were aged 55 and over (Carson & Golinelli, 2013). Although, there is no readily available data on the number of terminally ill prisoners in state and federal prisons, the mortality data in state and federal prisons give some idea about the extent of the problem. From 2001 to 2008 there were 2,801 deaths of prisoners under federal jurisdiction, 2,425 of which were illness-related deaths excluding deaths from AIDS (Bureau of Justice Statistics, 2009). During 2001–2011 35,317 prisoners died in state prisons. While the mortality data on federal prisoners (Noonan & Ginder, 2013 does not specify age of the deceased, the state data demonstrates that 15,111 of the deceased were prisoners aged 55 and older. Moreover, these data shows that prisoners aged 55 and older died from cancer, heart and respiratory diseases at least at a five times higher rate than prisoners in any other age group. Apart from highlighting the extent of the terminal illness in state and federal prisons, these data also demonstrate a strong correlation between the age of inmates and the cause of death (Noonan & Ginder, 2013).

In fact, the Bureau of Prisons (BOP) and the vast majority of state departments of correction have legal instruments at their disposal to deal with the issue of terminally ill prisoners in a civilized way: 46 states and the federal jurisdiction have developed polices allowing medical release of prisoners. Although these policies differ in terms of eligibility criteria and procedures, the federal jurisdiction and the vast majority of states include terminal illness as a release criterion (Demyan, 2013). Despite the availability of mechanisms to allow terminally ill prisoners to have a humane death at home or a community hospice surrounded by family and friends, only a few terminally ill prisoners are released each year (Chiu, 2010; Human Rights Watch, 2012). For instance, from 1990 to 2000 only 225 terminally ill federal prisoners were released under sentence modification provision (Price, 2001). This trend has continued also in recent years resulting in only 25 motions to courts for release of terminally ill prisoners by BOP in 2011 and 37 motions on combined medical grounds as of November 2012 (Human Rights Watch, 2012). The situation is not much different also in state jurisdictions. From 1999 to 2008 New Mexico released only 35 prisoners with Missouri releasing 236 from 1998 to 2008 under combined geriatric and terminal illness grounds (Chiu, 2010). In the period from 1995 to 2011 California released 276 terminally ill and permanently incapacitated prisoners (Demyan, 2013).

Apparently the available legal mechanisms for the early release of terminally ill prisoners have not had much impact on the situation of terminally ill prisoners. Several studies attempted to reveal the reasons behind the gap between the law and the practice of medical release in different jurisdictions identifying various grounds for the low impact of medical release laws. Although in the studied jurisdictions these laws were not similar, some common grounds responsible for the low impact can be identified such as political and public opinion considerations, narrow eligibility criteria, and procedural flaws of legal regulations (Chiu, 2010; Demyan, 2013; Human Rights Watch, 2012). This approach brings to the fore the question of proportionality of continued confinement of terminally ill prisoners under international human rights law in the United States and elsewhere.

Fundamental Principle of Proportionality of Punishment in the International Human Rights Context

It is widely accepted that the prohibition of cruel, inhuman, or degrading treatment or punishment at both national and international levels is aimed at protection of human dignity. In the view of majority of courts and legal scholars, human dignity can be degraded by application of *per se* cruel or unusual punishments (the issue of the type of punishment). However, it can also be degraded by application of an *excessive quantity* of punishment which is *per se* not cruel or unusual. The two versions of cruel punishments have been referred to as issues of type and quantity of punishment (van Zyl Smit & Ashworth, 2004). When the punishment is *per se* cruel and unusual its prohibition is absolute irrespective of any other factors (Rodley, 2009). However, when it comes to application of punishments that are not *per se* cruel or unusual, the quantity of punishment needs to be weighed against other factors, mainly the seriousness of the crime. Thus, for the later version a certain quantity of punishment may be cruel or unusual in relation to one crime, but not for another more serious crime (van Zyl Smit, 1995).

The fundamental principle of proportionality of punishment in human rights law[1] is concerned with situations where the quantity of *per se* not cruel or unusual punishment is (grossly) disproportionate in relation to the seriousness of a crime in question. According to this principle no person should be subjected to a disproportionate sentence on the ground that:

> Firstly, punishment, particularly imprisonment, constitutes a prima facie violation of an individual's right to liberty; secondly that in principle such a measure can be justified only where a person has been convicted of a serious offence; thirdly that respect for rights, and limitation on the arbitrary use of state power, requires that if substantial deprivations of an offender's liberty should only be permissible if the offender has committed a very serious offence; and finally that to allow states to impose substantial restrictions or deprivations of liberty where the offence was not serious would be to condone the use of individuals merely as a means to an end, which is inconsistent with fundamental respect for the dignity of each human being. (van Zyl Smit & Ashworth, 2004, p. 542)

This principle is observed both in international human rights instruments and national constitutions. The United States Federal Constitution following the English Bill of Rights of 1689 was among the first Constitutions to prohibit cruel punishment (Granucci, 1969). The Eighth Amendment of the United States Constitution prohibits excessive bail and fines and cruel and unusual punishments (United States Congress, 1791). Provisions similar to the Eighth Amendment of the United States Constitution can be found in international and regional human rights instruments. Article 5 of the Universal Declaration of Human Rights (hereinafter UDHR) prescribes that "No one shall be subject to torture or to cruel, inhuman or degrading treatment or punishment" (United Nations General Assembly, 1948). Following UDHR other international and regional human rights instruments adopted provisions with the same or slightly different wording (Council of Europe, 1950).

The prohibition of cruel, inhuman, or degrading treatment or punishment in human rights law is the primary source of prohibition of grossly disproportionate sentences (van Zyl Smit & Ashworth, 2004). In the United States until the recent Supreme Court cases[2] it was understood that the Eighth Amendment prohibits not only barbarous punishments but "all punishments which by their excessive length or severity are greatly disproportioned to the offenses charged" (Supreme Court of United States, 1910).

In legal scholarship both in the United States and internationally there has been much consideration of disproportionate sentences, including (grossly) disproportionate prison terms as human rights violations. Professors van Zyl Smit and Ashworth have convincingly demonstrated that the fundamental human rights principle of proportionality of punishment is widely practiced worldwide both by national and supra national courts (van Zyl Smit & Ashworth, 2004). However, when the proportionality of punishment and particularly prison terms was discussed the main focus was to look at the blameworthiness (harm caused or threatened and culpability of the offender) of the offender and the severity of punishment.[3] This means that personal sensibilities of the offender unrelated to her/his culpability are not taken into account while assessing the proportionality of the punishment. Furthermore, this would mean that, in general, once a proportionate or not (grossly) disproportionate sentence is imposed, it will remain proportionate as long as it remains in force irrespective of any changes in circumstances of the prisoner, including deterioration of existing illness or contraction of terminal illness in prison.

Although the fundamental human rights principle of proportionality of punishment does not explicitly mention that personal sensibilities of the offender shall be taken into the calculus of the proportionality, this chapter aims to demonstrate that some personal sensibilities, for example, terminal illness, should be taken into account in the assessment of proportionality of punishment. Moreover, it is argued that the fundamental principle of proportionality of punishment can be extended to the stage of execution of already imposed sentences, particularly to the situation of dying prisoners whose sentences were initially proportionate.

First, this chapter looks at the roots of the fundamental human rights principle of proportionality of punishment by briefly surveying the penal theory, the U.S. federal law, and some court cases in order to reveal whether personal sensibilities of the offender are taken into account in fixing a punishment for a particular offender. The chapter then undertakes analysis of jurisprudence and legislation in order to demonstrate that some personal sensibilities of offenders are taken into account as elements of the principle of proportionality, but not as exceptional acts of mercy. Finally, an examination of laws, legislative history, and court cases is conducted to substantiate the claim that this principle should be observed not only at the imposition stage but also at the stage of execution of already imposed sentences. The chapter subsequently concludes that there is a consensus among surveyed theories that terminal illness of the offender is an element of the principle of proportionality of punishment which indicates that the fundamental human rights principle that no one should be subjected to (grossly) disproportionate punishment must be interpreted to take it into account. Moreover, the legislative history of laws prescribing the early medical release of prisoners of the U.S federal and state jurisdictions and in Europe clearly suggest that in cases of definite and serious medical conditions, including terminal illness of the prisoner, this principle should be observed not only at the imposition stage, but also at the execution stage of already imposed sentences.

PROPORTIONALITY OF PUNISHMENT IN THEORY AND PRACTICE

The fundamental principle of proportionality of punishment stems from the penal theory. A large variety of punishment theories exist based on notions of desert and crime prevention which include both theories grounded only on the former or the latter idea and also integrative or "hybrid" theories that try to integrate both ideas on the way of coming up with plausible justifications for state-imposed punishment. Particularly in the United States up until the 1970s rehabilitation of offenders was regarded as the main purpose of criminal punishment in all jurisdictions (Frase, 2012). However, since that decade the emphasis has shifted from rehabilitation to retribution, deterrence, and incapacitation of high-risk offenders (Frase, 2012). Currently there is no uniformity in relation to punishment purposes among different U.S. jurisdictions with some states completely eliminating rehabilitation as a purpose of punishment, while others have kept it in a somewhat subsidiary role in relation to other purposes (Frase, 2012).

Although since 1970s the popularity of rehabilitation as a goal of punishment has fallen dramatically, other utilitarian goals such as general and specific deterrence and incapacitation are still quite popular. Against this backdrop punishment theories that are able to integrate and balance various prima facie conflicting goals have become popular. One such theory, the theory of Limiting Retributivism, is relatively well received both among theorists and practitioners (Frase, 2012). Limiting Retributivism allows utilitarian proportionality principles to be used alongside retributive proportionality to place limits on the imposition of state punishment. Its principles are widely accepted and explicitly or implicitly taken as a model in many sentencing guidelines systems in the United States and in other Western countries. Professor Frase considers Limiting Retributivism as a "de facto consensus theoretical model of criminal punishment" (Frase, 2012, p. 3). Another major theory of punishment which integrates utilitarian punishment goals – albeit to a lesser degree than Limiting Retributivism – into the otherwise retributive theory of punishment is the theory developed by Professor von Hirsch (von Hirsch, 1985, 1986, 1993; von Hirsch & Ashworth, 2005).

With reference to both traditional utilitarian and two major modern hybrid theories[4] this section aims to demonstrate that there is a universal acceptance that physical conditions and especially terminal illness of the offender are elements of the principle of proportionality of punishment and are used to make punishment proportional via equalizing the impact of punishment on otherwise similarly blameworthy offenders. Although there is a universal acceptance that conditions of the offender such as terminal illness are elements of the principle of proportionality of punishment, there is a disagreement among the theories about where to set the standard. On the one hand, utilitarian theories argue that *personal sensibilities* of the offender should be taken into account in the principle of proportionality of punishment setting a very broad standard (Bentham, 2007; Maestro, 1973; Walker, 1991). On the other hand, Morris included into proportionality principle only *depravations and undesirable collateral consequences for the offender and "others,"* which is probably a narrower standard than the pure utilitarian approach (1974). Although von Hirsch and Ashworth also accept that some personal conditions of the offender are elements of the principle of proportionality, they set the standard narrowly, limiting these conditions to so-called "*equity factors,*" which include only "unusual cases which diverge from the norm significantly" (von Hirsch, 2005, p. 172). Notwithstanding the disagreements among the theories on the issue of standard setting, the standard of all theories is wide enough to include terminal illness of the offender as an element of the principle of the proportionality of punishment. For demonstrating that there is a universal acceptance of the offender's physical conditions and especially terminal illness as elements of proportionality of punishment I will briefly discuss relevant propositions of these theories.

The possibility of applying unequal punishments on equally blameworthy offenders based on individual sensibilities has been long recognized by utilitarian theorists such as Cesare Beccaria (Maestro, 1973) and Jeremy Bentham. Bentham, for instance, came up with a list of 32 "circumstances influencing sensibilities" including grounds as extreme as health, radical frame of body, climate, rank, and religious profession (Bentham, 2007). According to Bentham based on individual sensibilities the sentence may be more or less severe for otherwise similar offenders. He viewed the principle of "equal impact" of punishment as a part of the requirement of the proportion between punishments and offences. He formulated this principle in the following way:

> Rule 6. It is further to be observed, that owing to the different manners and degrees in which persons under different circumstances are affected by the same exciting cause, punishment which is the same in name will not always either really produce , or even so much as appear to others to produce, in two different persons the same degree of pain: therefore that the quantity actually inflicted on each individual offender may correspond to the quantity intended for similar offenders in general, the several circumstances influencing sensibility ought always to be taken into account. (2007, p. 182)

A similar position was held by Walker, who stated that "the intensity of the suffering, hardship or inconvenience which a given penalty will inflict depends on the individual offender: on sex, age, social position, and so on" (1991, p. 102).

As was already mentioned the theory of Limiting Retributivism is one of the major hybrid theories of punishment. Its propositions have been articulated by many authors, but this theory was fully elaborated in the writings of Norval Morris (Morris, 1964, 1974, 1982; Morris & Tonry, 1990). This theory rejects indeterminate sentences with discretionary parole release based on coercive rehabilitative treatment explicitly linking punishment aims to human rights of offenders. According to this theory the upper limit of the sentence should be decided on the bases of proportionality of a sentence to the blameworthiness of the offender (harm caused or threatened and culpability of the offender; Morris, 1964). However, according to Morris it is impossible to precisely determine punishment based on desert. He rejects the idea of ordinal proportionality developed by von Hirsch which suggests that punishment for a particular crime should be decided as closely as possible based on three separate grounds:

> (i) **Parity**: offenders convicted of crimes of like gravity should receive punishments of like severity; (ii) **Rank-ordering**: punishing one crime more than another expresses more disapproval for the former crime, which is warranted only if it is more serious; (iii) **Spacing of penalties**: that is , the spacing between penalties of different severity should reflect the difference in the degree of seriousness of crimes: if the crimes C, D and E are ascending order of seriousness, there should be bigger space between punishments for crimes C and E, but the space crimes D and E should be less, regardless that the crime seriousness-gradations are likely to be matters of rather inexact judgement. (von Hirsch, 1993, p. 18)

Morris argues that it is impossible to precisely determine punishment based on desert, because there are big differences in a given society about a deserved punishment for a particular crime. In contrast, there is a general agreement that certain punishments are clearly undeserved. Thus, he suggests that desert is a limiting but not a defining principle allowing to apply a punishment from a range of not undeserved penalties (Morris, 1977). Within the limits of not undeserved punishments utilitarian goals are allowed to affect the amount of imposed punishment, but are subject to the general limiting principle of humanity and economy which Morris terms "parsimony." This principle provides that less burdensome and costly means should be preferred among equally effective means for nonretributive purposes within the overall desert limit (Morris, 1977).

Morris concedes that offenders of similar deserts (blameworthiness) may receive different punishments, because of the principle of parsimony; he viewed equality as only a guiding principle (with no strict parity requirement as suggested by von Hirsch) that applies unless there are substantial utilitarian reasons such as a need for parsimonious punishment (Morris, 1982). According to Morris when setting a penal sanction alongside with expected benefits, economic costs of the state, depravations, and undesirable collateral consequences for the offender and others must be taken into account (1974). The principle of parsimony requires that the expected utilitarian benefits are weighted against depravations and undesirable collateral consequences for the offender and others alongside economic costs of the state when setting a penal sanction for a particular offender. As a result of this balancing the sentencer is required to choose a penal sanction which is the least burdensome for the offender and costly for the state among equally effective penal sanctions (1974). Thus, the sentencer is required to choose a penal sanction which is the least burdensome for the offender. This brings us back to the issue of equal effect of sanctions based on personal sensibilities, because while choosing the least burdensome sanction for a particular offender the sentencer has to look at sensibilities of the offender and it is obvious that the least burdensome sanction for one offender (e.g., terminally ill) will be less than one for an equally blameworthy but healthy offender. This is the reason why Morris would allow offenders of similar deserts (blameworthiness) receiving different punishments.

Von Hirsh criticized Morris's theory for treating the principle of equal punishment for equally blameworthy offenders as not "essential" but only a guiding one (von Hirsch, 1981, p. 526). These according to von Hirsch could allow creation of a system where "the desert limits have been relegated to the margins and utilitarian grounds constitute the main basis for selecting penalties" (1981, pp. 526, 784–785). In defense Morris responded:

> My case for inequality is for mercy and clemency within an ordered system of justly deserved punishments; it aims at avoiding the severity amounting to tyranny that rigidly insists on equality and seeks to exorcise discretion and mercy from sentencing. It accepts the long tradition of justice as equality but seeks to moderate it by acceptance of the uncertainties attending our utilitarian purposes in the distribution of punishment and to allow for a slippage of inequality to achieve parsimony in punishment. (1982, pp. 203–203)

At the end let me reiterate that all this is within the desert limits of the punishment which means that the application of the principle of parsimony is a principle which places additional limits to the desert proportionality which means that utilitarian goals could not be used to punish the offender more than his/her desert requires (Morris, 1974).

As was already mentioned, in his earlier writing von Hirsh criticized the treatment of the principle of "like punishment for similarly blameworthy offenders" as not "essential" but only a guiding one (von Hirsch, 1981). However, it seems that von Hirsch's position on this issue has since evolved. In his later writing he indicated that he prefers his "living standard" analysis over the personal sensibility approach to equalize the effect of punishment on different offenders, because "sensibilities" are personal and subjective, while "living standard" is more objective[5] (von Hirsch, 1993). At this point the difference between the "living standard" and "individual sensibilities" is not important: the point here is to emphasize that von Hirsch's theory also gives room to factors other than those related to culpability of the offender and harm caused by the offence to play role in the calculus of the proportionality of punishment.

Furthermore, Ashworth and Player argued that fairness requires recognition of the principle of equal impact which is the only way to minimize a "disproportionate severe impact on certain offenders based on significantly different personal sensibilities" (Ashworth & Player, 1998, pp. 256–257). These authors further argued that it seems that the principle of equal impact is irreconcilable with the theory of von Hirsch because of the principle of "like punishment." This means that "any attempt to adjust proportionate sentences is bound to send inappropriate messages to the addressees of State punishment." However, they right away acknowledged that this is not necessarily true, because von Hirsch's theory treats offenders as moral agents capable of responding to punishment and thus if one of the two similarly blameworthy offenders would be given lesser sentence because of terminal illness, the other offender would be able to understand why it happened (Ashworth & Player, 1998, pp. 269–270).

Indeed, in his recent book von Hirsch together with Ashworth analyzed the issue in more detail and acknowledged that when certain handicaps of an offender make the punishment significantly more burdensome "the sanction should be adjusted in order to avoid its having an undue differential impact on him" (2005, p. 172). Von Hirsch found that it is justified to reduce the penalty for a disabled, wheelchair-bond offender to avoid the differential impact, because the imprisonment experience of this offender would be more onerous (2005).

This section attempted to demonstrate that both pure utilitarian and other major theories of punishment recognize that the same punishment may have more or less severe impact on different offenders based on personal sensibilities (broadly or narrowly defined depending on theory). Depending on theory, personal sensibilities to a certain extent are taken into account in the principle of proportionality of punishment and are used to equalize the impact of punishment on otherwise similarly blameworthy offenders and make punishment proportional. More importantly this section attempted to emphasize that, irrespective of the approach to which personal sensibilities shall be taken into account in the principle of proportionality of punishment, all theories agree that certain handicaps of an offender, including terminal illness shall necessarily be included in this principle. The next section will attempt to show that apart from being universally recognized in penal theory certain handicaps of an offender, including terminal illness, are taken into account by courts and legislators.

The Principle of "Equal Impact of Sanctions" in Legislation and Case Law

Apart from being universally recognized in penal theory the principle of equal impact is also practiced by courts. Indeed, English courts in several cases such as *R. v. Green* (Court of Appeal, 1992), *R. v. Bernard* (Court of Appeal, 1996), and *R. v. John Francis C.* (Court of Appeal, 1993) clearly imposed less punishment than otherwise appropriate referring to extraordinary health conditions and reduced life expectancy due to advanced age of the offender. Interestingly, at least on the legislative level the same approach seems to be emerging also in the United States. Until recently § 3553(b) of title 18 United States Congress (U.S.C., 1994) provided:

> ... the court shall impose a sentence of the kind, and within the range, referred to in subsection (a)(4) unless the court finds that there exists an aggravating an aggravating or mitigating circumstance of a kind, or to a degree, not adequately taken into consideration by the Sentencing Commission in formulating the guidelines" may provide grounds for departure. (U.S.C., 1994)

Furthermore, the policy statement of the U.S. Federal Sentencing Commission at the relevant time provided:

> Physical condition or appearance, including physique, *is not ordinarily relevant* to determining whether a sentence should be outside the applicable guideline range. However, an extraordinary physical impairment may be a reason to impose a sentence below the applicable guideline range .... (United States Sentencing Commission, 1993; § 5H1.4)

Interpreting the above-mentioned legislative provisions in the case of Thomas the Sixth Circuit explained that terminal illness and life-threatening conditions cannot be considered as grounds for imposing a sentence below the applicable guideline range, because the Sentencing Commission took them into account by explicitly stating that physical condition is not ordinarily a relevant ground for imposing a sentence below the applicable guideline range (United States Court of Appeals for the Sixth Circuit, 1995). Although the interpretation of the Court did not consider terminal illness and life-threatening conditions as circumstances making the sentence disproportionately severe for a particular offender, the legislation *per se* recognizes that a sentence can have a disproportionately severe impact on a particular offender based on a personal sensibility, for example "extraordinary physical impairment" (U.S. Sentencing Guidelines Manual § 5H1.4, 1993).

Moreover, the U.S. Federal Sentencing Commission has recently changed its position in relation to the physical condition, and other factors which previous policy statements considered irrelevant for downward departure from the guideline range stating that:

> Physical condition or appearance, including physique, ***may be relevant*** in determining whether a departure is warranted, if the condition or appearance, individually or in combination with other offender characteristics, is present to an unusual degree and distinguishes the case from the typical cases covered by the guidelines. An extraordinary physical impairment may be a reason to depart downward; e.g., in the case of a seriously infirm defendant, home detention may be as efficient as, and less costly than, imprisonment (U.S. Sentencing Guidelines Manual § 5H1.4, 2010).

Furthermore, the new policy statement apart from personal sensibilities related to physical conditions explicitly mentions old age *per se* and age-related physical conditions as possible reasons for a downward departure from the guideline range and even imposition of punishment such as home confinement where it "might be equally efficient as and less costly than incarceration" (U.S. Sentencing Guidelines Manual § 5H1.1, 2010). It remains to be seen where courts will fix the threshold in determining the relevant physical conditions, age, and degree of infirmity for application of the guideline's requirement, but it is clear that the principle of "equal impact" of punishment is taken into account in the U.S federal jurisdiction at least on a legislative and policy level.

With the reference to court cases and legislation it was indicated that following penal theory courts and legislatures recognized that certain handicaps of an offender, including terminal illness are taken into account by courts and legislators in law making and adjudication of court cases. As yet this chapter was concerned with demonstrating that personal sensibilities of the offender are taken into account as grounds for equalizing the effect of penal sanction on the offender in both penal theory and practice. Next it will be argued that some personal sensibilities of the offender, for example, terminal illness, indeed are taken into account as elements of the principle of proportionality of punishment and not as an exceptional act of mercy.

REFINING THE PRINCIPLE: AN EXCEPTIONAL ACT OF MERCY OR A GENERAL PRINCIPLE?

With reference to the penal theory, legislation, and case law this chapter has demonstrated that personal sensibilities are taken into account in sentencing in order to equalize the effect of punishment on otherwise similarly blameworthy offenders. However, the aim of this chapter is to argue that personal sensibilities are taken into account as an element of the fundamental human rights principle not to be subjected to (grossly) disproportionate punishment and not based on "genuine mercy," as defined by Smart (1968). According to Smart "genuine mercy" is "deciding not to inflict what is agreed to be just penalty, all things considered," which is different from mitigation or proportionality, because if they are not considered, the sentence could be criticized as "unjust" (Smart, 1968). Smart depicted "genuine mercy" as occasional leniency towards the offender for preventing suffering of innocent dependents caused by a just sentence (Smart, 1968).

In the view of Beccaria, mercy is something which is needed only because of imperfections of law (Beccaria, 1995). It might be assumed that he viewed mercy not as a provision of law but a virtue outside of it, called to fix its defects. Walker usefully has brought together and refined criteria suggested for distinguishing "genuine mercy" from other reasons, including those "which nowadays seems to be dictated by our motions of justice and proportionality" (1995). These criteria are:

a. compassion, it has been suggested, must be the main motive, not mere expediency;
b. it must not be merely whimsical or random;
c. it must not be improper in other ways (for example, the result of corruption);
d. it must not be so constrained by rules that it can be called "justice." (1995, p. 32)

It is obvious that personal sensibilities, which I argue are an element of the fundamental human rights principle not to be subjected to (grossly) disproportionate punishment, do not fit at least with the last criterion in the above list: as it will be demonstrated with reference to the legislative history these provisions have been adopted in the name of fairness and justice to prevent unequitable effects of punishment (Senate Committee on the Judiciary, 1983, p. 95). Walker explicitly acknowledges that personal sensibilities such as old age of the offender and illness are examples of reasons which are these days dictated not by "genuine mercy" but by "our motions of justice and proportionality" (1995).

This analysis has aimed to demonstrate that personal sensibilities are not elements of "genuine mercy," but elements of "our motions of justice and proportionality" and thus ought to be taken into account by the fundamental human rights principle of not being subjected to (grossly) disproportionate punishment. However, at this point it is useful to return to theories of Norval Morris and Andrew von Hirsch to clarify their position on the role of personal sensibilities of the offender in fixing the punishment for a particular crime.

Earlier in this chapter it was mentioned that in response to criticism for not treating the principle of like punishment for similarly blameworthy offenders as essential rather than guiding one, Morris has responded that his "case for inequality is for mercy and clemency" (Morris, 1982). This response seems to show that Morris's requirement of lenient sentences based on personal sensibilities is due to "genuine mercy" rather than to the general principle. However, the mentioning of "mercy and clemency" as a ground for taking into account personal sensibilities should not be confused with the type of "genuine mercy" which "must not be so constrained by rules that it can be called justice." It is evident from Morris's writings that his notion of mercy, which trumps the imperative principle of equal punishment, is wide enough to include both the "genuine mercy" and mercy dictated by "our motions of justice and proportionality." It is explicit that his case for mercy is motivated by the need to take into account his principle of parsimony while fixing the punishment for a particular offender, which requires choosing the least burdensome penal sanction for the offender and others (most probably of innocent dependents) (1974). Alongside with mercy dictated by "our motions of justice and proportionality," Morris's theory probably takes into account also "genuine mercy" as a reason for departure from the principle of equal punishment by mentioning that while choosing the least burdensome measure the interests of innocent dependents should also be taken into account. This, however, is not the place to elaborate this point. To put it plainly, it was important to clarify whether this theory treats offender's personal sensibilities as a reason "dictated by our motions of justice and proportionality" or as a "genuine mercy."

Now let us return to the theory of von Hirsch which was briefly discussed earlier in this chapter. I touched on this theory during my quest for the roots of fundamental human rights principle of not being subjected to (grossly) disproportionate punishment. In the previous section it was demonstrated that von Hirsch's theory accepts that the same punishment may have a more or less severe impact on different offenders based on personal sensibilities which need to be taken into account to equalize the impact of punishment on otherwise similarly blameworthy offenders and to make punishment proportional. However, for the sake of this chapter it is also important to clarify the status of this principle in this theory.

It should be mentioned from the beginning that von Hirsch and Ashworth explicitly acknowledged that the "equal impact" principle works within the proportionalist sentencing model, but applies only to unusual cases "that diverge from the norm significantly, that would speak for attending to those unusual features and, if appropriate, modifying the sentence – so as to ensure there is not an unequal impact" (2005, p. 172). However, it seems that von Hirsch and Ashworth did not regard the difference between the "genuine mercy" and reasons "which nowadays seems to be dictated by our motions of justice and proportionality" in substantive terms to be important. More important for them is the way in which the court applies this principle. These authors viewed the substantive difference between the above-mentioned two categories as the difference between two senses of a "just" sentence. When speaking of a just sentence this may refer to either a sentence which is just according to all "normal" criteria (which may be subsequently altered to take into account exceptional considerations such as mercy or equity factors); or it may refer to a sentence which is just, all considerations included. According to these authors in this context it is not significant whether mercy or equity factors regarded to be within or outside justice if the factors applied consistently. What is important here is treating cases which are like, considered all factors, alike (von Hirsch & Ashworth, 2005).

For von Hirsch and Ashworth the position of the English Court of Appeal in the case of Bernard, which held that reduction of the sentence due to the old age and poor health of the defendant, was made as "an act of mercy in exceptional circumstances of a particular case, rather than by virtue of any general principle," is "plainly objectionable": following this logic court can reduce the sentence in one case, but not in another with similar circumstances (2005). In their analysis of equity mitigation these authors abandoned the word "mercy" in favor of "equity factors," because "mercy" as in the case of Bernard above "tend to connote a highly exceptional, one-off exercise of a special dispensing power" (von Hirsch & Ashworth, 2005, p. 169).

Although von Hirsch and Ashworth did not explicitly state that they regard equity factors as reasons "dictated by our motions of justice and proportionality" rather than "genuine mercy," they plainly distinguished these factors from mercy which could be regarded as a sign of leaning towards the former. Another sign supporting this claim and ultimately the claim that physical conditions of the offender are constituting elements of the fundamental human rights principle of not being subjected to (grossly) disproportionate punishment is that these authors distinguish between "equity factors." They specified the "equal-impact" principle and compassion or sympathy related to the values underlying the desert rational as independent reasons for equity mitigation. Furthermore, they afford a special status to "equal impact" principle stating that:

> The equal impact principle does not actually function as true equity mitigation, because it actually does not call for qualifying defendants to suffer less punishment: it merely is a way of avoiding that such defendants be made to suffer *more*. Suppose the standard sentence for a given species of offence is there year' imprisonment. If this sanction is applied to a defendant in a wheelchair, he actually – under an interest analysis (living standard) – has his interests set back to a greater degree. Reducing the sentence under an equal – impact theory would be designed merely to eliminate this increment in severity. (2005, p. 173)

The recognition of the truly unique status of "equal impact" principle among equity mitigation factors is strongly supportive of the proposition of this chapter that some personal sensibilities, for example, terminal illness, of the offender are constituting elements of principle of proportionality of punishment. Therefore, it may be concluded that physical conditions of the offender, specifically terminal illness, shall also be taken into account in the fundamental human rights principle of not being subjected to (grossly) disproportionate punishment.

After presenting arguments in favor of one of its two central claims, this chapter will now turn to arguments supporting its second central claim.

EXTENDING FUNDAMENTAL HUMAN RIGHTS PRINCIPLE TO THE STAGE OF EXECUTION OF SANCTIONS

This section argues that the fundamental human rights principle of not being subjected to a (grossly) disproportionate sentence is also applicable at the stage of execution of already imposed sentences, particularly to the situation of dying prisoners whose sentence was initially proportionate. Following Ashworth and Player, it is argued that like in the sentencing stage the principle of equal impact should also be observed during execution of already imposed sentences in cases of a definite and serious medical condition, including continued imprisonment of terminally ill prisoners (1998, pp. 256–257). This argument is supported by laws, legislative history, and court cases in the United States and Europe which are discussed below.

In 1984 the United States Congress had adopted the Sentencing Reform Act (hereinafter SRA, 1984) announcing the beginning of the determinate sentencing era in the federal jurisdiction. The SRA 1984, codified in 18 U.S.C. §§ 3551–3742 and 28 U.S.C. §§ 991–998, among other innovations has introduced the United States Sentencing Commission with a mandate to promulgate sentencing guidelines for Federal Courts, and abolished parole release for federal prisoners. One of the main purposes of the shift from an indeterminate sentencing system to a determinate one was to limit sentencing disparities for similarly placed offenders by providing a framework within which the judges have to exercise their sentencing discretion (Senate Committee on the Judiciary, 1983).

Despite eliminating parole release, the SRA 1984 had introduced new provisions allowing modification of an already imposed prison term in exceptional cases. One of such provisions authorizes reduction of imprisonment to a term of probation or supervised release if extraordinary and compelling reasons warrant such a reduction (Title 18 § 3582(c)(1)(A)(i) U.S.C., 2002). Although Title 18 § 3582 (c)(1)(A)(i) of U.S.C. does not specify what are the extraordinary and compelling reasons for sentence modification, the legislative history of the SRA suggests that the legislators acknowledged that such situations include terminal illness and other changes in the circumstances of prisoners which can be deemed as extraordinary and compelling. Moreover, the legislative history of this provision clearly demonstrates why this provision was adopted. According to the Report of the Senate Committee on Judiciary this provision:

> Applies regardless of the length of sentence to the unusual case in which the defendant's circumstances are so changed, such as by terminal illness, that it would be *inequitable* to continue the confinement of the prisoner. (1983, p. 95)

This record explicitly acknowledges that the early release of a prisoner from an already imposed prison term regardless of the sentence length is motivated by the need to equalize the impact of the sentence on the offender, based on individual sensibilities, including terminal illness in cases where "it would be inequitable to continue the confinement of the prisoner." This is a clear recognition that the principle of equal impact shall be observed also at the stage of the execution of sentences.

This finding is also supported by the legislative history of early medical release legislation in California which has a rich legislative history of compassionate release and medical parole legislation. These laws are designed for early release of terminally ill and permanently incapacitated prisoners (Demyan, 2013). The notion that at some point continued imprisonment of terminally ill or permanently incapacitated prisoners becomes "unnecessary, and at times even cruel" is present throughout legislative bill files of 12 legislative attempts three of which were successful (Demyan, 2013, p. 102). The supporters of early medical release legislation including interest groups, the Legislature, and the California Department of Corrections substantiated the need for adoption of this legislation by arguing that circumstances such as terminal illness change the proportionality of punishment making continued imprisonment disproportionate (Demyan, 2013, p. 102).

The principle of equal impact at the stage of the execution of sentences is recognized not only in the United States, but also in Europe. The European Court of Human Rights observed that age in conjunction with other factors such as health may be taken into account as a ground for suspending the sentence of imprisonment or replacing it with house arrest. Furthermore the court noted that although the European Convention on Human Rights does not expressly prohibit imprisonment beyond a certain age, "under certain circumstances, the detention of an elderly person over a lengthy period might raise an issue under Article 3" (European Court of Human Rights, 2001, p. 8). The legislation authorizing early release on medical grounds, such as terminal condition or state of health incompatible with continued detention, is available in many European countries, such as France (Parliament of the French Republic, 2002).

The legislative history of SRA 1984 and California's compassionate release and medical parole legislation clearly demonstrate the legislatures' original intent of adopting these laws. By adopting these laws the legislatures created a legal mechanism that enables courts to modify an already imposed sentence releasing the prisoner whenever, due to reasons such as terminal illness of the prisoner, it would be inequitable to continue the confinement. This clearly demonstrates that these laws were adopted in recognition of the principle of equal impact for observing proportionality of punishment at the stage of execution of already imposed sentences.

CONCLUSION

Thirty seven thousand seven hundred forty two prisoners died from various illnesses in the period between 2001 and 2008 in the U.S. federal and state jurisdictions. Fifteen thousand one hundred eleven of these prisoners were aged 55 and older. The data from the Bureau of Justice Statistics indicate that illness-related deaths among prisoners aged 55 and over are five times higher than among prisoners in any other age group. These data also demonstrate a strong correlation between the age of inmates and the cause of death (Noonan & Ginder, 2013).

This situation prompted the current re-examination of the fundamental human right not to be subjected to (grossly) disproportionate punishment in order to answer two separate but interconnected questions. First, does this principle take into account serious medical conditions, including terminal illness of the offender in the calculus of the proportionality of punishment? And second, is this principle applicable also at the execution stage of sentences in cases of definite and serious medical conditions, including terminal illness of the offender?

In response to the first question, the chapter examined the roots of the fundamental human rights principle of proportionality of punishment by briefly surveying the penal theory, the U.S. federal law, court cases, and jurisprudence. This examination demonstrated that both pure utilitarian and two major hybrid theories of punishment recognize that the same punishment may have a more or less severe impact on different offenders based on personal sensibilities (broadly or narrowly defined depending on theory). Depending on the theory, some personal sensibilities are taken into account in the principle of proportionality of punishment and are used to equalize the impact of punishment on otherwise similarly blameworthy offenders in order to make punishment (more) proportionate. More importantly, it was found that irrespective of narrow or broad definitions of personal sensibilities, which are taken into account in proportionality assessment, all theories agree that certain handicaps of offenders, including terminal illness must necessarily be included in this principle. This examination has also revealed that certain handicaps of offenders, including terminal illness are taken into account as elements of the principle of proportionality, but not as exceptional acts of mercy.

In response to the second question, this chapter analyzed laws, legislative history, and court cases from the United States and Europe. This analysis clearly demonstrated that the legislatures' original intention of adopting these laws was to create a legal mechanism that enables courts to modify already imposed sentences releasing the prisoner whenever, due to reasons such as terminal illness of the prisoner, it would be inequitable to continue the confinement. This clearly demonstrated that these laws were adopted in recognition of the principle of equal impact for observing proportionality of punishment at the stage of execution of already imposed sentences.

Therefore, it is concluded that the fundamental human right not to be subjected to (grossly) disproportionate punishment must be interpreted to take into account terminal illness of the offender as an element of the principle of proportionality of punishment which shall be observed not only at the imposition stage, but also at the execution stage of already imposed sentences.

At the end it is relevant to specify that this chapter was concerned only with the role of the terminal illness of the offender in the fundamental human right not to be subjected to (grossly) disproportionate punishment. This by no means excludes other possible personal conditions of the offender which could be taken in the calculus of the proportionality principle. The reader of this chapter may have a feeling that the chapter remained inconclusive. The reason could probably be the lack of discussion related to issues of the impact of international human rights principle on the situation of terminally ill prisoners in the United States and other jurisdictions and the issues of practical application of the principle. In fact these and other related questions are discussed in the Ph.D. dissertation of the author which will be soon published.

Finally, it is important to note that the issues of equality of punishment in relation to race and wider issues of distribution and impact of punishment are well beyond the scope of this chapter.

NOTES

1. For the purposes of this chapter the terms "fundamental principle of proportionality of punishment" and the "fundamental principle of not to be subjected to (grossly) disproportionate punishment" are used interchangeably.
2. In the United States the principle was considerably weakened by the way the Supreme Court applied it in the most recent cases (*Harmelin v. Michigan* 501 US 957 (1991)); (*Ewing v. California* 538 US 11 (2003)).
3. The article by Professor Frase is an exception in this regard (2005).
4. Professor Frase considers both theories of Norval Morris and Andrew von Hirsch as hybrid theories (Frase, 2012).
5. The "living-standard approach" was developed by von Hirsch and Jareborg in relation to gauging criminal harm (von Hirsch & Jareborg, 1991).

ACKNOWLEDGMENTS

I thank Professors Hans-Jörg Albrecht and Dirk van Zyl Smit for their helpful discussions on the topic of this chapter. Of course they are in no way responsible for my errors and opinions. Funding is provided by the Max Planck International Research Network on Aging (MaxNetAging).

REFERENCES

Ashworth, A., & Player, E. (1998). Sentencing, equal treatment, and the impact of sanctions. In A. Ashworth & M. Wasik (Eds.), *Fundamentals of sentencing theory: Essays in honour of Andrew von Hirsch, Oxford monographs on criminal law and justice* (1. publ., pp. 251–272). Oxford: Clarendon Press.

Beccaria, C. (1995). *On crimes and punishments and other writings, Cambridge texts in the history of political thought* (1. publ.). Cambridge: Cambridge University Press.

Bentham, J. (2007). *An introduction to the principles of morals and legislation, Dover philosophical classics.* Repr. der Ausg. Oxford, 1907, Mineola, NY: Dover.

Bureau of Justice Statistics. (2009). *Deaths of prisoners under federal jurisdiction, by case of death, 1999–2008.* Retrieved from http://www.bjs.gov

Carson, A. & Golinelli, D. (2013). Prisoners in 2012: Trends in admissions and releases, 1991–2012. Retrieved from http://www.bjs.gov/content/pub/pdf/p12tar9112.pdf. Accessed on March 21, 2014.

Chiu, T. (2010). It's about time: Ageing prisoners, increasing costs, and geriatric release.

Council of Europe. (1950). Convention for the Protection of Human Rights and Fundamental Freedoms: ECHR.

Court of Appeal. (1992). R. v. Green, *Criminal Appeal Reports, 13*(S), 613.

Court of Appeal. (1993). R. v. John Francis C., *Criminal Appeal Reports, 14*(S), 562.

Court of Appeal. (1996). R. v. Bernard *(Basil Mortimer), Criminal Appeal Reports, 1*(S), 135.

Demyan, A. L. (2013). *What compassion got to do with it? An empirical examination of medical release in California prisons.* Ph.D. dissertation, Department of Criminology, Law and Society, University of California, Irvine, Irvine, 2013.

European Court of Human Rights. (2001). *Papon v. France (dec.)*, HUDOC.

Frase, R. S. (2005). Excessive prison sentences, punishment goals, and the eighth amendment: 'Proportionality' relative to what? *Minnesota Law Review, 89*, 571–651.

Frase, R. S. (2012). *Just sentencing: Principles and procedures for a workable system.* Oxford: Oxford University Press.

Granucci, A. F. (1969). "Nor cruel and unusual punishments inflicted": The original meaning. *California Law Review, 57*(4), 839–865.

Human Rights Watch. (2012). The answer is no. Too little compassionate release in US federal prisons.

Maestro, M. (1973). *Cesare Beccaria and the origins of penal reform.* Philadelphia, PA: Temple University Press.

Morris, N. (1964). *Studies in criminal law.* London: Oxford University Press.

Morris, N. (1974). *The future of imprisonment.* Chicago, IL: Chicago University Press.

Morris, N. (1977). Towards principled sentencing. *Maryland Law Review, 37*(2), 267–285.

Morris, N. (1982). *Madness and the criminal law, studies in crime and justice.* Chicago, IL: University of Chicago Press.

Morris, N., & Tonry, M. (1990). *Between prison and probation: Intermediate punishments in a rational sentencing system.* New York, NY: Oxford University Press.

Noonan, M., & Ginder, S. (2013). *Mortality in local jails and state prisons, 2000–2011 – Statistical tables.* Retrieved from http://www.bjs.gov/index.cfm?ty=pbdetail&iid=4757. Accessed on March 21, 2014.

Parliament of the French Republic. (2002). *Code of Criminal Procedure: Art. 720-1-1, Criminal Procedure Code 2002.*

Price, M. (2001). The other safety valve. Sentence reduction motions under 18 U.S.C. § 3582 (c)(1)(A). *Federal Sentencing Reporter*, *13*(3–4), 188–191.

Rodley, N. S. (2009). *The treatment of prisoners under international law* (3rd ed.), Oxford: Oxford University Press.

Senate Committee on the Judiciary. (1983). *S. Rep. No. 225, 98th Cong., 1st Sess. 1983, 1983 WL 25404 (Leg. Hist.)*. Retrieved from http://www.fd.org/docs/select-topics—sentencing/SRA-Leg-History.pdf. Accessed on August 23, 2013.

Smart, A. (1968). Mercy. *Philosophy*, *43*(166), 345–359.

Supreme Court of United States. (1910). *Weems v. United States*, 217 US 349.

United Nations General Assembly. (1948). Universal Declaration of Human Rights: UDHR.

United States Congress. (1791). Eighth Amendment to the United States Constitution.

United States Congress. (1994). *Sentencing Reform Act*: 18 U.S.C. § 3553(b).

United States Congress. (2002). Sentencing Reform Act: 18 U.S.C. § 3582(c)(1)(A)(i).

United States Court of Appeals for the Sixth Circuit. (1995). *United States v. Garland D. Thomas*, U.S. App. LEXIS, Vol. 5034.

United States Sentencing Commission. (1993). Sentencing Guidelines Manual, § 5H 1.4.

United States Sentencing Commission. (2010). Sentencing Guidelines Manual, § 5H 1.1.

van Zyl Smit, D. (1995). Constitutional jurisprudence and proportionality in sentencing. *European Journal of Crime, Criminal Law and Criminal Justice*, *3*(4), 369–380.

van Zyl Smit, D., & Ashworth, A. (2004). Disproportionate sentences as human rights violations. *The Modern Law Review*, *67*(4), 541–560.

von Hirsch, A. (1981). Utilitarian sentencing resuscitated: The American bar association's second report on criminal sentencing. *Rutgers Law Review*, *33*(3), 772–789.

von Hirsch, A. (1985). *Past and future crimes: Deservedness and dangerousness in the sentencing of criminals, crime, law, and deviance series*. New Brunswick, NJ: Rutgers University Press.

von Hirsch, A. (1986). *Doing justice: The choice of punishments*. Boston, MA: Northeastern University Press.

von Hirsch, A. (1993). *Censure and sanctions, Oxford monographs on criminal law & justice*. Oxford: Clarendon Press.

von Hirsch, A., & Ashworth, A. (2005). *Proportionate sentencing exploring the principles*. New York, NY: Oxford University Press.

von Hirsch, A., & Jareborg, N. (1991). Gauging criminal harm: A living-standard analysis. *Oxford Journal of Legal Studies*, *11*(1), 1–38.

Walker, N. (1991). *Why punish?* Oxford: Oxford University Press.

Walker, N. (1995). The quiddity of mercy. *Philosophy*, *70*(271), 27–37.

SENTENCING AND INCARCERATION IN A DEMOCRATIC SOUTH AFRICA

Willem F. M. Luyt

ABSTRACT

Purpose – *In this chapter, the author analyzes sentencing and incarceration practices in South Africa during the last 20 years, a period which saw the country transforming into a fully flexed democracy.*

Design/methodology/approach – *The concepts of sentencing, mandatory minimum sentencing, sentencing of children and incarceration are discussed. The past 20 years of democracy serve as a point of departure for this discussion. The retrospective nature of the adopted approach necessitates a heavy reliance on existing literature, but a statistical analysis is also relied upon. The author also reflects on research conducted during the last 20 years.*

Findings – *While it is almost impossible to duly consider all sentencing-related developments in democratic South Africa, important advances have been made but they were not always systematically followed through. Well-intended policies have at times been poorly executed.*

Punishment and Incarceration: A Global Perspective
Sociology of Crime, Law and Deviance, Volume 19, 203–225

ISSN: 1521-6136/doi:10.1108/S1521-613620140000019009

Specially, the correctional system destroyed all types of staff motivation through poor human resource practices.

Originality/value – *Few scholars have considered the influence of sentencing practices on the South African inmate population, more particularly during the period of democracy that has been running for 20 years. This influence in the South African criminal justice system will be highlighted. The contribution of sentencing in the democratization of the country may be drawn from this discussion. The study may contribute to policy implementation for decades to come and through that, strengthen the South African democracy. At the same time, lessons from South Africa may serve as a roadmap for other young and established democracies.*

Keywords: Sentencing; mandatory sentencing; incarceration; correctional centers; awaiting-trial inmates; unit management

INTRODUCTION

South African law can traditionally be divided into public and private law. Public law organizes (in principal) the relationship between government and the citizens. The state will therefore always be one of the parties in public law. Under public law a person would commit a crime. Under private law, in contrast, any wrongdoing would damage private interest and is called a delict. Crimes will lead to sentencing, while delicts would lead to compensation (Snyman, 2012).

Sentencing will form the first main theme of the discussion in this chapter. The second main theme to be discussed in the chapter is the correctional system. The origin of the South African correctional system can be traced to Britain (Venter, 1959). Since 1990 (after the release of Nelson Mandela) various transformation practices were introduced into the correctional system. These include becoming an independent Government department (1990), the release of political inmates, introducing community corrections (1991), integrating whites-only and blacks-only inmate populations (1993), incorporating five Bantu State correctional systems into one (1993), allowing inmates to vote (1994), adapting to Constitutional dictates, addressing representation amongst management (since 1995), demilitarization (1996), implementing new legislation (since 1998), introducing a judicial inspectorate (1998), opening super maximum correctional centers (1999), implementing unit management (since 2000), introducing private correctional facilities (2001) (Luyt, 2001), implementing changed management policies with rehabilitation as the core (Department of Correctional Services, 2005), and, recently, developing remand detention management policies (Department of Correctional Services, 2012).

For the first couple of years after the election the Department of Correctional Services (the Department; DCS) shared the same top-management as was the case during the dying years of Apartheid. One could argue that the release of Nelson Mandela triggered the transformation agenda in 1990. Van Zyl Smit (2004) indicated that "when major political changes took place at the beginning of the 1990s, it was common cause that elementary human rights of prisoners were not being respected." He noted that "the sad reality is that, in late 2002, there is no evidence of overall prison conditions having improved significantly for the bulk of prisoners in the eight years since the first democratic elections."

After 20 years of democracy it may be time to reevaluate the situation. In doing so, and without disregard for the positive influences of the past 20 years, this chapter will evaluate crime, certain sentencing practices, and elements of incarceration that originated during the democratic dispensation. Despite successes, one could not ignore factors that are hampering progress. The question to be answered is whether the country is still in the 1994 starting blocks (where it has been in 2002, according to Van Zyl Smit, 2004), or whether it has indeed advanced in the quest for improved criminal justice and an improved correctional system. In analyzing the situation, crime statistics during the democratic era, the awaiting-trial inmate population, minimum sentencing practices, and certain concerns regarding sentenced inmates will be discussed. It is not the intention to dwell on theories of sentencing or discuss law, but to focus on the identified areas of sentencing that have a direct bearing on inmate population management.

CRIME IN SOUTH AFRICA

Crime and Crime Statistics

Snyman (2008, 2012) describes South African criminal justice as dysfunctional. Crime statistics normally arise from police reports. Crime increased by 30% between 1994 and 2004, levels never experienced before. South Africa has a low conviction rate and a high (estimated) recidivism rate.

The Constitution and the abolition of the death penalty could not, according to Snyman (2008), secure adequate personal safety.

Despite seasonal changes, there is an ever upward trend in South African crime and incarceration statistics. The average number of murders between 1950 and 1990 was around 7,000 per year. It increased to an average of 24,000 per year in the first eight years of democracy (1994–2002). In the first decade after the death penalty was abolished nearly 250,000 people were murdered. Since 2004, more than 160,000 people have been murdered in South Africa, an average of 43 persons per day. The world murder rate stands at 7.6 per 100,000 and for South Africa at 36.5 per 100,000. The worst country, Honduras, stands at 60.9 per 100,000 (Crime Stats SA, 2014).

Between 1994 and 2007 robbery with aggravating circumstances (being armed) increased by 49.3%. This category comprises seven subcategories, including street robbery, house robbery, robbery at nonresidential premises, car-hijacking, truck-hijacking, cash-in-transit robbery, and bank robbery.

Assault with intent to cause grievous bodily harm made up 31% of the total of violent crime during 2011/2012, but has maintained a slow downward trend for the last eight years. Statistics for aggressive crime are constantly higher than those for economic crime. According to experts (IRIN, 2013) the armed struggle against Apartheid and the following violent backlash have led to the normalization of violence.

The Criminal Law (Sexual Offences and Related Matters) Amendment Act 32 of 2007 created "new" sexual offences other than "conventional" rape. For example, marital rape and raping of men were now sexual offences (IRIN, 2013). The new law made it impossible to compare sexual offence statistics before and after December 2007. The new police crime report category named "total sexual crimes" contains 59 offences ranging from sex-work-related offences to rape and is not useful for comparison with statistics before 2007. Sexual offences show low reporting rates. Medical Research Council research during 2010/2011 has shown that rape levels are unusually high (Institute for Security Studies, 2012). Underreporting of rape is experienced in the male-dominated inmate population (Luyt, 2013).

Commercial crime as a statistical category includes all forms of corruption, money laundering, fraud, embezzlement, and forgery. It has increased by 63% between 2004/2005 and 2010/2011. Public and private sectors are reportedly notoriously bad at reporting crime. The actual number is understood to be far greater than that recorded in crime statistics (Institute for Security Studies, 2012).

Policing and prosecution is ineffective and statistics are untrustworthy. There is one-sided emphasis on the rights of accused and convicted persons and little on the rights to safety of law-abiding citizens (Snyman, 2008). Perceptions of police inability are also noted abroad. The Overseas Security Advisory Council of the Bureau of Diplomatic Security in the United States noted that "for residential and commercial properties in the more affluent neighbourhoods, the use of private security companies has become the norm for first response to crime. The police have proven incapable of providing this service" (Ford & Snyder, 2013). The incapability of police is also observed in informal settlements. It is reported that "crimes occur with great frequency throughout neighbourhoods" (Ford & Snyder, 2013).

Since 2002/2003, when crime levels peaked, the overall crime rate has decreased by 21% (Institute for Security Studies, 2012). One should not ignore the influence of the 2009 and 2010 soccer tournaments in South Africa. During these tournaments crime was at an all-time low, which may have influenced the decrease in crime rates reported in the media. Edwards (2010) reported that crime dropped by 70% in Johannesburg during the soccer world cup, but returned to former levels thereafter in some provinces. Nonetheless, for statisticians, the decrease created new, lower benchmarks from which crime was measured and reported.

Crime Rates and Incarceration Figures

Decreasing crime rates (per police statistics) contradict sentencing statistics (portrayed by the sentenced inmate population) over the democratic period. Between 1991 and 2000, prosecutions decreased by 23%, while convictions decreased by 19% (Steinberg, 2005). Yet the inmate population increased as discussed later. South Africa is ranked ninth globally with overpopulated correctional centers (Snyman, 2012). The awaiting-trail inmate population also shows that crime is not decreasing.

What can we learn from crime and incarceration statistics? Crime statistics deal with individual incidences. Incarceration statistics deal with a specific number of people. For example, if there were five police reports of housebreaking and the same person is arrested for all five, he is counted once in terms of correctional crowding, while reflected five times under crime statistics.

Another difference is that crime statistics are counted for one year. The same inmate may have a long-term effect on correctional statistics as each inmate contributes to the annual inmate population for the total length of incarceration. This may seem unimportant at first glance, but one cannot ignore the growing effect of long sentences on the inmate population. The more long sentences you have, the more the correctional population will show an upward trend over time. This is one of the outcomes of the minimum sentencing legislation in South Africa, posing major long-term inmate population challenges. In 2011, 88,095 inmates served sentences longer than two years to life, compared to only 23,140 in 1994. This increase is not sustainable over time. Sentences less than two years decreased dramatically since 1994, as illustrated below from the writings of by Bruyn (1994) and the Department of Correctional Services (2011) (Table 1).

Manipulation of Inmate Populations

Before 1994 inmate population manipulation occurred through flexible release policies and amnesties. During 1994, President Mandela appointed the Kriegler Commission to investigate correctional crowding, unrest, and inmate release. A reviewed release policy emanated from it (Van Zyl Smit, 2004).

Constitutional dictates ensured new correctional legislation in 1998, which was fully implemented in 2004 (Luyt, 2008). While not fully implemented, inmates were released under the 1959 legislation. Simultaneously,

Table 1. Sentence Length Breakdown (1994 and 2011).

Sentence Length (1994 (Bruyn, 1994) and February 2011 (Department of Correctional Services, 2011))		
Sentence length	1994 number	2011 number
< 6 months	62,500	4,405
> 6–12 months (6–23 months, 1994 statistics)	16,961	3,725
> 12–24 months		3,661
2–3 years (24 months and longer, 1994 statistics)	23,140 (all categories including life)	
3–5 years		11,987
5–7 years		8,086
7–10 years		14,773
10–15 years		20,060
15–20 years		12,168
> 20 years		10,712
Life		10,349
Other (including 1994 unsentenced)	8,332	525
Total sentenced (1994 figure included unsentenced)	*110,933*	*112,467*

sentencing was investigated (Van Zyl Smit, 2002), resulting in minimum sentencing legislation and an increased inmate population. Today, repeatedly revised release policies remain the main source of inmate population manipulation since 1998.

Awaiting-Trial Confrontation

Crime remains a growing, complex social phenomenon thriving on historical and current socioeconomic–political dictates, compounded by ineffective offender rehabilitation (Herbig & Hesselink, 2012). DCS finds itself at both ends of the criminal justice supply chain. The Department receives alleged offenders on remand, while the South African Polices Service is liable to investigate crimes and ensure court appearances. Remand inmates have unique rights enshrined in Sections 12 and 35 (2) of the Constitution (Republic of South Africa, 1996).

During democracy, awaiting-trial inmates increased by 164% from 24,265 in 1995 to 63,964 in 2000 (Fagan, 2001). Simultaneously, the sentenced population increased by 17% from 92,581 to 108,307. The awaiting-trail inmate population stabilized due to what Van Zyl Smit (2004) described as creative use of release policies. The main decline happened in 2000 by applying Section 66 of the Correctional Services Act 8 of 1959 to release 8,451 awaiting-trail inmates who were granted bail of less than R1,000, but were unable to pay (Steinberg, 2005). Fagan (2001) motivated that their release was "justified and urgent" under Section 66, as conditions of detention were inhumane and disregarded human rights.

In 2000, 11,924 minor offenders out of 59,275 inmates received bail below R1,000.00, but could not pay it, while 40,315 inmates were denied bail for serious crimes. Those with bail of less than R1,000.00 were released on their own responsibility to alleviate overcrowding (Fagan, 2001). A further challenge concerning awaiting-trail inmates is the long periods they are incarcerated. Those who were incarcerated for more than three months increased from 4,000 in 1995 to 27,000 by 2000 (Fagan, 2001).

Overcrowding remains critical, despite an increase in design capacity. With a design capacity of 118,154 beds the Department reserved 93,154 beds for sentenced inmates. The benchmark for awaiting-trail inmates was 25,000. February 2011 figures showed a total inmate population of 162,262, of which 49,695 were awaiting-trial (Department of Correctional Services, 2014). This was double the awaiting-trail benchmark and nearly one third of the total inmate population. The sentenced population

(112,476) increased by less than 2% over 10 years (2000–2010) (Herbig & Hesselink, 2012).

SENTENCING

Sentencing may be that part of the law in action most closely observed by the public. In this discussion sentencing refers to punishment of convicted offenders by a criminal court. Sentences finalize (apart from appeals/reviews) criminal cases against offenders.

Courts must find the most appropriate sentence (Republic of South Africa, 1977). Judge Chetty, in *S v. Mtshabe* (62/05) (2005) ZACHC 81, reiterated this principle (finding appropriate sentences), explaining that: "In determining an appropriate sentence, it is perhaps apposite to commence by restating the guidelines to sentencing which have consistently been applied and followed in our courts. These sentencing principles were succinctly articulated by Holmes, J.A. in *S v Rabie* 1975 (4) SA 855 (A) at 862G as: '*Punishment should fit the criminal as well as the crime, be fair to society and be blended with a measure of mercy according to the circumstances*'."

Sources of Sentencing

The South African law of sentencing primarily originates from criminal law, criminal procedure, and important influences from the Constitution. Three other sources give origin to sentencing, namely, legislation, case law, and common law (Snyman, 2012). English law may also be regarded as an important influence on our sentencing law, rather than being a source of law itself. English law influence is particularly strong in the naming and categorizing of offences and requirements for these offences (Snyman, 2012).

Legislation: The Constitution

The Constitution is the supreme law of the country. The Constitution contains the Bill of Rights in chapter 2, which affected sentencing through various rights. The right to life and the right to dignity, for example, have lead to the abolishment of the death penalty and corporal punishment. Principles and values in the Bill of Rights cause courts to interpret legislation to ensure that the rights of offenders are protected (Terblanche, 2007).

Specified rights include cruel, inhuman, or degrading punishment, human dignity, and the right to a fair trial. No right is absolute, but limitations may apply (Republic of South Africa, 1996).

Legislation: Statutes

Offences are created by law. A vast number of statutory offences are created in South African legislation, but cannot be discussed within the scope of this chapter. All statutes are subject to the Constitution (Snyman, 2012). Concerning criminal procedure, the Criminal Procedure Act 51 of 1977 is the primary source of sentencing. In 1997 the Criminal Law Amendment Act 105 of 1997 (Republic of South Africa, 1997) started to regulate mandatory and minimum sentencing.

Other important sentencing statutes are the Child Justice Act 75 of 2008 (Republic of South Africa, 2009), dealing with offences by children and youth in conflict with the law, and the Correctional Services Act(s) 8 of 1959 and 111 of 1998 (Republic of South Africa, 1959, 1998), regulating how sentences of community corrections and incarceration must be executed. The 1959 Act has only limited influence on inmates sentenced before 1998 and 2004 (when various sections of the 1998 Act were implemented). Sentencing of children and youth will be discussed later.

Case Law

The interpretation of legislation and the general principles of sentencing are influenced by case law. The principle of precedent (*stare decisis*) applies to sentencing in South Africa. The (previous) decisions of higher courts are binding on lower courts and courts on the same level. Previously imposed sentences should be considered as guidelines during sentencing.

Common Law

Common law refers to those rules of law not captured in law by Parliament or provincial legislators. The origin of common law is mainly in the Roman-Dutch law. The influence of the Dutch-Roman law on South African sentencing is decreasing (Snyman, 2012). The general principles of sentencing are important when considering common law. Sentencing should always be placed in proper context. Too much importance should not be attached to common law in relation to sentencing. Common law hardly influences criminal procedure (Terblanche, 2007).

Types of Sentences

Types of sentences are regulated by law. Section 276(1) of the Criminal Procedure Act 51 of 1977 largely codifies sentencing options. A court may generally impose any one or a combination of sentences discussed below. *Historically (regarding (a) and (f) below)*, but also today, subject to the provisions of the Act, any other law and the common law, the following sentences were passed upon conviction:

(a) Death penalty [was deleted by Section 34 of Act 105 of 1997 and is unconstitutional.]
(b) Imprisonment, including for life or for an indefinite period as referred to in section 286B (1); [Par. (b) substituted by Section 3 of Act 107 of 1990 and Section 20 of Act 116 of 1993.]
(c) Periodical imprisonment;
(d) Declaration as a habitual criminal;
(e) Committal to any institution established by law;
(d) A fine;
(f) Corporal punishment [deleted by Section 2 of Act 33 of 1997 and is unconstitutional.]
(g) Correctional supervision; [Para. (h) added by Section 41 (a) of Act 122 of 1991.]
(i) Imprisonment from which such a person may be placed under correctional supervision in the discretion of the Commissioner or a parole board. (Republic of South Africa, 1977)

Imprisonment is the most common punishment. A district court can normally impose a sentence of up to 3 years imprisonment, but in terms of the Drugs and Drug Trafficking Act 140 of 1992 (Republic of South Africa, 1992), a district court can impose up to 25 years. A regional and high court can sentence an accused to life imprisonment. A court may impose any term of imprisonment up to the maximum prescribed by law (courts are discussed in more detail below).

Correctional supervision is a community sentence subject to prescribed conditions such as the court may deem fit. They include house arrest, community service, and submission to various programs aimed at training and rehabilitation. The objective is to enable offenders to lead a socially responsible and crime-free life during their sentence and thereafter..

A court can sentence qualifying offenders to periodical imprisonment for not less than 100 hours and not more than 2000 hours. An offender would normally report to a correctional center on a Friday afternoon and would be released on a Monday morning. Periodic imprisonment has existed in law since 1959. Relatively minor, nonviolent crimes with no minimum sentences attached would qualify for a sentence of periodic imprisonment, for example traffic violations and driving while intoxicated (Rossouw, 2010).

Mandatory Minimum Sentencing

The Criminal Law Amendment Act 105 of 1997 compelled courts to impose mandatory minimum sentences for specific crimes, unless substantial and compelling circumstances justify the imposition of a lesser sentence (Cilliers, 2002). Judges must provide reasons for deviations.

The legislature intended to reduce serious and violent crime, using as motivation *S v. Malgas* when the Supreme Court of Appeal declared: "In short, the legislature aimed at ensuring a severe, standardized and consistent response from the courts to the commission of such [serious] crimes" (Sloth-Nielson & Ehlers, 2005). The provisions were initially intended to be in effect for two years. This period was extended and today mandatory minimum sentencing remains the dominant approach to sentencing.

The Act provides for minimum incarceration in a relatively small range of serious offences, including murder, rape, robbery, and serious economic crimes. The least severe mandatory sentence is 15 years imprisonment, rising to 20 and 25 years for offenders with previous convictions for the same offence. The Act provides for progressively harsher penalties for repeat offenders (Van Zyl Smit, 2000).

Terblanche (2007) argues that South African courts dislike *mandatory* sentencing. Judge Corbett in *S v. Toms*; *S v. Bruce* regarded it as "an undesirable intrusion by the Legislature upon the jurisdiction of the courts." In comparison, *minimum* sentencing leaves the court with discretion to impose a sentence higher than the lower limit set by the Legislature. In such cases, maximum sentences are determined by court jurisdiction and any other prescribed maximum sentence, but would still mean a minimum term of incarceration.

The Criminal Law Amendment Act 105 of 1997 is not the first to deprive courts of their sentencing discretion. Previous attempts by the Legislature to limit sentencing discretion through mandatory minimum sentences have evoked strong protest from the legal fraternity. The Viljoen Commission of Inquiry into the Penal System of the Republic of South Africa, 1971, argued that prescribed minimum sentences were undesirable and that erosion of sentencing discretion of courts could lead to grave injustice (Neser, 2001). The following (Neser, 2001) are previous examples of sentencing deprivation:

- Mandatory imposition of corporal punishment under particular circumstances (1952).
- Imprisonment for corrective training (minimum of 2 and maximum of 4 years) and the prevention of crime (minimum of 5 years and maximum

of 8 years), which were mandatory penalties where the criminal record of the accused met certain requirements (1959).

- Act 41 of 1971, prescribing mandatory sentences for drug-related offenses.

On recommendation of the Viljoen Commission, mandatory minimum sentences for corrective training and prevention of crime have been scrapped. Chief Justice Corbett commented in *S v. Toms*; *S v. Bruce* (1990 2 SA 802 [A] 817 C-D):

> … the imposition of a mandatory minimum prison sentence has always been regarded as an undesirable intrusion by the Legislature upon the jurisdiction of the courts to determine the punishment to be meted out to persons convicted of statutory offenses and as a kind of enactment that is calculated in certain instances to produce grave injustice.

The Constitutional Court tested the Constitutionality of Act 105 of 1997 (*S v. Dzukuda*; *S v. Dodo*). Concerns included whether the Act (*inter alia*) breached the separation of powers and the right not to be punished in a cruel, unusual, or degrading manner. In judgment it was maintained that the Act does not compel courts to do anything unconstitutional (Terblanche, 2007). The constitutionality of mandatory minimum sentencing was again confirmed in the 2013 case of the *Minister of Justice and Constitutional Development and Another v. Masingili and Others*. This case also addressed the imposition of a lesser sentence.

Bernick and Larkin (2014) argued that the proliferation in recent decades of mandatory minimum penalties for federal crimes in the United States, along with increased prison populations, has forced those concerned with criminal justice in America to reconsider. They maintain that mandatory minimum sentences are the product of good intentions, but do not always make good policy. Bernick and Larkin (2014) provide full arguments against minimum sentencing in the American setup.

South African criminal justice is in the same predicament. Sloth-Nielson and Ehlers (2005) argued that it is difficult to find substantive evidence that mandatory minimum sentencing laws have had any general deterrent effect or reduced crime. Altbeker (2005) concluded similarly, noting discrepancies in reporting of different crime categories. Terblanche (2003) argued that minimum sentences legislation has worsened the inconsistencies that prevail in relation to targeted offences. In addition, research examining the effects of mandatory minimum sentencing suggests it has not achieved South Africa's sentencing goals (Berg & Schärf, 2004).

Giffard and Muntingh (2006) maintain that blame for the increased inmate population has been placed on minimum sentencing legislation. The major driver is the growing proportion of long-term inmates. Inmates sentenced under minimum sentences legislation may be considered for parole only after serving a minimum of four fifths (previously one third) of their sentence, while inmates serving life are considered after 25 years (previously 20 years).

Roth (2008) proposed that South Africa should renovate sentencing approaches. Mandatory minimum sentencing has failed to address sentencing problems. It has not deterred violent crime or reduced sentencing disparities. Instead, the Act has led to procedural delays, victimization, and overcrowding (Roth, 2008; Terblanche & Mackenzie, 2008).

Sentencing of Children

In South Africa, children are persons under the age of 18 years. Sentencing principles for offending children changed fundamentally since the Constitution was adopted in 1996. Section 28 introduced rights specifically aimed to protect children. Some of these rights directly affected offending children. Concerning sentencing, important rights include that the best interests of children are paramount, and that children should not be incarcerated unless incarceration is unavoidable (Terblanche, 2012).

The South African Law Commission investigated child justice, which culminated in the Child Justice Act 75 of 2008. The Act establishes a child criminal justice system separate from adult criminal justice. The Act aims to avoid child incarceration and, through diversion, keeps children away from the formal criminal justice system. The Act also provides for child offenders to be tried and sentenced in child justice courts (Republic of South Africa, 2009). Child justice courts are different from children's courts, which are established in terms of the Children's Act 38 of 2005.

The following two aims of the Child Justice Act are important:

1. Whenever "appropriate circumstances" prevail, child offenders should be diverted from the criminal justice system, and;
2. When diversion is not possible or advisable, child offenders should be dealt with "in the criminal justice system in child justice courts" (Republic of South Africa, 2009).

Under diversion accused children do not enter formal criminal proceedings, but are subjected to alternative processes without a formal trial, conviction, and sentencing. Alternative processes may require the person to perform determined services/tasks, or to undergo training. These tasks may be perceived as punitive (Gallinetti, Muntingh, & Skelton, 2004).

According to the Child Justice Act 75 of 2008 (Republic of South Africa, 2009) children who commit an offence while under the age of 10 years do not have criminal capacity and cannot be prosecuted. Such children must be dealt with in terms of Section 9 of the Act. Children 10 years or older, but under 14 years, who commit an offence are presumed to lack criminal capacity, unless the State proves that they have criminal capacity in accordance with Section 11 of the Act.

Experts (Gallinetti et al., 2004; Terblanche, 2012) correctly point out that the Child Justice Act does not establish child justice courts. Children could appear before any court under the Criminal Procedure Act. The intention of the legislature is that all courts involved in criminal procedure are child justice courts when dealing with provisions under the Child Justice Act. Terblanche (2012) argues that it is unfortunate that child justice courts were not created. "Mixed responsibilities" of adult courts may not create ideal child justice.

Sentencing in child justice courts is regulated by chapter 10 (Section 68) of the Child Justice Act. The sentences are the following: community-based sentences, restorative justice sentences, a fine, correctional supervision, residence in a child and youth care center, and imprisonment. Most sentences may be imposed as suspended sentences (Republic of South Africa, 2009). Periodical imprisonment and committal to a treatment center are not applicable to children.

When offenders *under* 18 years old are sentenced, courts must sentence them in terms of Section 68 of the Child Justice Act, while applying all principles relevant to sentencing of children (Republic of South Africa, 2009). Some offenders, being children when offending, may be *older* than 18 years during sentencing. Offenders who (despite being children offending) are older during sentencing pose particular challenges. The Child Justice Act attempts to solve the problem of offenders turning older than 18 by focusing on the age of the offender when the criminal proceedings *are instituted.*

Section 4(1) (b) of the Act regulates these matters. By implication Section 4(1) (b) indicates that when these proceedings *are instituted* before the offender turns 18, the provisions of the Act apply. These provisions read as follows:

> Subject to subsection (2), this Act applies to any person in the Republic who is alleged to have committed an offence and …
>
> (b) was 10 years or older, but under the age of 18 years when he or she was-
>
> i. handed a written notice in terms of section 18 or 22;
> ii. served with a summons in terms of section 19; or
> iii. arrested in terms of section 20, for that offence.

For persons aged between 18 and 21 the provisions of the Child Justice Act will apply for sentencing. Section 4(2) of the Child Justice Act permits subsequent prosecution (after age 18), as long as the accused is under the age of 21 (also considering the National Department of Public Prosecution directives). When the offender is 21 years or older when criminal proceedings are *instituted*, regardless of whether the crime was *committed* while under eighteen, the Child Justice Act cannot find application. In such cases the accused can *only* be charged, tried, and sentenced in terms of the provisions of the Criminal Procedure Act (Terblanche, 2012).

In 2009 Justice Edwin Cameron, in the *Center for Child Law v. Minister for Justice and Constitutional Development and Others*, changed the approach to sentencing of youth under the minimum sentencing law. In terms of the Criminal Law (Sentencing) Amendment Act 38 of 2007 (Republic of South Africa, 2007) minimum sentences for certain serious crimes were made applicable to 16- and 17-year-old children. Justice Cameron remarked that "the Constitution requires an individuated judicial response to sentencing for children that focuses on the particular child who is being sentenced." The court held that the new law, coming into effect in 2008, forced sentencing officials to impose incarceration as a minimum sentence in some cases, taking away their discretion when dealing with people the Constitution regards as children. The Constitutional Court ruled that 16- and 17-year-olds affected by new minimum sentencing laws could have their sentences reviewed (Sapa, 2009).

Children under the age of 14 may not be remanded in a correctional center. For children older than 14 years, correctional remand is only possible if charged with a Schedule 3 (serious) offence and referral to a place of safety is not possible (Erasmus & Jonker, 2011).

Sentencing and Incarceration of Women

There is no separate legal basis for the sentencing and incarceration of women in South Africa. Sentencing laws apply to men and women alike (Luyt & Du Preez, 2013). The female inmate population in South Africa is small, which may lead to marginalization. Sentenced women are obliged to wear correctional clothes. Incarcerated women face various challenges. Inadequacies persist in various areas. The Department of Correctional Services (2005) expressed that rehabilitation will be at the center of activities, but it is not always the case considering rehabilitation of women (Luyt & Du Preez, 2013).

South African Courts as Sentencing Mechanism

The judicial authority of South Africa vests in the courts (Republic of South Africa, 1996). Courts are independent and subject only to the Constitution and the law, which must be applied impartially. An order or judgment (including sentencing) issued by courts binds all persons and State organs to which it is applicable.

South Africa administers three *levels* of courts. Jurisdiction refers to the authority or competence of a court to hear a matter validly brought before it and to grant relief or judgment in respect of that matter. District (magistrate) courts are presided over by magistrates and have jurisdiction over all cases apart from murder, rape, and high treason. Sentencing is limited to a maximum of three years' incarceration (drug offences may be dealt with differently) or a maximum fine of R60,000.00. Regional courts are presided over by regional magistrates and have jurisdiction over all cases apart from high treason. Sentencing is limited to a maximum of 15 years' incarceration or a maximum fine of R300,000.00 (Anon, 2011; Terblanche, 2007).

High courts are presided over by judges and have jurisdiction over all cases, including high treason. Sentencing is unlimited for both incarceration and fines, except for statutory fine limits. There is no limit to the jurisdiction of the courts concerning the number of offences (a court can give the maximum sentence 20 times should an offender be guilty of 20 offences).

The Supreme Court of Appeal is the highest court of appeal for all matters that are not constitutional. It is not a trail court, but may impose sentences if the sentence of a lower court is invalid. Cases may also be referred back to the lower court for resentencing. The Constitutional Court only deals with constitutional matters and is not a sentencing court (Anon, 2011; Terblanche, 2007).

The Role of Correctional Services in Sentencing

The DCS is exclusively responsible for sentenced inmates under incarceration and community corrections sentences. Most offenders are sentenced to incarceration, compared to community corrections. Fines remain popular, sometimes combined with incarceration or *alternative* incarceration as regulated through Section 287(1) of the Criminal Procedure Act (Republic of South Africa, 1997). In these cases, fines may be paid at correctional centers. Periodic incarceration is served in correctional centers. According to Rossouw (2010) periodic incarceration is an effective and constitutional alternative sentence for minor crimes that should be applied more widespread.

Although two private correctional centers are operative, they only receive inmates from the Department and not from courts. Inmates in private correctional centers have to be transferred back to DCS before they may be released. The duties of the Department are stipulated in the Correctional Services Act 111 of 1998 (Republic of South Africa, 1998).

Correctional Management and Financial Planning

Inmate population growth remains a correctional management challenge in South Africa. In 1985 South Africa incarcerated on average 108,955 inmates, increasing to 110,069 during 1995. Since 1997 the inmate population exploded, as illustrated below (Table 2).

The Department is managed according to seven programs, which are used for budgetary purposes. Programs address broad responsibilities aimed at meeting the statutory mandate of the Department.

Program 1: Administration has the purpose to provide administrative, management, financial, information and communication technology, research, policy coordination, and good governance support functions that are necessary for all areas of service delivery, including the functions of the ministry.

Program 2: Security is used to provide safe and healthy conditions for all incarcerated persons, consistent with their right to human dignity and in support of personnel and public security.

Table 2. Inmate Population (Department of Correctional Services, 2011; Luyt, 2008).

Year	Design Capacity	Inmates on 31/12	% Overcrowding
1995	94,381	112,572	19.3
1996	96,329	125,750	30.5
1997	99,407	142,410	43.3
1998	99,294	146,287	47.3
1999	99,834	162,638	62.9
2006	115,344	160,198	38.9
2007	115,327	163,049	42.35
2011	118,154	162,162	37.25
2014	Not available	157,170 (28 March)	

Program 3: Corrections aim at providing needs-based correctional sentence plans and interventions through individual assessment of security risk and criminal profiles. Corrections target elements associated with offending behavior and focus on the offence for which a person was sentenced.

Program 4: Care – The purpose of care is to provide needs-based care programs and services that are aimed at maintaining the personal well-being of incarcerated persons.

Program 5: Development provides needs-based personal development programs and services to all offenders, including educational, skills, and other development-related programs to facilitate the reintegration of offenders into communities.

Program 6: Social Reintegration provides services focused on release preparation, effective parole and correctional supervision, and social reintegration into communities.

Program 7: Facilities is aimed at providing physical infrastructure that supports safe and secure custody, humane conditions, corrective services, care, development, and general administration.

All programs can be linked to the sentencing mandate. Without proper facilities, for example, sentences may be served in unconstitutional conditions. However, the programs corrections, development, and social reintegration are specifically linked to sentence execution by the State and may be used more creatively to counter overcrowding.

Unit and Case Management in Relation to Sentencing

The above seven programs are implemented within the unit management philosophy. Individual case management forms one of the pillars of unit management and is directly linked to sentence management (Luyt, 1999). Unit management is the comprehensive correctional management philosophy in South Africa. It is defined as decentralized inmate management that divides correctional populations into small, manageable entities for improved inmate control, good relationships, and inmate development service delivery for effective reintegration. It ensures proper supervision, control, and job satisfaction for officials. For inmates, unit management facilitates personal development and safe, normalized environments (Luyt, Jonker, & Bruyns, 2010).

Case management means organizing the advancement of sentenced offenders through the correctional system, linking correctional resources to inmate needs. Case management facilitates desired change in offenders to improve security and reduce relapses into crime (Luyt, 1999). Case management is a statutory duty prescribed in Section 42 of the Correctional Services Act (Republic of South Africa, 1998). The purpose is productive sentences to ensure successful reintegration into communities. Each inmate sentenced to more than 12 months must have a sentence plan, which should be executed meticulously and reviewed regularly (Luyt, 2008).

Despite excellent policies, the correctional system suffers from an inability to implement and maintain unit and case management (Luyt, 2008). The Judicial Inspectorate for Correctional Services reported that "*general systemic problems found during audit, which suggested that the infrastructure of prisons was not conducive for rehabilitation, there was an over emphasis on security in medium prisons, accommodation was not adequate and admissions of prisoners had not been administered appropriately.*" It further stated that 11% of inmates participated in rehabilitation. The rest spent 23 hours inside cells (Parliamentary Monitoring Group, 2007). Staff members illustrate low levels of productivity and motivation, partly to the lack of career opportunities and promotion (Luyt, 2008). Productive execution of sentences cannot happen under these circumstances.

FINDINGS

It is almost impossible to duly consider all sentencing-related developments (some positive, other negative) during the South African democratic era. Lessons were learnt and international best practices were implemented, but not refined and followed through. With well-intended policies comes poor execution. A weak political setup will turn part-time sentencing solutions into long-term horrors of overcrowding, aging inmate populations, extreme idleness, poor rehabilitation efforts, and extreme financial consequences. Additionally, the correctional system destroyed all types of staff motivation through poor human resource practices.

Sentencing in South Africa is under severe pressure. Mandatory minimum sentencing is creating more problems than solutions. Rehabilitation participation is already extremely low. Long sentences are counterproductive to rehabilitation and will adversely affect the inmate population in future. This policy must be reviewed urgently to avoid tragic consequences.

The children justice system is growing in stature, but the absence of dedicated children courts is causing a gray area. For the judiciary to put on different hats all the time may not come naturally, particularly when adult adjudication, child age during the crime, age during sentencing, and also age when proceedings are started are different all the time. Child justice may be served better within a dedicated child justice system, including children courts.

The implementation of sentences within the correctional system is cumbersome. Correctional staff members do not contribute optimally to sentence planning and case management implementation, irrespective of the statutory duty to do so. They have extremely low levels of motivation and expectations for the future, brought about through the lack of a fair, dedicated, and workable promotion policy that promotes positive attitudes.

Female inmates remain marginalized, as confirmed from research by Luyt and Du Preez (2013). The relatively small female inmate population contributes to marginalization and should be the catalyst why alternatives should be considered. Not only corrections (executing sentences), but also the judiciary (during sentencing) should think differently about offending women. Reinstating sentencing discretion lost through mandatory minimum sentencing may make a difference in this regard. Community alternatives and even diversion as applicable to children should be strong considerations.

The sentenced population have little gains from well-intended policies grinded to a halt through inability of poorly trained staff to implement them. Free society is also on the losing side, having to see additional taxes spent on long, unproductive sentencing terms at an increased rate. All of this occurs while career opportunities are diminishing, poverty is increasing, and more resources are needed for a growing group of people who become subjected to criminal justice.

South Africa has made positive strides to strengthen the democracy. Developments at legislative and policy level need mentioning, but implementation remains problematic. As long as this trend continues, true democracy will remain a dream. Lack of motivation and promotion opportunities are at the core of policy implementation problems. Criminal justice and positive sentencing outcomes will continue to suffer without a comprehensive system in which all role-players feel their contribution is valued. South Africa failed in this regard.

REFERENCES

Altbeker, A. (2005). The impact of the introduction of the minimum sentencing legislation on levels of crime and crime prevention. Presentation at the OSF-SA Workshop Report on Minimum Sentencing, January, 6 and 7.

Anon. (2011). *Jurisdiction of South African courts and tribunals: A guide for the legal practitioner*. Retrieved from http://www.northernlaw.co.za/important_information_for_members/constitutional_court_judgment/Jurisdiction.LSSA.pdf. Accessed on April 4, 2011.

Berg, J., & Schärf, W. (2004). Crime statistics in South Africa 1994–2003. *Southern African Journal of Criminal Justice*, *17*, 57.

Bernick, E., & Larkin, P. (2014). *Reconsidering mandatory minimum sentences: The arguments for and against potential reforms*. Retrieved from http://www.heritage.org/research/reports/2014/02/reconsidering-mandatory-minimum-sentences-the-arguments-for-and-against-potential-reforms. Accessed on April 2, 2014.

Bruyn, H. J. (1994). *Department of correctional services report for 1 January 1994 to 31 December 1994*. Pretoria: Department of Correctional Services.

Cilliers, A. (2002). *Minimum sentences in South African Law*. Retrieved from http://jurist.law.pitt.edu/world/foreignmay02.php. Accessed on April 2, 2014.

Crime Stats SA. (2014). *Crime stats simplified*. Retrieved from http://www.crimestatssa.com/didyouknow.php. Accessed on February 17, 2014.

Department of Correctional Services. (2005). *White paper on corrections*. Pretoria: Department of Correctional Services.

Department of Correctional Services. (2011). *Sentence length breakdown as on the last day of 2011/02*. Retrieved from http://www.dcs.gov.za/AboutUs/StatisticalInformation.aspx. Accessed on March 18, 2014.

Department of Correctional Services. (2012). *Draft white paper on remand detention management in South Africa*. Pretoria: Department of Correctional Services.

Department of Correctional Services. (2014). *Statistical information. Incarceration levels as on the last day of 2011/02*. Retrieved from http://www.dcs.gov.za/AboutUs/StatisticalInformation.aspx. Accessed on February 12, 2014.

Edwards, G. (2010). *Increase in crime after world cup*. Retrieved from http://www.news24.com/SouthAfrica/News/Increase-in-crime-after-World-Cup-20100913. Accessed on February 17, 2014.

Erasmus, H., & Jonker, J. (2011). Legislation relevant to youth in corrections. In N. Du Preez & W. F. M. Luyt (Eds.), *Fundamentals and development psychology in youth corrections*. Pretoria: Unisa Press.

Fagan, J. J. (2001). *The judicial inspectorate of prisons annual report for the period 1 April to 31 December 2000*. Cape Town: Office of the Judicial Inspectorate.

Ford, P. D., & Snyder, J. (2013). *South Africa 2013 Crime and Safety Report*. Retrieved from https://www.osac.gov/pages/ContentReportDetails.aspx?cid=13642. Accessed on February 17, 2014.

Gallinetti, J., Muntingh, L., & Skelton, A. (2004). Child justice concepts. In J. Sloth-Nielsen & J. Gallinetti. (Eds.), *Child justice in Africa: A guide to good practice*. Cape Town: Community Law Center.

Giffard, C., & Muntingh, L. (2006). *The effect of sentencing on the size of the South African prison population*. Retrieved from http://www.osf.org.za/wp/wp-content/uploads/2012/09/The-effect-of-sentencing-on-the-South-African-prison-population1.pdf. Accessed on March 29, 2014.

Herbig, F. J. W., & Hesselink, A. E. (2012). Seeing the person, not just the number. Needsbased rehabilitation of offenders in South African prisons. *SA Crime Quarterly*, *41*(September), 29–37.

IRIN. (2013). *South Africa's rape problem: Why the crime remains under-reported.* Retrieved from http://www.theguardian.com/global-development/2013/nov/04/south-africa-rape-problem-crime. Accessed on February 17, 2014.

Luyt, W. F. M. (1999). *Unit management in prisons.* Unpublished doctoral thesis,University of South Africa, Pretoria.

Luyt, W. F. M. (2001). The transformation of corrections in the new South Africa. *Southern African Journal of Criminology, 14*(3), 26–33.

Luyt, W. F. M. (2008). Contemporary corrections in South Africa after more than a decade of transformation. *Acta Criminologica, 21*(2), 176–195.

Luyt, W. F. M. (2013). Preventing and managing sex crimes inside correctional centers. *Southern African Journal of Criminology, 26*(2), 30–63.

Luyt, W. F. M., & Du Preez, N. (2013). *Women, families and imprisonment in South Africa. Wagadu, Volume 11.* Retrieved from http://appweb.cortland.edu/ojs/index.php/Wagadu/article/view Article/396/985. Accessed on April 3, 2014.

Luyt, W. F. M., Jonker, J. J., & Bruyns, H. J. (2010). *Unit management and legal principles in prisons* (3rd ed.). Pretoria: Unisa Press.

Neser, J. J. (2001). Mandatory minimum sentences in the South African context. *Crime Research in South Africa, 3*(3), 1–7.

Parliamentary Monitoring Group. (2007). *Judicial Inspectorate of Prisons Annual Report 2006/07 briefing.* Retrieved from http://www.pmg.org.za/minutes/20071105-judicial-inspectorateprisons annual-report-200607-briefing. Accessed on February 18, 2008.

Republic of South Africa. (1959). *The Correctional Services Act 8 of 1959.* Pretoria: Government Printer.

Republic of South Africa. (1977). *Criminal Procedure Act 51 of 1977.* Pretoria: Government Printer.

Republic of South Africa. (1992). *The Drug and Drug Trafficking Act 140 of 1992.* Pretoria: Government Printer.

Republic of South Africa. (1996). *Constitution of the Republic of South Africa 108 of 1996.* Pretoria: Government Printer.

Republic of South Africa. (1997). *The Criminal Law Amendment Act 105 of 1997.* Pretoria: Government Printer.

Republic of South Africa. (1998). *The Correctional Services Act 111 of 1998.* Pretoria: Government Printer.

Republic of South Africa. (2007). *Criminal Law (Sentencing) Amendment Act 38 of 2007.* Pretoria: Government Printer.

Republic of South Africa. (2009). *The Child Justice Act 75 of 2008.* Pretoria: Government Printer.

Roth, S. M. (2008). South African mandatory minimum sentencing: Reform required. *Minnesota Journal of International Law, 17*(1), 155–182.

Rossouw, H. (2010). Alternatives to traditional sentencing methods – The efficacy and constitutionality of periodic imprisonment in South Africa. *COLR* (9th ed., pp. 10–26). Ireland: COLR.

Steinberg, J. (2005). Prison overcrowding and the constitutional right to adequate accommodation in South Africa. Paper commissioned by the Centre for the Study of Violence and Reconciliation, January. Retrieved from http://www.csvr.org.za/index.php/publications/1356-prison-overcrowding-and-the-constitutional-right-to-adequate-accommodation-in-south-africa.html. Accessed on April 3, 2014.

Sapa. (2009). *Court rules on minimum sentences for teens.* Retrieved from http://www.iol.co.za/news/south-africa/court-rules-on-minimum-sentences-for-teens-1.449820. Accessed on April 3, 2014.

Sloth-Nielson, J., & Ehlers, L. (2005). Assessing the impact: Mandatory and minimum sentences in South Africa. *SA Crime Quarterly No, 14*(December), 15–22.

Snyman, C. R. (2008). *Criminal law* (5th ed.). Durban: LexisNexis.

Snyman, C. R. (2012). *Strafreg. 6 de Uitgawe.* Durban: LexisNexis.

Terblanche, S. S. (2007). *Guide to sentencing in South Africa* (2nd ed.). Durban: Lexis Nexis.

Terblanche, S. S. (2003). Sentencing guidelines for South Africa: Lessons from elsewhere. *South African Law Journal*, 120(4), 194.

Terblanche, S. S. (2012). The Child Justice Act: A detailed consideration of Section 68 as a point of departure with respect to the sentencing of young offenders. *PER/PELJ, 15*(5), 436–475.

Terblanche, S. S., & Mackenzie, G. (2008). Mandatory sentences in South Africa: Lessons for Australia? *Australian and New Zealand Journal of Criminology, 41*(3), 402–420.

Van Zyl Smit, D. (2000). Mandatory sentences. A conundrum for the new South Africa? *Punishment and Society*, *2*(2), 197–212.

Van Zyl Smit, D. (2002). Mandatory sentences in a New South Africa. In C. Tata & N. Hutton (Eds.), *Sentencing and society: International perspectives.* Aldershot: Ashgate.

Van Zyl Smit, D. (2004). Swimming against the tide: Controlling the size of the prison population in the new South Africa. In B. Dixon & E. Van der Spuy (Eds.), *Justice gained? Crime and crime control in South Africa's transition.* Devon: Willan Publishing.

Venter, H. J. (1959). *Die Geskiedenis van die Suid-Afrikaanse gevangenisstelsel 1652–1958.* Kaapstad: H.A.U.M.

CASES

Center for Child Law v. Minister for Justice and Constitutional Development and Others 2009 (11) BCLR 1105 (CC).

Minister of Justice and Constitutional Development and Another v. Masingili and Others (CCT 44/13) (2013) ZACC 41; 2014 (1) BCLR 101 (CC).

S v. Dodo 2001 (2) SACR 594 (CC).

S v. Dzukuda and Others 2000 (2) SACR 443 (CC).

S v. Malgas 2001 (1) SACR 469 (SCA) par 25.

S v. Mtshabe 2005 (62/05) ZACHC 81.

S v. Toms; S v. Bruce 1990 (2) SA 802 (A) at 806J-807A.

S v. Toms; S v. Bruce 1990 (2) SA 802 (A) 817 C-D.

PUNISHMENT AND INCARCERATION IN JAPAN: A NET-WIDENING OF CRIME CONTROL AND A NEW PRIORITY SYSTEM OF PROSECUTION

Shinichi Ishizuka

ABSTRACT

Purpose – *The number of reported cases for Japanese Penal Code offenses amounted to 2.5 million in 1997 and increased every year, reaching 3.6 million in 2002 and 2003. However, the number decreased from 2004 to 2008 to 2.5 million. Almost throughout the same period, the number of cases and persons cleared remained comparatively steady between 1.3 and 1.5 million and 1 and 1.2 million respectively, but the latter finally fell below one million in 2011. In this chapter I describe such a rise and fall as a "Mt. Fuji-line" that appears as a mountain-shaped curve on a graph.*

Design/methodology/approach – *The Japanese government reacted to the increase of crimes, which was seen as a reflection of a weakened or broken security and safety. The most effective policy, it was thought*

Punishment and Incarceration: A Global Perspective
Sociology of Crime, Law and Deviance, Volume 19, 227–253

ISSN: 1521-6136/doi:10.1108/S1521-613620140000019010

therefore, was to increase the number of policemen. This policy followed the strategy of New York City, made famous by its then Mayor Giuliani, who declared "A War on Crimes" and increased the number of police officers by ten thousand to revive New York from "A Crime City." As criminologists have experienced so-called "labeling shocks" and learned from the approach of symbolic interactionism, criminologists can no longer simply accept that statistical data reflect weakened or broken security issues. Agencies of criminal justice, especially police officers, use such data as statistical evidence to show that the crime situation got worse.

Findings – *I argue that the rise and fall of crimes, especially the increasing and decreasing number of reported cases, reflects changes of crime control policies. I analyze the Mt. Fuji-line from 1998 to 2011. The increase of crimes as well as the weakened or broken security and safety functioned as evidence that justified the reinforcement of police power and a new criminal justice shift for a lay judge system in the rising phase (1998–2003). Since the concept of a bigger justice system needs, however, lots of personnel and material sources, the Japanese government eventually gave up sustaining it. Agencies used their discretion to skip petty crimes and divert suspects because of a reduction of excessive burdens and inappropriate prison population, but they stepped into a new stage to adjust their burdens, keeping their own empowered framework of criminal justice system. These changing policies resulted in the reduction of crime in a falling phase (2004–2011).*

Originality/value – *These phenomena are explained from the viewpoint of Jürgen Habermas' crisis theory. I conclude that the framework and capacity of the Japanese criminal justice system grew far bigger and that original functions of crime control through criminal procedure became weaker by being outsourced to other peripheral social systems and agencies. Thus the crime control system has been successful in bringing about a net-widening effect.*

Keywords: Increasing and decreasing crimes; safety and security; penal populism; crisis theory; police power; net-widening

INTRODUCTION

The number of reported crimes as specified in the Japanese Penal Code (JPC) (Act No. 45 of 1907) amounted to 2.5 million in 1997, increasing over 3.6 million in 2002 and 2003, and then returning to 2.5 million in 2008 again. The number of criminal cases cleared varied between 1.2 and 1.5 million and the number of persons cleared between 0.9 and 1.2 million. In this chapter, such a mountain-shaped curve is referred to as a "Mt. Fuji-line."

Increases in crime are typically explained by causality and attribution theories. According to the causality theory, a rise in reported crimes signifies a crisis of security, hence it leads to increasing numbers of policemen, if it is necessary to manage the crisis. According to the attribution theory, this is a reason to justify a policy of increasing numbers of policemen, because a majority of a society supports the policy. This chapter is based on the latter and analyzes the "Mt. Fuji-line" of criminal statistics from 1997 to 2011 on the hypothesis that a rise and fall of crimes reflects changes in crime control policies instituted by the Japanese government.

The Japanese government used the increasing crimes and the weakening security and safety as evidences, which justified reinforcement of police powers (increasing police officers and reducing burdens per person) and a new shift towards a lay judge system in criminal justice (reducing burdens through a new priority system) in a rising phase (1998–2003). Since the concept of a bigger justice system needs, however, lots of human and material resources, the government soon gave up sustaining it. The national agencies used their discretion to skip out petty crimes and divert suspects causing a reduction of excess burdens and inappropriate prison population, but they stepped into a phase to adjust their burdens while keeping their own empowered framework of a criminal justice system. Changes of policies resulted in the reduction of crimes in a falling phase (2004–2008).

I examine these phenomena from the viewpoint of Jürgen Habermas' crisis theory. My analysis concludes that the framework and capacity of a criminal justice system grew up faster at first and then that original functions of crime control powers through the criminal procedure became lesser by being outsourced to other peripheral social agencies. Thus, the Japanese crime control system has been successful in bringing about a net-widening effect.

QUANTITATIVE CHANGES OF CRIMES AND PUNISHMENTS

Crimes and Criminals

The number of reported crimes for JPC has increased after World War II. The number amounted to about 2.5 million in 1997, increasing every year, reaching over 3.6 million in 2002 and 2003. It has, however, suddenly decreased since 2004, reaching about 2.5 million in 2008 again. In this chapter a mountain-shaped curve based on these increasing and decreasing numbers of reported crimes is called the "Mt. Fuji-line" (Fig. 1). The number of crimes cleared varied between 1.3 and 1.5 million and the number of persons cleared between 1 and 1.2 million. No one could find the "Mt. Fuji-line" here (Fig. 2). All three numbers continue decreasing, reaching

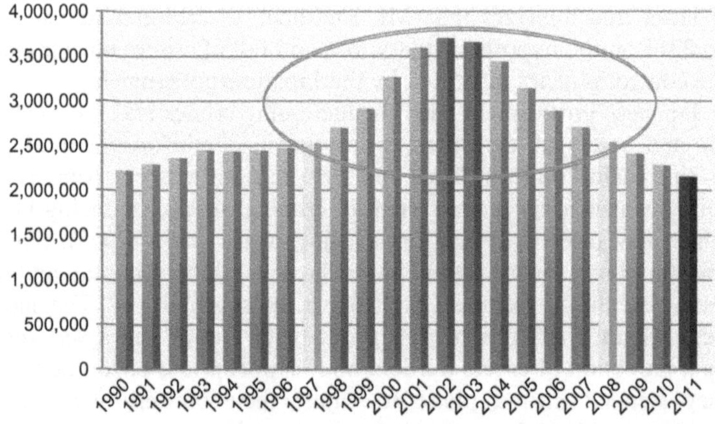

Fig. 1. The "Mt. Fuji-Line" of a Trend of Reported Crimes in JPC (1990–2011).

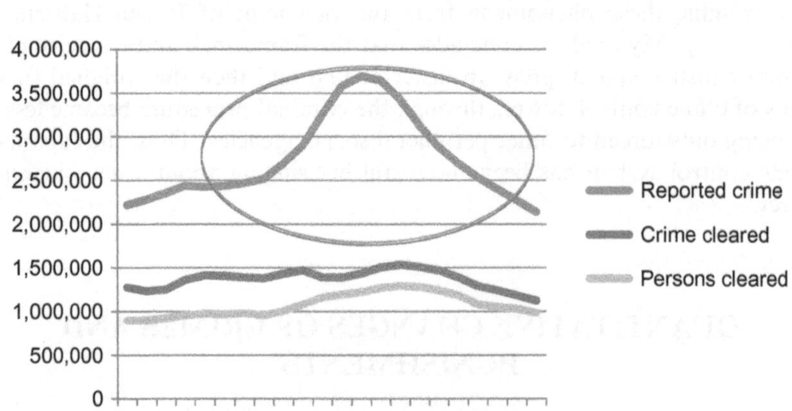

Fig. 2. Trends of Reported Crimes, Crimes Cleared, and Persons Cleared (1990–2011).

2,139,725 of reported crimes, 1,121,500 of crimes cleared, and 986,068 of persons cleared in 2011. They return to the same levels: 2,518,074 of reported crimes, 1,378,119 of crimes cleared, and 957,460 of persons cleared in 1997[1] (Table 1).

Prisons and Inmates

The total number of prisoners has increased gradually by some hundreds per year since 1994, drastically by few thousands every year since 1997, and then reached more than 80,000 in 2006, when the rate of incarceration was more than 100% (115% for prisoners and 70% for suspects and defendants) (Table 2; Fig. 3).

Increasing harsher sentences and lengthening imprisonments cause overcrowded prisons. However, the parole rate remained relatively stable.

Table 1. Numbers of Reported Crimes, Crimes Cleared and Persons Cleared (1990–2011).

	Reported Crime	Crime Cleared	Persons Cleared
1990	2,217,559	1,273,524	899,650
1991	2,284,401	1,231,062	899,023
1992	2,355,504	1,249,428	922,953
1993	2,437,252	1,359,712	958,475
1994	2,426,694	1,410,106	974,158
1995	2,435,983	1,406,213	970,179
1996	2,465,503	1,389,265	979,275
1997	2,518,074	1,378,119	957,460
1998	2,690,267	1,429,003	1,006,804
1999	2,904,051	1,469,709	1,080,107
2000	3,256,109	1,389,410	1,160,142
2001	3,581,521	1,388,024	1,195,897
2002	3,693,928	1,432,548	1,219,564
2003	3,646,253	1,504,436	1,269,785
2004	3,427,606	1,532,459	1,289,416
2005	3,125,216	1,505,426	1,278,479
2006	2,877,027	1,466,834	1,241,358
2007	2,690,883	1,387,405	1,184,336
2008	2,533,351	1,288,720	1,081,955
2009	2,399,702	1,241,357	1,051,838
2010	2,271,309	1,182,809	1,029,117
2011	2,139,725	1,121,500	986,068

Source: Ministry of Justice, 2013.

Table 2. Total Average Number of Inmates in Prisons and Police Detentions (1997–2011).

	Prison	Detention	Total
1997	50,091	7,696	57,787
1998	51,986	8,388	60,374
1999	53,947	9,504	63,451
2000	58,747	10,572	69,319
2001	63,415	11,554	74,969
2002	67,354	12,641	79,995
2003	71,889	13,539	85,428
2004	75,289	14,149	89,438
2005	77,932	13,959	91,891
2006	80,335	13,196	93,531
2007	80,684	11,901	92,585
2008	78,533	11,070	89,603
2009	76,019	11,235	87,254
2010	74,232	10,274	84,506
2011	71,378	9,559	80,937

Source: Ministry of Justice, 2013.

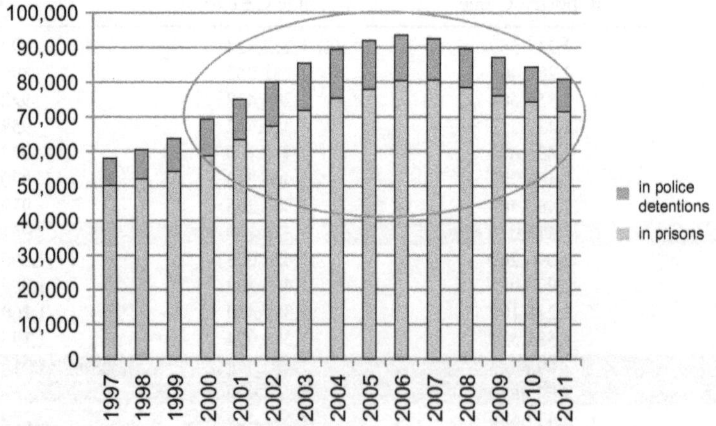

Fig. 3. Trends of Total Average Number of Inmates in Prisons and Police Detentions (1997–2011).

The Act to reform JPC (Act No. 156 of 2004) on December 8, 2004, confirmed harsher punishments to increase the limit of a determinate sentence from 15 to 20 years for a single case and from 20 to 30 years for more than one case; a new standard of sentences was established among judges.

EXPLANATIONS OF A RISING PHASE (1998–2003)

A Weakened or Broken Security and Safety Resulting in "Law and Order"

The Japanese government reacted to the increase of reported crimes, which was thought to reflect a weakened or broken security and safety in society. The most effective policy was thought to be to increase the number of policemen. The policy followed the model of New York City, instituted by the then Governor Giuliani (Rudolph William Louis Rudy Giuliani III). Giuliani declared "A War on Crimes" to increase the number of policemen by ten thousands and to revive "A Crime City" to a safe town.

Agencies of states and local governments, especially the National Police Office, in that term used these data as statistical evidence to show that juvenile delinquencies increased and that the perpetrators had become younger. They legitimated their policies under a series of campaigns, "a crash of the safest society," "against AUM-sect and terrorisms," "For rights of victims," etc., by using the crime data as evidence.

As criminologists have experienced so-called "labeling shocks" and learned an approach of symbolic interactionism, no criminologist can believe in such statements that statistical data would reflect a weakened or broken security. Agencies of criminal justice, especially police officers, used these data as statistical evidences to show that the situation of crimes got tough. Criminologists have learned about "dark figures" and have to adjust official data using self-reports or victim research. Official crime statistics are seen as one kind of indices representing activities of crime control agencies.

Relations between the Labor Market and Prisoners

Generally speaking, economic depressions induce a rising rate of unemployment, resulting in increasing property crimes being committed by poor persons and delinquents in early modern and liberal capitalist societies. After the foundation of "correction houses" in Amsterdam, the situation in the labor market relates closely to the number of prisoners (Rusche, 1933; Sellin, 1944). Economic systems require inputs of work and capital and the output consists of consumable values. A crisis that derives from inadequate input is not typical of a capitalist mode of production but disturbances of liberal capitalism caused output crises (Habermas, 1973/1975).

It is indeed definite that the financial crisis post a bubble economy resulted in a higher rate of unemployment and problems of irregular employment (non-fulltime) in the 1990s, but it is questionable whether disturbances of the labor market related directly to the increasing inmates and worsening circumstances in prisons. Despite the drastic increase of reported crimes, the number of suspects and defendants remained relatively stable. Prosecuting and sentencing policies related much more effectively to the number of inmates than economical disturbances. Additionally it is a definite fact that the composition of the population in Japan has changed rapidly. Cohorts of high-risk offenders decreased, while cohorts of vulnerable potential victims increased. In the 20th century, when systems for social welfare and security had been developed, the relation between labors and crimes became so complicated that criminologist should analyze it carefully and precisely (Liszt, 1882; Rusche & Kirchheimer, 1939) (Fig. 4).

A number of cross-sectional surveys based on complicated factors related to criminal, economical, political, cultural, etc., make it clear that differences in the imprisonment rate cannot be explained by differences in crime. "Penal severity instead is closely associated with public sentiments (fears, levels of trust and punitivity), the extent of welfare provision, differences in income equality and corporatist political culture" (Lappi-Seppaelae, 2008).

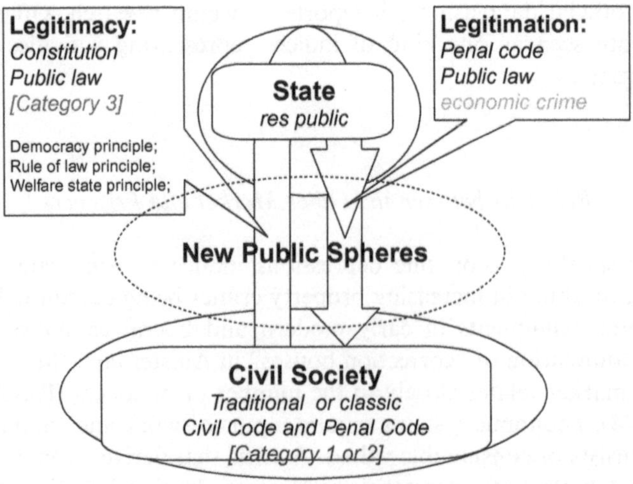

Fig. 4. Relationship between a State and Society in Modern Societies.

Penal Populism Resulting in Harsher Punishments

During the last century, penal affairs were largely addressed and managed by civil servants and bureaucratic organizations working in conjunction with governments, and drawing on advice from academic experts and similar elites (Garland, 2001; Pratt, 2008). From the early 1990s, however, "it has been possible to see increasingly strong relationship being developed between governments and extra-governmental forces – law and order lobby groups, the tabloid press, talk back radio hosts and callers and so on – which claim to speak on behalf of public or which in some way represent their feelings about crime and punishment matters" (Pratt, 2008). Habermas called the same area as "the public sphere" (Fig. 4)[2].

Representations of public opinion have become significantly more embedded in policy development. "[T]he criminal justice 'establishment' has had increasingly less influence on government policy. These twin developments – more public influence at the expense of that of the establishment – are now usually referred to as 'penal populism'" (Pratt, 2008). In Japan, "the growing power of the victims' lobby and press coverage of police investigative incompetence scandals, forced policing policy changes. Many previously unreported and/or relatively trivial crimes were formally recorded under the new police policy. This, in turn, produced a sudden and drastic increase in overall rise in recorded crime and decrease clearance rate. The Japanese press, inaccurately, raised the notion that the current 'moral panic', or 'the myth of the collapse of security society', has in turn contributed to increasingly punitive public view about offenders and sentencing in Japan" (Hamai & Ellis, 2008).

EXPLANATIONS OF A FALLING PHASE (2004–2011)

A Victory of Struggle for Justice

Some police officers comment that strict crime control and harsher punishment lead to the decrease of reported crimes because these policies deter potential criminals from committing crimes and furthermore high-risk offenders are incarcerated in prisons and detention centers. In my opinion, however, the explanation is doubtful because the criminals cleared remained relatively stable and the prison population considerably declined and reached a low level.[3] The large part of prison capacity was not occupied by younger and stronger dangerous offenders but rather older or weaker poor people (Table 3).

It is questionable whether a policy of increasing policemen results directly in a decrease of reported crimes, because between 1998 and 2002 the number of policemen was increased to 13,000 (5.7%) despite which there was an increase in reported crimes from 2,465,503 to 3,693,928 (48.8%) (Table 4).

Table 3. Number of Police Officers (1995–2012).

	Capacity	Difference
1995	221,000	0
1996	225,000	4,000
1997	226,000	1,000
1998	226,000	0
1999	225,000	−1,000
2000	230,000	5,000
2001	233,000	3,000
2002	238,000	5,000
2003	242,000	4,000
2004	244,900	2,900
2005	248,500	3,600
2006	251,900	3,400
2007	253,500	1,600
2008	253,400	−100
2009	254,305	905
2010	255,156	851
2011	255,911	755
2012	257,367	1,456

Table 4. Numbers of Retired Persons, New Employees, Capacity, and Difference (2002–2011).

	The Retired	Rookies	Capacity	Difference
2002	7,300	15,376	238,000	5,000
2003	8,300	15,241	242,000	4,000
2004	9,200	15,346	244,900	2,900
2005	9,000	15,724	248,500	3,600
2006	10,800	16,138	251,900	3,400
2007	12,100	16,027	253,500	1,600
2008	11,400	14,505	253,400	−100
2009	11,100	15,018	254,305	905
2010	10,500	14,464	255,156	851
2011	10,100	14,704	255,911	755

Source: National Police Agency, 2014.

Changing Policies of Police Offices

In varying opinions increasing the number of policemen between 2001 and 2008 had an influence on increases of crimes, criminals, and prisoners. A special committee for renovation of police systems prepared a report, "Rationalization and Reinforcement of Police Power (RRPP)" on July 14, 2000. The report planned a policy increasing ten thousand policemen resulting in a total of more than fourteen thousand policemen in that term.[4]

It is important in bureaucratic systems that leaders are able to acquire surplus budgets for human and material resources and their discretionary powers. The National Police Agency required budgets in 1990s on the grounds that human resources were necessary to investigate or prevent specified types of dangerous crimes, for example, AUM-sect's terrors, juvenile crimes, sexual offenders, etc., and to protect victims' rights and curb their revenge sentiments. Furthermore the drastically increasing number of reported crimes could justify easily surplus budgets for policemen by reasoning that "A Security Myth" had collapsed and that we had to revive it. The National Police Agency did not need those old fashioned justifications post-RRPP, because the number should increase totally to ten thousand (13%), that is 3,500 in 2005, 3,500 in 2006, and 3,000 in 2007 (Fig. 5). A new index is the number of residents per policeman.[5] Thus the number of reported crimes is not a definitive determinant any more.[6]

Police offices became also interested in the increasing number of retiring policemen who belonged to so-called "baby boomers."[7] Since every police academy at local levels had to invest its manpower into training rookies, it

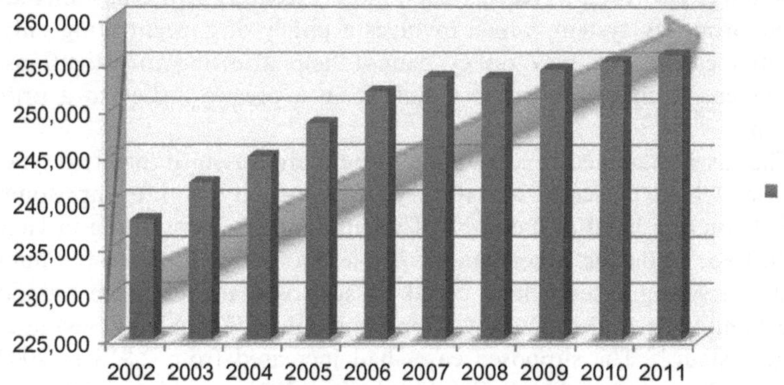

Fig. 5. A Trend of Police Officials Capacity (2002–2011).

was impossible to recruit a surplus. The police officials have their discretional powers to accept cases. If a policeman arrests a suspect who commits some crimes, he/she has to decide how many crimes he/she investigates for the suspect. Of utmost importance in the Japanese criminal justice system is whether a defendant is prosecuted based on a single or multiple crimes. Policemen sometimes indeed select crimes to send to prosecutors, though it is illegal for policemen to screen out criminal cases. Such handling by policemen is called "maesabaki" in Japanese[8].

Changing Policies of the Prosecutors Office

The Japanese government introduced a new lay judge system (SAIBANIN-SAIBAN), which consisted of three professional and six lay judges.[9] Prosecutors would not handle so many cases in new procedures and they could suggest implicitly to investigators to screen out inappropriate cases, because the process was complicated and more expensive than normal trials.

Prosecutors can control directly the sorting of accused offenses. For example, a robbery resulting in bodily injury should be examined employing a lay judge process on one hand. However, if the case was separated out as a theft and an injury, it could be handled in a normal trial on the other hand. The harsher sentences prosecutors in the era of harsher punishment would demand, the heavier offenses they should accuse the prosecuted for. Police officers under the control of such prosecutors had investigated and collected evidences in order to send serious offences as far as possible. However, in recent years, the Prosecutors Office has introduced a new propriety system, which involves a policy of concentrating only on essential cases. The new policy cannot help affecting investigations by policemen. A change is called a shift from a precise justice to a priority system.

The cases examined in a lay judge system are classified into two types of offenses which prescribe a statutory death penalty or life imprisonment (No. 1) on one hand and consist of intentional crimes resulting in victim's death (No. 2) on the other hand.[10] Table 5 and Fig. 6 depict the number of the targeting cases, which could be supposed to be trialed (supposed cases) and were trialed actually after being enforced (trialed cases) in a lay judge system.[11] The supposed cases had increased from 2,818 in 2002 to 3,231 in 2005, but suddenly decreased since 2006, reaching 2,208 in 2008 (68.3%). The number in 2009 was a mixture of supposed and trialed cases.

Table 5. The Number of Sentences Examined by a Lay Judge System (SAIBANIN-SAIBAN) (2002–2011).

	Sentences
2002	2,818
2003	3,089
2004	3,008
2005	3,231
2006	2,878
2007	2,436
2008	2,208
2009	2,070
2010	1,530
2011	1,570

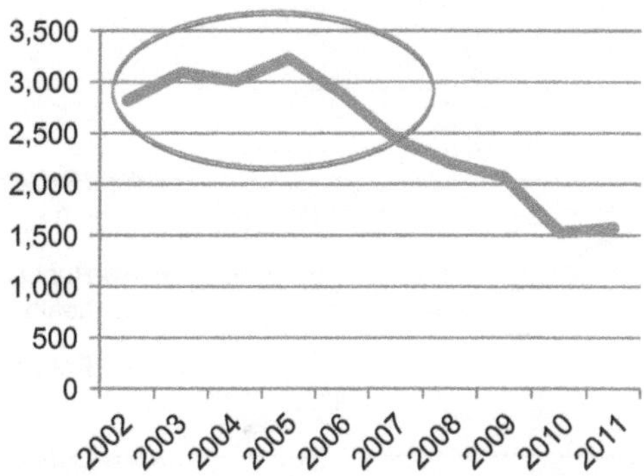

Fig. 6. A Trend of Sentences Examined by a Lay Judge System (SAIBANIN-SAIBAN) (2002–2011).

The trialed cases are reduced to 1,570, which is about a half of the peak (48.6%) (Table 6).

Concerning types of crimes, homicides are reduced from 795 in 2002 to 345 in 2011 (43.4%); robberies resulting in death from 126 to 42 (33.3%); injury resulting in death from 277 to 134 (44.8%), and dangerous driving resulting in death from 50 to 17 (34%).[12] Exceptionally smuggling of stimulants, which possibly is punished with life imprisonment, has increased from 80 to 163[13] (Fig. 7).

Prosecutors are the most powerful legal experts in the Japanese criminal justice system. They were disposed to harsher punishment and increased

Table 6. Numbers of Initial Cases in Lay Judge Systems (SAIBANIN-SAIBAN) (2002–2011).

	Homicide	Robbery Resulting in Death	Robbery Resulting in Injury	Dangerous Driving Resulting in Death	Dealing Stimulants
2004	795	126	277	50	80
2005	795	130	219	42	55
2006	675	112	231	51	23
2007	590	72	153	50	99
2008	557	78	201	29	56
2009	505	83	175	20	158
2010	359	51	115	20	113
2011	345	42	134	17	169
	(43.4%)[a]	(33.3%)[a]	(48.4%)[a]	(34%)[a]	(211.3%)[a]

[a]Numbers in 2011 are compared with those of 2004.

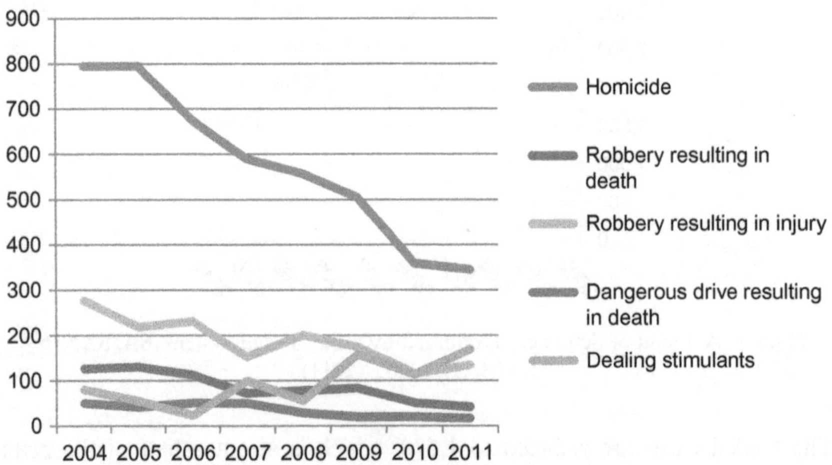

Fig. 7. Trends of Initial Cases in Lay Judge Systems (SAIBANIN-SAIBAN) (2002–2011).

security seemingly so covered by the public in a rising phase of the Mt. Fuji-line (Hamai & Ellis, 2008).[14] On the contrary they carried out important tasks to reduce reported crimes and serious sentences. A prosecutor can control accused cases, because he has wide discretion to indict for attempted murder or injury in the case of physical damage. In the case of death, it is possible for them to demand capital punishment or life imprisonment because of homicide or shorter imprisonment because of manslaughter and theft. Since it depends on subject factors to prosecute for attempted murder or injury, prosecutors' discretion is definitive here. Prosecutors have indicted carefully and unobtrusively in a falling phase, since they were afraid of their failures (Fig. 8).

Additionally defense lawyers start working at earlier stages of a criminal justice system after a public defender system for suspects was introduced on May 28, 2004 (Act No. 62 of 2004) and came into force on October 2, 2006. Since they can settle their case pretrial, numbers of suspensions of indictment or prosecution for lighter crime increase. The Prosecutors Office inclines to invest human and material resources into lay judge trials. This practice leads to some tendencies that prosecutors avoid lay judge trials and that they deal simply and speedily with non-lay-judges' cases. Prosecutors who indicted previously suspects for serious crimes and demanded harsher punishment for defendants are now ready to deal with cases simply and speedily, because trials that consisted of three professional and six lay judges are so difficult that procedures pre- and in-trial become complicated and need to be handled carefully. The images of prosecutors are changed from authoritative to kind ones under a new priority system.

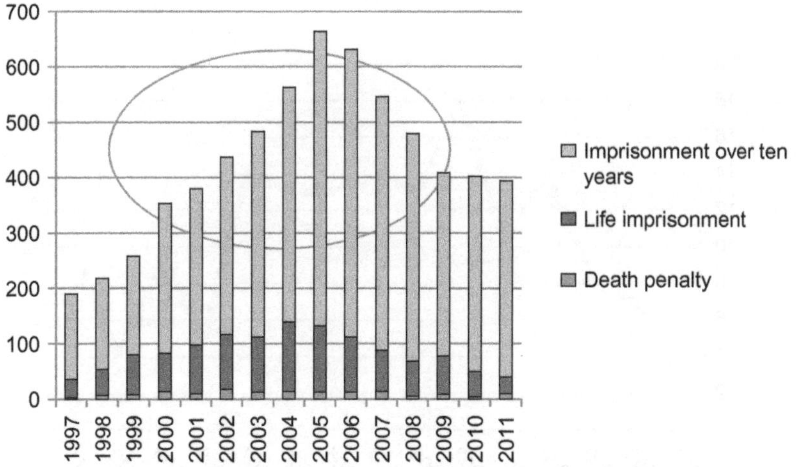

Fig. 8. Numbers of Death Penalty, Life Imprisonment, and Imprisonment over 10 Years in District Courts (1997–2011).

Changing Sentencing Standards in Courts

The Japanese government introduced a protection system for the witnesses in 1999, two acts for victims in 2000, a Basic Act on Crime Victims in 2004, a Law to revise a part of the Criminal Procedure Codes to protect rights of victims in 2007. Recently victims' families can participate in criminal procedures and examine witnesses, give statements, or demand penalties for defendants. New policies for victims influence standards of sentences.

Most lawyers had foreseen that lay judges would sentence much harsher against defendants than professional judges. In addition "the Act for partial amendment of the Criminal Code" (Act No. 156 of 2004) passed for the purpose of harsher statutory penalties on December 8, 2004, came into force on January 1, 2005. The Act raised the maximum limit of imprisonment from 15 to 20 years and the aggregative maximum from 20 to 30 years (150%). Lawyers feared for incredible sentences. Capital punishments (see Fig. 9) and life and long-term imprisonments (see Fig. 10 and Fig. 11), however, decreased in comparison to before the Act came into force.[15] The Supreme Court had developed a PC-system concerning sentence precedents, preparing for a lay judge system. If lay judges would acquire an appropriate sentence in similar cases, they could find it by using the PC-system. Legal professions could not show their own opinions but refer to judicial precedents. The Supreme Court would maintain their control powers skillfully and effectively by using the system.[16]

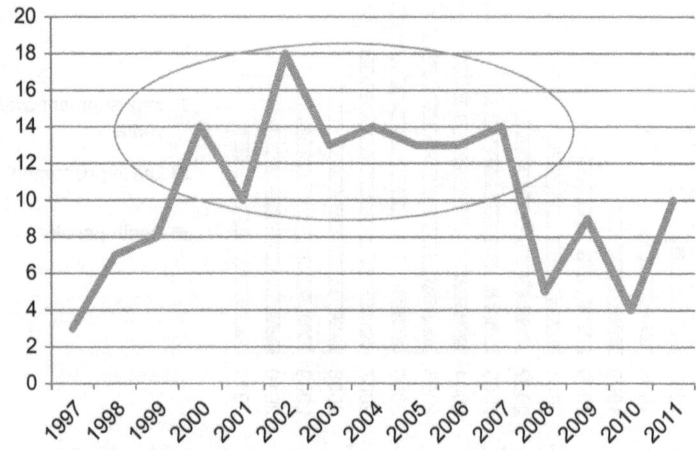

Fig. 9. A Trend of Death Penalty in District Courts (1997–2011).

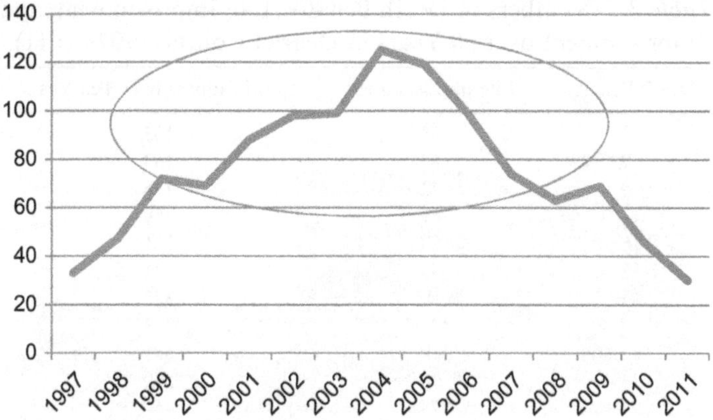

Fig. 10. A Trend of Life Imprisonment and in District Courts (1997–2011).

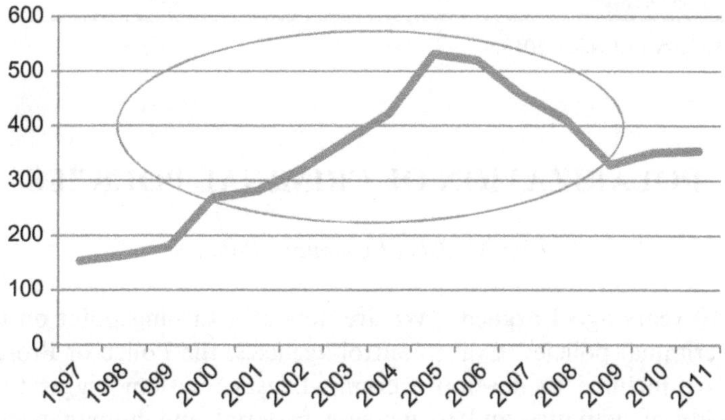

Fig. 11. A Trend of Imprisonment over 10 Years in District Courts (1997–2011).

Before a lay judge system started in 2009, district judges had sentenced over 10 death penalties (2000–2007) and more than 70 life imprisonments per year (2001–2007). Long-term, more than 10 years, imprisonments had amounted to more than 400 (2004–2008). In the meantime the Prosecutors Office and Supreme Court shifted obviously the criminal justice toward harsher punishments.

In spite of their anxiety and fears there are no evidences that lay judges emotionally make sentences harsher. Death penalties and life imprisonments return to previous levels before the harsher punishment era (Table 7).

Table 7. Numbers of Death Penalty, Life Imprisonment, and Imprisonment over 10 Years in District Courts (1997–2011).

	Death Penalty	Life Imprisonment	Imprisonment over Ten Years	Total
1997	3	33	153	189
1998	7	47	163	217
1999	8	72	178	258
2000	14	69	269	352
2001	10	88	281	379
2002	18	98	321	437
2003	13	99	372	484
2004	14	125	423	562
2005	13	119	531	663
2006	13	99	520	632
2007	14	74	457	545
2008	5	63	411	479
2009	9	69	329	407
2010	4	46	351	401
2011	10	30	354	394

Source: Ministry of Justice, 2013.

POLARIZATION OF CRIMINAL POLICIES

Two Models of Criminal Policies

About 10 years ago I argued, "We are now at a turning point on the history of criminal policies. Crime control agencies, the Police or Prosecutors Office, are inclined to develop a criminal justice system bigger to widen their fields of activities and to increase material and human resources." "The rhetoric connects the increasing number of reported crimes and a lowering of clearance rate with security and safety in order to justify increasing policemen. It is leading to more reported crimes and overcrowded prisons. Inhuman circumstances in prisons produce new offenses and sensational crime news create exceeding demands for safety." "If we want to escape such a spiral of overcrowding prison population, we have to avoid useless and harmful labeling on weak, poor and low-risk offenders to control resources for a criminal justice system and to support criminals and prisoners to rehabilitate and integrate into a society. Criminologists should consider a criminal justice not as a closed system but as a complicate whole of medical, welfare, educational and other agencies. A criminal justice is only one part of a whole, and always 'ultima ratio'. From this standpoint I will choose not a bigger criminal justice for security but a smaller and appropriate one based on self-determination of individuals" (Ishizuka, 2003).

A Rising Phase of Criminal Statistics

Japanese criminal justice had chosen a bigger system in 1990s. Schematically speaking, an entrance of a system opened from 2.5 million to 3.6 wider (plus 44%), and length of incarceration grew up from maxims 20 to 30 years (plus 50%), therefore the total capacity of management (plus 116%). If one would make the capacity full, one should invest human and material resources into it. Though the government usually had to cut down personnel and expenses post a bubble economy, policemen and budgets for crime control were exceptionally increasing almost every year. A fall of "Safety Myth" was a simple and clear slogan that symbolized and legitimated the reinforcement of police powers.

In that term the government campaigned for struggle against juvenile crimes and delinquencies. The campaign was supported by using criminal statistics, especially numbers and types of reported crimes. Indeed numbers of cleared cases and arrested suspects were relatively stable. The concurrent campaign of victims' rights accelerated campaigns against monsters. Police officers accepted most cases that victims notified. They picked up dark figures most of whom were involved in petty property crimes and officers used to screen them out.[17] This resulted in the drastic increase of reported crimes, but the number of crimes cleared was relatively stable. This unbalance led to the lower rate of clearance, which made citizens fear crimes, in spite of the fact that the rate of serious crime kept getting lowered and the number of juvenile delinquencies decreased.

A Falling Phase of Criminal Statistics

In December 2003 the government released an action plan to revive "the Safest Country, Japan,"[18] that aimed to maintain security and safety. It was, however, measured not by using quantitative parameters of reported crimes and clearance rate but burdens of a policeman. Police offices did not need to increase numbers and raise rates any more. They would not pick up unnecessary crimes and intervene in civil disputes. In 2008 the number of reported crimes returned to the same level, about 2.5 million in 1998.

The Ministry of Justice and Correctional Bureau tried to revive an appropriate number of inmates in prisons to resolve problems of overcrowding. The harsher standards of sentences might retain the high rate of incarceration and overcrowded prisons; hence policies of diversion were accepted by authorities. The targets were drug users, old and mentally retarded criminals. A criminal justice system could divert and release them for medical and welfare fields. We can name the new policies as "a priority system."[19]

In December 2008 the government proposed "the action plan for a strong society against crime 2008" which aimed to reduce crimes further in five years and to remove citizens' fear on crimes for the purpose of reviving security and safety. After two regime changes the coalition government of the Liberal Democratic Party and the KOMEI released "a fundamental action plan for a strong society against crimes" on May 28, 2013. The number of reported crimes inclined to increase and the security became better to a certain degree. Despite the decrease in reported crimes, 40% of nationals felt, however, still unsafe regarding crime problems.[20]

The Japanese government emphasizes fear of cyber crimes and terrorisms, which threaten nations and a society. In order to revive "the securest and safest state," Japan's government enforces policies to protect nations' lives, bodies, and properties against risks of crimes and terrors and to maintain environments of security and safety which is based on sustainable economic development and corporate activities. In contrast, policies against street crimes differ from policies in the post-bubble economy. In order to construct a strong society against crimes, the government is acting across ministries and cooperating with various civil sectors to prevent ex-prisoners from recidivisms to let members of communities realize about crimes and criminals and to include people who will live without offenses in their own communities and make their rehabilitation sustainable. The conservative government has changed crime policies from a model of the post-bubble economy to a model of new liberalism, which orientates toward free labor markets and strong corporations on one hand and prepares safety nets for weak and poor but law-abiding people willing to work without committing any crimes. People who have committed crime are accepted by a society, if they are able and willing to work without new offenses too.

FISCAL CRISIS AND CRIME CONTROL

Consequences of a Fundamental Contradiction

It is a consequence of the fundamental contradiction of the capitalist system that either (a) *the economic system* does not produce the requisite quantity of consumable values, or (b) *the administrative system* does not produce the requisite quantity of rational decisions, or (c) *the legitimacy system* does not provide the requisite quantity of generalized motivations, or (d) *the socio-cultural system* does not generate the requisite quantity of action-motivating meaning (Habermas, 1973/1975) (Fig. 12).

Japanese society and government have experienced economic crises five times in recent history, in 1929, 1945, 1972, 1993, and 2008. In this context only 1993 can be considered as that of an economic crisis, because exceeding output led to a fall of the economic system. Disturbances of systems integration endanger continued existence only to the extent that social integration was at stake, that is, when the consensual foundations of normative structures are so much impaired that the society becomes anomic (Habermas, 1973/1975).

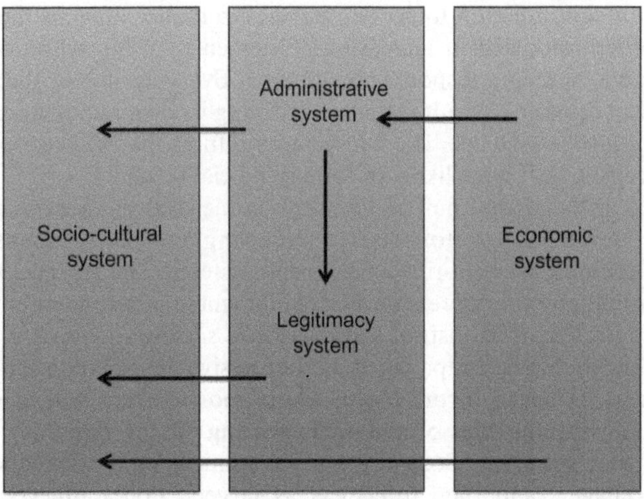

Fig. 12. Relations between Economic, Administrative, Legitimacy, and Socio-Cultural Systems in a Modern Society based on Habermas' Crisis Theory.

Fiscal Crisis Post-Bubble Economy in a Rising Phase

The Japanese government in the 1990s declared a crisis not only in the economic system but also in the political system, which was believed to influence the socio-cultural system too. At that time the prosecutors and police intervened in the socio-cultural and economic systems, leading to reactions such as the AUM-sect prosecutions and financial witch-hunting. The mass media also fueled such tendencies. In parallel they had to maintain the foundation of a liberal capitalist society (commercial exchanges and private law systems) and to keep the existing social identity (rooted in feeling of safety and social security). They also tried to answer victims' complaints and to give the impression they were struggling for justice. This resulted in a drastic rise in the number of reported crimes, especially property crimes. People showed their mercilessness against enemies.

From this perspective, one could explain the Mt. Fuji-line as responses to the economic crisis after a crash of bubble economy in Japan round the changing century. Generally speaking, in aging or aged societies where teenagers and young adults who belong to "high-risk" cohorts of crimes and delinquencies decrease, and aged people increase, total numbers of crimes tend to be reduced. As a criminal justice system, however, is likely to maintain functions of homeostasis, it absorbs relatively petty offenses into itself. It was in a rising phase (1998–2003) that these functions worked actively. In contradiction to general policies to reduce officials the national Police Office succeeded in increasing policemen by using sensational press releases and exceeding responses by citizens. Every agency of the Japanese government appealed simultaneously regarding its own importance in order to reform justice systems. The Prosecutors Office, the Ministry of Justice, and Supreme Court were likely to form a judicial scrum.

At first in the second half of the 1990s crime control agencies cooperating with various civil sectors started struggling mercilessly against AUM-sect and enemies of authoritative financial systems. The struggle for a free society would give an impression that the Japanese government enforced its powers to protect an industrial and developed society and sustain identities with the social membership. The more impressive image made sure that the government protected victims, with whom most citizens will identify and struggled against enemies of a state; increasing crimes, especially property offenses were reported. Secondly the government chose free and uncontrolled teenagers and then foreigners as targets. Police officers involved with communities campaigned the "security and safety" in order to support a plan for an increase in policemen.

Diversion from a Criminal Justice to a Welfare System

Some dissonances rang here and there inside a criminal justice system. Though the Correctional Bureau prepared for treatment programs for aggressive sexual offenders, a great part of inmates were weak and poor people who committed petty crimes, such as property crimes, drug abuse, and others. Most sexual offenders are perverts in crowded trains in Japan. A few aggressive sexual offenders sentenced with death cannot take part in these programs, since they are sentenced with the severest punishments, such as a capital punishment or life imprisonment and have rare chances to be released. Specialists have planned new programs for delinquents of asocial type, because only few juveniles come to juvenile detention centers and training schools.

The ideology of the security and safety revealed that it did not conform to real problems, and then disturbances in a socio-cultural system came to fear on legitimacy and administrative systems. Some economic contradictions after a fall of the bubble economy, for example, increasing problems of unemployment and non-fulltime workers, could not be solved inside an administrative system; the dysfunction of the system actualized a crisis of its legitimacy. Policy makers had to propose criminal policies for resolutions of these disturbances. It is a new idea of judicial welfare that should divert petty crime offenders and illegal drug abusers from a criminal justice system into welfare fields. Thus reported crimes started decreasing.

Crisis Theoretical Analysis in a Falling Phase

Since an administrative system cannot maintain a bigger criminal justice on the ground of fiscal reasons, it is necessary to reduce budgets as much as possible but to preserve a lay judge system as legacy of a late bigger criminal justice. Diversion policies are so convenient that agencies, especially prosecutors, could cut inappropriate costs for punishment by using wide discretional powers. In a fundamental contradiction the government has to get simultaneous support from the public and mass media in the public sphere. The Japanese government separated good offenders who are weak and poor or willing to work without any criminals from bad ones who are aggressive and clever or unwilling to work with diligence. The good ones can be diverted into welfare fields but the others should be accused strictly and punished severely. The majority of society sympathized with the weak but in contrast hated social enemies. The political coalition always needs justifications and ideologies of political ruling inside a legitimacy system.

CONCLUSION

This chapter assumes that a "Mt. Fuji-line," namely the rise and fall of reported social crimes, cleared crimes and criminals, and population of prisons, reflects the changes of crime control policies. A rising phase (1998–2003) can be explained by (1) a broken society or "Law and Order," (2) labor market and prison population, and (3) penal populism. It is, however, difficult to explain the falling phase (2004–2011) from perspectives such as (1) a victory of struggle against crimes (deterrence and incapacitation) and (2) changing policies of the national police officers, prosecutors, and the Supreme Court.

It is concluded that the increase of crimes and the broken security and safety functioned as evidences which justified the reinforcement of police power (increasing police officers and decreasing population per police officer) and setting a new criminal justice shift in preparation for the lay judge system (reducing burdens through a new priority system) in the rising phase (1998–2003).

If one takes a straight look at realities of inmates, most of them are drug addicts, and the old, handicapped, or poor. Harsh punishments give them just pain, in spite of the fact that they need to be supported by medical and welfare services. Policies of diversion should be recommended, because they will be able to cut burdens of inappropriate sources in the administrative system and to screen out the weakness in a socio-cultural system.

The agencies such as the National Police Agency and Prosecutors Office used their discretion to skip petty crimes and divert suspects because of reduction of excessive burdens and inappropriate prison population. Suddenly in 2003 they stepped onto the next stage to adjust their burdens while keeping their own empowered framework of a criminal justice system. These changing policies resulted in the falling phase (2004–2011).

There are two concepts of criminal policies, that is, a bigger and smaller criminal justice system. The Japanese government in a rising phase orientated toward a bigger one. Since this concept, however, needs a number of personnel and material resources, the government was not able to sustain it. The phenomena happened mainly inside the administrative system, whose disturbances were input into legitimacy and socio-cultural systems.

Behind the "Mt. Fuji-line" there is a fundamental contradiction, which results in economical, administrative, legitimacy, and socio-cultural crisis in the sense of Habermas' crisis theory. The framework and capacity of a criminal justice system grew too big in a rising phase and their original functions of crime control through the criminal procedure are weakened by being outsourced to other peripheral social systems and agencies. The committee of cabinet ministers for policies against crimes decided in July 2012 "a comprehensive policies for prevention of recidivisms," which promised to reduce 20% of re-entering ex-prisoners within two years.[21] Thus the crime control system is successful in net-widening.

NOTES

1. The data are cited basically from *White Paper on Crime in Japan 2012* (Ministry of Justice, 2010/2013) and *The White Paper on Police 2013* (National Police Agency, 2014).

2. The public sphere is conceptually distinct from the state: it is a site for the production and circulation of discourses that can in principle be critical of the state. It is also distinct from the official economy; it is not an arena of market relations but rather one of discursive relations, a theater for debating and deliberating rather than for buying and selling (Habermas, 1962/1989).

3. The National Police Office commented concerning the increasing capacity of policemen, "The increased number of policemen in local level in cooperation with other policies stopped increasing crimes and then recovered the security and safety in Japan" (Police Office, 2012).

4. The Reformative Committee of Police System in 2004 decided on a concept of increasing ten thousand policemen. http://homepage2.nifty.com/takauchi/kougi/police.htm

5. The number of residents per policeman declined from 557 in 2000 to 511 in 2008. The number of residents depends on statistics of population as on March 31, 2007.

6. The capacity of policemen was maintained as stable at 221,085 from 1991 to 1995. After that a series of sensational affairs happened almost every year. This resulted in increasing the capacity, namely increasing 3,900 officials because of the Han-Shin Awaji Earthquake disaster, AUM-sect's sarin gas attacks on Tokyo subway, and a juvenile murder case in Kobe in 1996; 1,416 against foreign offenders and economic crimes in 1997; 4,355 against juvenile criminals in 2000; and 1,835 to preserve the social security in 2001.

7. 12,100 policemen left their own official businesses in 2007 (National Police Agency, 2012, *Police of Japan: White paper of police agency* 2010).

8. "Maesabaki" is dominating the opponent by preventing a frontal attack in sumo wrestling in Japan.

9. The Committee for Reformative Justice System proposed a general plan in 2001, and then the Ministry of Justice confirmed a bill and then the Act on

Criminal Trials Examined under the Lay Judge System (Act No. 63 of 2004) was passed on May 21 and proclaimed on May 2004. The Act came into force on May 21, 2009, and the first trial was held on August 3, 2009.

10. Article 2 No. 1 is typified of a murder and robbery resulting in injury or death on one hand and No. 2 is of dangerous driving or abandonment by a person responsible for protection both resulting in death. These offenses are so-called "serious crimes."

11. The Act came into force on May 2006. The cases between 2002 and 2005 were only imaged, ones since 2007 were trialed indeed, and ones in 2006 used mixed procedures.

12. It is remarkable to see the decrease in cases of dangerous driving resulting in death from 50 to 17, because it depends on subject factors whether defendants are accused for dangerous driving or involuntary manslaughter by car.

13. Smugglers are arrested at airports in Chiba and Osaka Prefectures. Some cases are found to be not guilty.

14. The tendency is called as "genbatsuka," which means "increasing the severity of punishment" or "harsher punishment" controlled by the Prosecutors Office (Miyazawa, 2008).

15. Before a lay judge system was introduced, it was an implicit consensus inside layers that sentences were decided according to professional standards. Prosecutors should demand severe penalty compared to normal standards for defendants, to whom judges should sentence between 70% and 80% of the demanded penalty. Prosecutors should be satisfied with average sentences and then defense lawyers also could not complain in appeal courts. Since these standards, however, were valid only in a closed circle of lawyers, they were anxious about lay judges who would not follow precedents in courts and would ignore professional advices. Especially bureaucrats and officials of courts feared that they could not control lay judges.

16. When prosecutors demand death penalty for defendants, they refer to "NAGAYAMA-case" (Judgments of Supreme Court on criminal cases, July 8, 1983, vol. 37, No. 6, p. 609) and propose a list of cases in which courts had accepted capital punishment as evidences.

17. See note "maesabaki."

18. http://www.kantei.go.jp/jp/singi/hanzai/index.html

19. However, the total capacity of management is maintained at about 50% higher than in the 1990s. PFI prisons are kept in rooms for inmates occupied only 70%. The "maesabaki" by policemen, prosecutions by prosecutors, and sentences by judges are all typified of discretional powers. Since prisons stand at the end of criminal justice, they ought to maintain their capacities.

20. The public-opinion poll by the Cabinet Office in July 2012.

21. See http://www.moj.go.jp/hisho/seisakuhyouka/hisho04_00005.html

REFERENCES

Garland, D. (2001). *The culture of control: Crime and social order in contemporary society*. Chicago, IL: University of Chicago Press.

Habermas, J. (1962/1989). *Strukturwandel der Öffentlichkeit. Untersuchungen zu einer Kategorie der bürgerlichen Gesellschaft* [trans. T. Burger & F. Lawrence (1989), *The structural transformation of the public sphere: An inquiry into a category of Bourgeois Society*].
Habermas, J. (1973/1975). *Legitimationsprobleme in Spaetkapitalismus*. Frankfurt am Main: Suhrkamp Verlag [trans. by T. McCarty (1975), Legitimation crisis, Beacon Press, 1975].
Hamai, K., & Ellis, T. (2008). Genbatsuka: Growing penal populism and the changing role of public prosecutions in Japan. *Japanese Journal of Sociological Criminology, 33*, 67–92.
Ishizuka, S. (2003). *Gendai 'shiminhou'-ron to atarashii shimin undoh* [*Japanese: Contemporary Civil Society Theory and New*]. Tokyo: Gendaijinbun.
Lappi-Seppaelae, T. (2008). Explaining national differences in the use of imprisonment. *Japanese Journal of Sociological Criminology, 33*, 93–121.
Liszt, F. V. (1882). Der Zweckgedanke im Strafrecht. In ders (Ed.), *Strafrechtliche Vortraege und Aufsaetze, Bd.I.* (pp. 126–179). Berlin: Walter de Gruyter & Co., 1905.
Ministry of Justice. (2010/2013). *White paper on crime in Japan 2009/2012*. Retrieved from http://hakusyo1.moj.go.jp/jp/nendo_nfm.html
Miyazawa, S. (2008). Will penal populism in Japan decline: A discussion. *Japanese Journal of Sociological Criminology, 33*, 122–132.
National Police Agency. (2012/2014). *The white paper on police 2010/2012*. Retrieved from http://www.npa.go.jp/hakusyo/h25/english/Contents_WHITE_PAPER_on_POLICE2013.htm
National Police Agency. (2014). *The white paper on police 2013*. Retrieved from http://www.npa.go.jp/hakusyo/h25/english/Contents_WHITE_PAPER_on_POLICE2013.htm
Pratt, J. (2008). Penal populism in New Zealand and its future: Is penal populism inevitable? *Japanese Journal of Sociological Criminology, 33*, 30–45.
Rusche, G. (1933). Arbeitmarkt und Strafvollzug. *"Zeitschrift für Sozialforschung", Bd.2*, 63–78. [trans. G. Dinwiddie, "Labor market and penal sanction," Crime and Social Justice, vol. 10, 1978, pp. 2–8].
Rusche, G., & Kirchheimer, O. (1939). *Punishment and social structure*. New York, NY: Columbia University Press.
Sellin, T. (1944). *Pioneering in penology: The Amsterdam houses of correction in the sixteenth centuries*. Philadelphia, PA: University of Pennsylvania Press.

GENDER AND IMPRISONMENT IN HONG KONG

Maggy Lee and K. Joe Laidler

ABSTRACT

Purpose – *This chapter aims to examine the ways in which gender has featured in Hong Kong's prison system from its colonial origins to its contemporary form as a politically autonomous region of China. We conclude with a discussion on the reasons for these recent trends of imprisonment.*

Design/methodology/approach – *We draw from the concepts of patriarchy and colonialism to examine how gender has operated and shaped Hong Kong's prison system. Our analysis is based on historical and contemporary government reports and other documents and secondary data.*

Findings – *Similar to other locales around the world, Hong Kong's prison system was designed for and by men in its early colonial days, as expected given that most prisoners were male. Although a few prison administrators attempted to provide some programs for women and voiced concern over the conditions of women's imprisonment to colonial authorities during the latter part of the 1800s, it was not until the 1930s that the first female prison was established. Since then, Hong Kong prison authorities have faced the challenge of a phenomenal and rapid*

Punishment and Incarceration: A Global Perspective
Sociology of Crime, Law and Deviance, Volume 19, 255–273

ISSN: 1521-6136/doi:10.1108/S1521-613620140000019011

growth in women's imprisonment, which resulted in a historical reversal of shifting male prisoners to alternate accommodation to make room for their female counterparts.

Originality/value – *This study is among the few which have examined how gender operates in the context of imprisonment in a colonial and postcolonial context. This chapter does this by examining how colonial authorities managed competing political debates about the purpose of punishment and cultural understandings of race and difference, and the limited recognition of gender and difference. It also examines how, in postcolonial Hong Kong, authorities have placed gender center stage and the reasons for this in coping and dealing with the growth in women's imprisonment.*

Keywords: Gender; race; imprisonment; colonialism; Hong Kong

INTRODUCTION

Since its inception in 1841, Hong Kong's prison system has faced challenges similar to those around the globe. From its beginnings, it was tasked with managing the incarceration of those convicted of crimes, meting out varying levels of punishment, ensuring public safety, and later the treatment and rehabilitation of prisoners. Its character and policies were, at one level, a broad reflection and adaptation to international debates and reforms, in part, because of its colonial administration for 150 years. But at the same time, given its colonial history, it has developed many distinct characteristics and faced specific challenges that continue to evolve with Hong Kong's return to China in 1997 and becoming an autonomous region of China.

This chapter looks at the development of Hong Kong's prison system, with a particular focus on gender.[1] Similar to other locales around the world, Hong Kong's prison system was designed for and by men in its early colonial days, as most prisoners were indeed male. Authorities responded to the increasing numbers of male prisoners at its one/prison by moving females off site to make room for their male counterparts. Although a few prison administrators attempted to provide some programs for women and voiced concern over the conditions of women's imprisonment to colonial authorities during the latter part of the 1800s, it was not until the 1930s that the first female prison was established. Since then, Hong Kong prison authorities have been faced with the challenge of a phenomenal and rapid growth in women's imprisonment, which resulted in a historical reversal of shifting male prisoners to alternate accommodation to make room for their female counterparts. We conclude with a discussion on the reasons for these recent trends of imprisonment.

THE EARLY YEARS – IT'S A MAN'S WORLD

While the progressive views of the Enlightenment period – reason, rationality, equality – took hold in Europe, the Hong Kong colonial government, along with various members of the European and Chinese communities, remained steadfast in its adherence to the principle that punishment must be punitive (Dikotter, 2004). This principle was based on the longstanding view of the deterrent value of the punitive approach. At that time in Hong Kong, there was also the consideration of differential levels of punitiveness since Europeans were assumed to be fundamentally different from Chinese (e.g., physically, mentally, and morally) (Dikotter, 2004). It is in this context of punitiveness and difference that, in 1841, Hong Kong's first prison, Victoria Gaol (renamed in 1899 as Victoria Prison), opened under the direction of the Chief Magistrate, Captain William Caine. Given his military background, Caine subscribed to and enforced a punitive approach to crime in Victoria Gaol (Dikotter, 2004). Caine, in these initial years, also believed flogging to be an effective form of punishment – swift, harsh, public, and certain (held every Wednesday) for Chinese. The public display was a message for all, but not long after its introduction, Europeans and Chinese alike opposed its sheer brutality for minor offenses and inconsequential acts. Transportation was also a preferred method to long-term incarceration, but its use waned as colonial authorities faced difficulties in finding locations to send prisoners to and the considerable monies necessary for transportation (Chan, 1994). From available government records and histories, it is unknown whether and how these two forms of popular punishment – used principally on Chinese male offenders – were meted out to any female offenders.

Victoria Gaol, on its opening, was a relatively small and contained unit with one-day room and 12 single cells for European prisoners, and three large cells with an opening courtyard for Chinese prisoners (Chan, 2012). Not long after opening, the prison population far outstripped its capacity, with authorities speculating that the convicted refused or had no means to pay fines and so, opted for a period of imprisonment, ranging from a few days to several years. The increase in prison admissions led to numerous extensions, the first occurring in 1845. These extensions were necessary to accommodate the growing numbers of and segregation of prisoners – Europeans from Chinese, and males from females. In 1846, the Superintendent reported that the one-day count of prisoners at the year's end was 13 white males, no white females, 114 Chinese males, and 1 Chinese female (HK Blue Book, 1847). Extensions and renovations continued throughout the 1850s and 1860s, and included renovation of Victoria Gaol, and the construction of a new prison on Stonecutter's Island complete with the new radial design developed in the United States. During the renovations of Victoria Gaol and the building of the new facility on Stonecutter's Island, prisoners lived on the ship, "Royal Saxon." Prisoners moved back into Victoria Gaol by 1867 but the Stonecutter's project, which would have accommodated 600 prisoners, was ultimately abandoned by the new Governor MacDonnell (Chau & Siu, 2011). It is unclear where female prisoners stayed during this period, but very likely they remained in the rented building near Victoria Gaol.

As Table 1 suggests, the prison population grew steadily from the 1870s onward and rather rapidly by the turn of the century. The colonial government continued to hold firm in its punitive approach, and on more than one occasion, reiterated that the main goal of punishment was deterrence. Personal reformation was at best, a wishful secondary goal, unlike the view taking hold in Europe. According to the Gaol Committee (HK Government Gazette, 1877, p. 116):

> Important as the mental and moral training of criminals may be, and satisfactory as it may be to make a prison self supporting by employing prisoners in remunerative labour, these objects must be considered of secondary importance and must be put

Table 1. Prison Admissions by Sex (1874–1934).

Year	Male *N* (%)	Female *N* (%)	Total
1874	2,819 (90.4)	300 (9.6)	3,119
1884	3,670 (95.6)	168 (4.4)	3,838
1894	3,739 (97.4)	101 (2.6)	3,840
1904	6,911 (93.2)	503 (6.8)	7,414
1914	3,803 (95.3)	187 (4.7)	3,990
1924	7,063 (97.0)	218 (3.0)	7,281
1934	11,382 (85.5)	1,922 (14.5)	13,304

Source: Hong Kong Blue Book (1874–1934).

> aside if they have the effect of rendering punishments lighter and therefore more tolerable and less deterrent.

Personal reformation required time and understanding of individual "dispositions and character," and therefore, would be relevant only to the few long-term European prisoners in custody. Most European prisoners were in custody for short to medium terms for "breaches of military and naval discipline," and therefore would have limited time to reflect and grow from moral training (*ibid.* p. 116). Having limited understanding of the language and disposition of Chinese prisoners, colonial authorities believed reformation to be "hopeless," and therefore,

> The only resource is to make the life of prisoners in Gaol, and of Chinese prisoners especially, as distasteful as it can possibly be made, consistently with reason and humanity, by hard labour, hard fare and strict physical discipline. (*ibid.* p. 116)

It should be noted here that although the hard line attitude and practices prevailed in the colony, the 1870s were a time of great debate. In 1877, the new Governor, Hennessey, arrived, and set off to introduce a balance of prison discipline and reformation. Hennessey was a controversial figure because of his "radical attempts to pursue a policy of racial equality wherever he was governor" (McLaughlin & Lowe, 1992, p. 223). Although he encountered organized opposition from colonial authorities and European and Chinese community members – who feared increased crime from liberal policies – he was able to stop the use of public flogging and other severe forms of punishment (Dikotter, 2004). Mainly, however, the British attitude toward punishment and its management (e.g., space, mental and physical abilities, labor) in the colony continued to be based on the fundamental differences of the races. Throughout the prison's development, dialogue and debates in this period, little is said about differences between the sexes.

In the 1870s, prisoners, both men and women alike, were required to work from 7 a.m. until 4:30 p.m., with an hour break for dinner. Annual gaol reports during this period consistently document the nature of penal labor men faced while imprisoned. European men would need to complete a maximum of 15,300 revolutions per day, at a shot drill three hours per day in 30-minute intervals with stone breaking or oakum picking during those breaks. Chinese men were to do four hours in a day with 30-minute intervals for stone breaking, stone carrying, or oakum picking. Other forms of labor were generally geared toward the maintenance of the gaol. There is little mention of the nature of labor for female prisoners in the 1870s, but very likely it was of a domestic nature as reflected in later periods.

Subsequent records indicate that female prisoners "shall be employed at No. 2 Hard Labor with regard to washing their own clothes and at No. 3 Light Labour" (HK Government Gazette, 1890). No. 1 Penal or Rigorous Hard Labour – shot drill, stone carrying, crank labor, or tread wheel – was reserved for male prisoners only, but with due consideration for race. No. 2 Industrial Hard Labour included employment on public works, combinations of shot drill and oakum picking, or laundry for the gaol or making coir mats. No. 3 Industrial Light Labour included ironing and mending of clothes, mat making, carpentry, tinsmith's work, tailoring, cooking cleaning, printing, oakum picking, and other miscellaneous work.

In the midst of debates about the need for labor as discipline and whether it should be redemptive in nature, authorities were concerned with the rise in prison admissions. Various superintendents tried to find ways to reduce and address crowding with ever increasing numbers of male prisoners. Among the initial steps, in 1885, Superintendent Stewart oversaw the removal of female prisoners to a rented location nearby, so that the eight cells and yard for women at Victoria Gaol could be used for the men (HK Administrative Reports, 1886). A government committee on prison accommodation was among the first to call for a completely separate institution for female prisoners, even providing authorities with an architectural plan for a two-story prison to replace the ill-suited rented building (HK Sessional Papers, 1892). The committee pointed to the growing number of female admissions with the average daily population growing from nine in 1888 to 16 in 1891. For the same period, for males – European and Chinese – the average daily population remained relatively steady at about 547, but conditions within the men's facilities remained crowded. A separate institution made sense with female prisoners' daily routines of work and cleaning, and the resident matron, who from, the gaol's opening, was already fully aware of the specific security and discipline issues of female prisoners. The matron was tasked with ensuring the strict separation of male officers and prisoners from female prisoners, searches, supervising personal cleanliness and dress, overseeing food distribution, and inspecting the ward. Although, we can find little discussion of the differential needs of female prisoners during this period, authorities were aware of the need to segregate the sexes. Importantly, authorities also recognized the importance for female prisoners as mothers. Regulations state:

> 258. The child of a female prisoner may be received into prison with its mother, provided it is at the breast, and any such child shall not be taken from its mother until the Surgeon certifies that it is in a fit condition to be removed.

> 259. Such child may be supplied with such diet and clothing as may be necessary, at the public expense; but except under special circumstances, no such child shall be kept in prison after it has arrived at the age of twelve months. (HK Government Gazette, 1890)

Governor Hennessey and Superintendent Gordon believed that one reason for the increase in prison admissions was due to the belief that life in Victoria Gaol – its routines, accommodation, space, and diet – was far superior than life outside the gaol for poor laboring Chinese coolies. Superintendents' reports frequently made mention of the "benefits" of a good diet while in custody as compared to daily life for many Chinese. The prison diet for Europeans included bread and water for those with a short term, with a portion of meat and vegetables for long-term prisoners. The Chinese diet included water and rice for those with a short sentence, and a portion of fish and vegetables for those committed for longer stays. Women received the same portions as the men. Gordon argued,

> In this Gaol, as far as my observation goes, Chinese convicts are better fed, better clothed and better lodged than free coolie labourers, and the labour exacted from them is less. The deterrent effects of imprisonment are therefore almost limited to loss of liberty and its accompanying pleasures – a loss more acutely felt by Western races than those we have to deal with here. (HK Administrative Reports, 1886, p. 265)

This view of a too liberal and generous term of imprisonment led to dietary cuts for all classes of prisoners, Europeans, Chinese, male and female, on the rationale of its deterrent effects. But it had no impact on prison admissions. The main strategy to address crowding was to further extend prison space.

In 1894, Superintendent Lethbridge acknowledged that the colonial government's provision for an extension of Victoria Gaol would help to alleviate crowding for men, but did little to address the ongoing problem of housing female prisoners:

> The unsuitableness of the building in which they are now located is well known. There are only two associated wards and two punishment cells so that in order to keep prisoners on remand separate from convicted prisoners, all classes of convicted prisoners must be placed together in one ward. The only place where the prisoners can exercise in the open air is 24 feet long and 9 feet wide, a totally inadequate space for the purpose. (HK Administrative Reports, 1894, p. 150)

It is not clear as to what were the main offenses driving the increase in prison admissions, as available court and prison records do not specify the nature of offenses by sex. It can be gleaned from magistrates' diaries and reports however that a range of colorful and gray behaviors resulted in convictions and imprisonment. Among those involving men, they included misadventures, robberies, piracy, and even murder involving the poor, the ordinary, the elite, sailors and soldiers, gamblers, and teachers in the European and Chinese communities. There are fewer reports about women coming before the courts, but when they did, it often involved prostitution and insubordination as a domestic servant. The sentence sometimes involved a fine or a term of imprisonment. In some instances, however, as in the case of ill treatment of a child or burglary, imprisonment was accompanied by hard labor (Bickley, 2005).

THE FIRST WOMEN'S PRISON IN HONG KONG – INTERRUPTED BY WAR

With the advent of the new century, Hong Kong continued to witness a rise in the prison population. Prison crowding resulted in further expansion of Victoria Gaol as well as a new workshop for productive work, intended to generate income. Printing was among the top industries of the Gaol, generating in 1932, the sum of HKD 1,877 (HK Administrative Reports, 1933). Prison industries were to become a lasting hallmark of Hong Kong's prisons – providing services internally and externally to the community. To address the long-term problems of capacity, authorities built a new men's facility, in 1924, Lai Chi Kok – a relatively remote area of Kowloon where gardening and coir mat making were among the main vocational activities there.

It was not long after, in 1932, when the first fully dedicated institution for women opened in an adjacent space to the men's prison in Lai Chi Kok. Authorities described this new women's facility as "a model establishment of its kind, and a step in the right direction for the better accommodation of prisoners in Hong Kong" because it was designed to house prisoners on a classification system (e.g., short- and long-term, remand) and styled with local features (e.g., Chinese style pitched roof and tiles) (HK Administrative Reports, 1933, p. L2). Oddly, authorities envisioned the women's facility at Lai Chi Kok to be a temporary arrangement until a permanent site could be completed at another location adjacent to the soon to open Stanley – a male facility on Hong Kong Island. The facility was crowded within the first year of its opening, with the annual prison report indicating that, "although it was constructed to accommodate 120 (about double the daily average in custody in the old female prison), the number in the new prison has frequently been over 200" (HK Administrative

Reports, 1933, p. L2). Despite the crowding, over the next few years, female prisoners were industriously employed in laundry and mending, and weaving, although the latter could only be done on a small scale due to lack of space. Although Lai Chi Kok was in a remote area, volunteers provided female prisoners with basic education and religious instruction.

> The administration has again to thank the visiting ladies, both English and Chinese, for their valuable services in giving free instruction and elementary education to the prisoners. Now that the prison is at Lai Chi Kok, many of these ladies have to travel a long way to attend. That they do so regularly and willingly is a proof of their continued interest. It is difficult to estimate the results of their efforts as the majority of the prisoners in whom they are interested are banished for terms of 5 years and upwards, but their visits are much appreciated and it is to be hoped that the Lady visitors' endeavors assist the women to become useful members of society upon their release. (*ibid.*)

It should be noted that in these early days, records suggest that no formal education was offered in male and female prisons, but do indicate that female prisoners benefitted from this informal arrangement with "visiting ladies."

By 1937, plans for a new large prison complex were realized, and all male prisoners at Victoria Gaol and Lai Chi Kok were transferred. Although Stanley was designed with single cells to accommodate 1,559 prisoners (with segregation for European and Chinese prisoners), cells were shared as the population at the opening was 2,215 (Hong Kong Administrative Reports, 1938). The intention to build a permanent site for female prisoners at Stanley was abandoned as Hong Kong, and Stanley prison, became a site of the Japanese occupation.

Subsequent to the war, in the mid-1940s, Hong Kong's prison authorities were faced with postwar challenges, including refurbishing the deterioration of its facilities, resource and staffing shortages, the destruction of prisoner and government records, and an increase in prison admissions, especially of young males (Chan, 2012). But its biggest challenge was to manage overcrowded conditions in both male and female prisons as increasing numbers of short-term prisoners were admitted, often for less than three months for minor offenses like, "spitting, obeying a call of nature, and hawking without a license" (Chan, 2012, p. 58). Although fewer women were admitted than men for these short sentences (35% of 8,254 prisoners in 1948/1949), the crowding problem was particularly acute for females given capacity differentials. The governor ordered early release of more than 1,400 male and female prisoners sentenced to six months or less as a mechanism to relieve crowding in the latter half of 1948. Over the next decades, Hong Kong's prison population continued to rise as the colony's population grew at a rapid pace – with the development of a manufacturing economy and increasing numbers of migrants crossing the border to escape political turmoil in China. The colonial government opened additional facilities to accommodate this increase in male and female inmates, and in doing so, began introducing programs to address inmate needs, in particular, age (youth training and detention centers), and narcotic addiction.

CONTEMPORARY TRENDS

Organizational Features

Through the years, Hong Kong's prison population has fluctuated, with some period of marked growth or gradual declines. Such fluctuations impact prison management, especially in relation to accommodation. As we saw in the early period, Hong Kong was facing continual expansion. Currently, Hong Kong's Correctional Services Department (CSD) manages 30 facilities, which are designed to address the needs of different types of offenders in relation to age, gender, and security level (e.g., committing offense, prior histories). Adult male prisoners, who constitute the largest custodial population, may be in a remand center pending court or at one of its minimum, medium, or maximum security prisons. Young male inmates can be sent to the correctional institution or one of three centers – training, detention, or rehabilitation. Adult females may be incarcerated at one of two CSD facilities – a maximum security facility or in one of the units at its newest correctional facilities which has adopted an integrated management approach for holistic care. Young female inmates may be incarcerated in either a minimum security correctional institution or in a rehabilitation center. CSD also operates Drug Addiction Treatment Centres (DATCs), classed as an alternative to prison, and provides court-mandated treatment in a secure, controlled, and segregated setting for male and female drug users. In addition to these main facilities, CSD also operates halfway houses as part of the reintegration process and custodial wards in two public hospitals.

Regime

From our visits over the past 20 years, one consistent feature of daily life in Hong Kong's prisons, from its inception through to the present, is the level of order and discipline. Prisoners, whether male or female, young or old, white, African, Chinese, Hispanic, South Asian, and others appear tidy and clean in their uniforms – which are usually color-coded to indicate the type of inmate. Prisoners move in a highly ordered manner, from one activity to the next, sitting quietly in classrooms and workshops. There is a kind of militaristic tradition in interactions – when staff and visitors' paths cross, inmates are especially at attention, waiting for the call to return to their duties be it work or study. Staff hold a respectful and traditional stance with each other as well, saluting colleagues and superiors, and serving as a role model to inmates. Dormitories and cells also exude discipline and order with a barren and clean appearance. Bed linens are precision rolled and inmates' few personal belongings (e.g., usually essential toiletries, and occasionally a book) are neatly stored in a corner. There is no time for boredom or idleness within the prison walls. The day begins early at daybreak with inspection of one's personal space – having tidied one's possessions. This is followed with exercise and breakfast, and then the morning begins with work or lesson. Mid-day lunch lasts for one hour, after which prisoners return to work or study until dinner. For a few hours after dinner, inmates might spend time in recreation, evening classes, or other organized activities.

As we noted of earlier periods, the hard penal labor of the early colonial days was gradually abandoned by the 20th century, but the idea of purposeful activity and self-improvement has continued into the 21st century. Young offenders – male and female – are legally required to spend at least one-half of their day in educational or vocational training, and can take local and international examinations. Inmates can choose to study a course full time or through a distance-learning program to attain a professional qualification in a range of vocational oriented subjects such as plumbing, electrical, data processing, hairdressing, and beauty therapy. In accord with the law, adults – male and female – must work for a minimum of six to a maximum of ten hours, with an average of eight hours per day. An internal unit, the Correctional Services Industries (CSI) organizes training and work with the aim of fostering individual and team responsibility, confidence, and employable skills. In 2013, an estimated daily average of 4,639 inmates worked in a trade, providing goods and services for government agencies, charitable organizations, and other public sectors. The goods and services provided range from making government furniture, staff uniforms, hospital linen, filter masks, fiberglass litter containers, production of various metal parts for infrastructure projects, traffic signs, laundry services for hospitals and clinics, bookbinding for libraries, and, as in the early 20th century, printing jobs (e.g., envelopes, publications) (Hong Kong Correctional Services Department [HKCSD], 2014).

In the late 1990s, CSD took steps to begin strengthening its rehabilitation division, focusing especially on treatment and training for eventual community reintegration. Vagg (1991, p. 143) observed that CSD's "vigorous" rehabilitation agenda, [was] made all the more distinctive as it took place in the "context of strict and paternalistic discipline, surveillance and control." Its' campaign, "We Care" was built on a commitment to rehabilitation through custody and care. Today, rehabilitation and preparation for release are central to the daily regime. As part of its rehabilitation program, CSD has developed training programs to provide inmates with employment skills consistent with the current market. Prerelease vocational training is available for male and female prisoners, providing an opportunity to train in a variety of employable areas, including language and IT, bookkeeping and accounts, printing and desktop publishing, culinary, food and beverage services, hairdressing, beauty therapy, and mechanical craft. In conjunction with this training, CSD holds a series of public awareness campaigns on the importance of employment to successful reintegration. For CSD, community engagement is an essential part of the rehabilitation process, and promotes this view in a variety of ways, from lunch symposiums with the business sector to television programs and other public events (Joe Laidler, 2009).

In reflecting on Hong Kong's penal system – from Victoria Gaol, to the Prison to Correctional Services – order and discipline have governed an inmate's daily life, and become part of its institutional culture. But its articulation has been tempered by ideas of reformation and productive labor, and later by rehabilitation and education as the means for reintegration. Order, discipline, work, and study comprise the bulk of an inmate's daily life with little time for idleness. This correctional regime may, in part, account for the very limited and rare instances of prison violence. The only major incident in recent decades was in 2000 when ongoing tensions between local Chinese and Vietnamese male prisoners led to a violent attack, the setting of a fire, and the filing of grievances of perceived preferential treatment (Joe Laidler, 2009).

EXPANSION OF WOMEN'S IMPRISONMENT

The rarity of these types of disturbances is due to numerous factors for which CSD has taken proactive control, including the regime and discipline of daily life, and the various monitoring and quality assurance mechanisms that have developed over the years. Yet there are some aspects of operating a correctional institution in which it has little control. Imprisonment represents the near end point of the criminal justice system as those who are convicted are sent to a correctional institution to serve their sentence. Consequently, CSD has virtually no control over the number and types of offenders placed in their care and custody.

In reflecting on contemporary trends, this "operational flow" has led to a distinct challenge for Hong Kong's correctional authorities, namely the significant and rapid rise in female prison admissions. In the late 1990s, public concern about the rise of women's imprisonment was voiced when the Hong Kong Human Rights Monitor (HKHRM, 1999), on behalf of a number of local NGOs, submitted a shadow report in response to the government's report to the United Nations, Convention to Eliminate All Forms of Discrimination against Women (CEDAW). For CEDAW, women's imprisonment was an important area of consideration under women's issues related to laws and their enforcement. At the time of the report, two of the main issues raised had to do with the custody and care of women in prison (CEDAW, 1999).

First, correctional authorities had witnessed a significant rise in the number of female admissions to prison, such that the proportion of females to the overall total prison population had reached 12% – a ratio higher than the international range of 2–9%. This growth in the female prison population led to unprecedented crowding, with one facility's population standing at 414 despite its capacity of 278, and led to its ranking as first, in a global survey of female imprisonment, with the largest proportion of incarcerated females of the total prison population in the mid-2000s. This ranking remains high, as the second highest, in the most recent global survey in 2011 (International Centre for Prison Studies [ICPS], 2006, 2011).

How did this growth occur? As Fig. 1 shows, female prison admissions grew at a much faster rate than compared with their male counterparts. The first signs of a rise in the female prison population appeared in the late 1980s. In 1982, women sentenced and admitted to correctional services constituted a relatively small proportion of all admissions (4%). A decade later, female admissions more than doubled to 1,287, accounting for 9% of all admissions. But after another 10 years, by 2001, the proportion of females admitted to CSD grew to 7,955 representing 38% of all admissions. A second CEDAW report (2004) raised similar concerns to those five years previously, in particular noting the "sharp upsurge" in the female prison population since the latter part of the 1990s. At the time of the report,

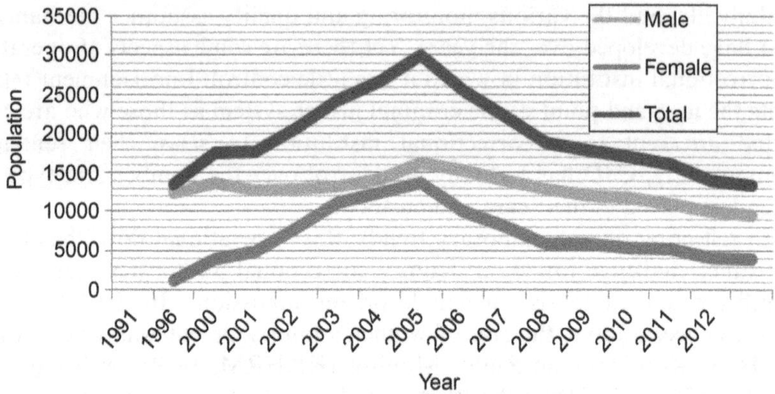

Fig. 1. Admissions to HK Correctional Services by Sex (1991–2012). *Source:* HK Annual Digest of Statistics.

female admissions had reached an all-time high, with 13,775 women being admitted to CSD in 2004. For three consecutive years (2002–2004), female admissions represented 46% of all CSD admissions.

There has been a gradual but significant decline from 2006 onward with CSD reporting admission of 8,147 female prisoners in that year to 3,946 in 2012. Although admissions decreased from 2006 onward, authorities still required short- and long-term plans to accommodate the changing nature of its prison population. These strategies included the redevelopment of the Tai Lam Female Correctional Institution (additional 260 places) in 2002 to the conversion of a male facility to a female institution (220 places) in 2003. One of the DATC's annex was also converted to accommodate 196 inmates in 2002, and expanded to 276 spaces in 2004. In 2006, CSD opened the Lai Chi Kok Correctional Institution to accommodate 650 inmates as a mechanism to alleviate crowded conditions in its female institutions and Ma Hang Prison and the DATC annex were converted back to accommodate male offenders and female drug users respectively (Joe Laidler, 2009). Despite these shifts, CSD's annual report (2007) stated that its capacity remained problematic with an average daily population of 1,964 female prisoners. More recently, CSD's newest correctional institution for women has led to a consolidation into two main female facilities.

What accounts for this growth? As we have described elsewhere (Joe Laidler, Emerton, & Petersen, 2007; Lee, 2007), this rise has been largely driven by the large numbers of mainland Chinese women who have been convicted and imprisoned in Hong Kong. Mainland Chinese women proportionately have represented between 70% and 88% of the total female prison population since 2000. At its peak, in 2006, mainland Chinese women represented over three fourths of all female prisoners admitted to CSD. The majority of these mainland women have been sentenced to prison for offenses against local laws, in particular, activities related to their engagement in sex work, including soliciting and breach of conditions of their visa stay under the immigration ordinance.

Sex work is not a crime but soliciting is an offense – many of these women are charged and convicted for this. Yet their main violation resulting in prison is one related to their immigration status. Visitors are not permitted to engage in any form of employment, including sex work, despite the fact that sex work is not officially considered an occupation. Elsewhere we describe the process and problems associated with the imprisonment of these women, but here we note that many women cross the border to engage in sex work and for those who are arrested through police raids and undercover operations, most are quickly processed through the criminal justice system, serving an average sentence length of two to three months; imprisonment may serve as a means of control (Joe Laidler et al., 2007; Lee, 2007).

What effect has this increase in female prisoners had on prison operations? Most immediate is the issue of crowding for which CSD created additional capacity through modifications of existing and new facilities, and the shifting of male prisoners to accommodate this growth. This is, paradoxically, a reversal of the early colonial period with female prisoners being moved to make way for male prisoners. Moreover, it is worth noting that the greater numbers of female prisoners has required a corresponding increase in female staffing.

A second concern raised in the shadow report had to do with the nature and objectives of work, education, and training for female prisoners, especially in light of CSD's rehabilitation goals and the changing nature of Hong Kong's economy. Given the shift from a manufacturing to a knowledge-based economy, training and work in such fields as sewing, laundry, and stationary production would not be sufficient to equip female prisoners upon release into the community, although it was observed that some young female prisoners were training in cosmetology. The educational curriculum for women could be strengthened with the adoption of compulsory literacy classes and a systematic curriculum, particularly for young women below 21 years of age, who because of the serious nature of their committing offense, were incarcerated in an adult facility and young illegal immigrants (mainly from mainland China) held in a minimum security prison.

RESPONDING TO CHANGING FEMALE PRISONER POPULATION

CSD developed a number of strategies in response to the significant changes in the nature and types of females imprisoned, broader economic shifts, and commitment to rehabilitation. At the most immediate level, crowding has been addressed with the opening of a new female institution, Lo Wu, which opened in July 2010. This facility is designed to cater to women's needs, including a health clinic and accommodation for mothers and their babies – who can stay up to three years of age. Given the colonial authorities' commitment to allowing mothers to nurse their babies, perhaps this contemporary arrangement is not so surprising.

In total, there are seven facilities for female prisoners and inmates. Yet challenges remain with the increase in female foreign prisoners, most of who are serving short sentences for breach of conditions of stay; the ideal of rehabilitation, work, and training may be at difficult to achieve given their circumstances. Nevertheless, correctional authorities have responded to the differential needs of incarcerated women, including the development of a gender-specific treatment approach that adopts a holistic frame of reference to promote reintegration, a personal growth and emotion treatment center for women (PSY GYM). In designing the women's treatment program, there has been recognition of gender-specific risks including emotional/psychological problems, parenting stress, and self-harming behaviors. As such, programs are centered around crisis management, cognitive behavioral therapy for emotional problems and trauma, and structured treatment groups. Importantly, at its newest facility is a unit for mothers and their babies.

CONCLUSION

Hong Kong's penal system – from the gaol to the prison to correctional institutions – has been shaped by its unique political, economic, and cultural position first as a colony and more recently as an autonomous region of China. Our goal here has been to examine how gender did and did not feature in its development. It appears from early colonial records that there was some limited acknowledgment and attempts to address the needs of women in prison, but the challenge at that time was based more centrally on differences among Europeans and Chinese and moral debates about punitiveness and reformation. The latter of which was part of broader discourses in Europe.

It is in more recent times that women's imprisonment became an urgent issue, a pattern seen elsewhere in the world (Reynolds, 2008). From our examination, CSD has been responsive to many of the challenges it faces as the "last stop" in the criminal justice tunnel, developing an infrastructure to work toward its goals of rehabilitation and at the same time accommodate to a changing female prison population. It has managed to address the issue of crowding, first with short-term measures of converting male accommodations suitable for female prisoners, and the construction of a new modern and up-to-date facility. It has also developed relevant programming in a changing environment. With this developing infrastructure, gender-sensitive monitoring will be important.

One of the central aims of the Bangkok Rules is the protection of human rights. Perhaps then, it is worth considering existing policies and laws governing sex work. In 1999, CEDAW's concluding observations stated, "The Committee recommends that adequate regulations to protect women sex workers be put in place and enforced. It also recommends that the Government monitor the links between the presence of migrant women, a regulatory approach to prostitution and trafficking in women."

Finally, the Hong Kong experience sheds some light on the practical constraints of some of the Bangkok Rules. Hong Kong, like many other locales around the world, has witnessed the rise in women's imprisonment. Increasingly many women who are imprisoned are not residents or citizens of that locale, caught in the circuit of migration. While the Bangkok Rules encourage transfers for foreign nationals to their native country with the prisoner's consent, what are the difficulties in practice? In addition, what are relevant strategies for short-, medium-, and long-term imprisonment?

NOTE

1. Our discussion draws from colonial and contemporary government reports and documents, and various scholars' attempts including our own, to make sense of

Hong Kong's prison system, historically and today. It should be noted that during the period of the Japanese occupation in Hong Kong, 1941–1945, many government records, including those from the prison, were destroyed, resulting in an incomplete and sketchy understanding of that period and the years before it. In the postwar period, prison authorities encountered difficulties in classifying newly admitted prisoners without knowing their previous criminal and penal histories.

ACKNOWLEDGMENTS

We wish to acknowledge our appreciation of the Hong Kong Correctional Services Department for their continued support of our research.

REFERENCES

Bickley, G. (Ed.). (2005). *A magistrate's court in nineteenth century Hong Kong*. Hong Kong: Chinese University Press.

CEDAW. (1999). Concluding comments on the initial report of the Hong Kong SAR under the convention on the elimination of all forms of discrimination against women. Point 76.

CEDAW. (2004). *Second report on the Hong Kong Special Administrative Region under the convention on the elimination of all forms of discrimination against women*. Retrieved from http://www.lwb.gov.hk/UNCEDAW/documents/CEDAW_2nd_report_E.pdf. Accessed on August 25, 2014.

Chan, S. (1994). *Development of the Hong Kong Penal Policy and Program under the British Administration (1841–1945)*. MA Dissertation, University of Leicester.

Chan, S. (2012). *Colonial penality: A case study of Hong Kong's Penal Policy and Programs under British Administration (1945–1997)*. Unpublished Ph.D. thesis, University of Hull.

Chau, H. W., & Siu, L. K. S. (2011). *Custody and correction: Development of Hong Kong's penal system, 1921–2011*. Hong Kong: Hong Kong Correctional Services.

Dikotter, F. (2004). "A paradise for rascals": Colonialism, punishment and the prison in Hong Kong (1841–1898). *Crime, History and Societies*, *8*(1), 1–11.

Hong Kong Administrative Reports. (1938). *Report of the superintendent of prisons for 1937*. Hong Kong.

Hong Kong Correctional Services Department. (2014). *Hong Kong fact sheet for correctional services*. March. Hong Kong: Hong Kong Government Printing.

Hong Kong Human Rights Monitor. (1999). Submission by HKHRM in respect of the Hong Kong Special Administrative Region's initial report on the HKSAR under Article 18 of the Convention on the Elimination of All Forms of Discrimination against Women. Retrieved from http://www.hkhrm.org.hk/english/reports/cedaw.html. Accessed on August 25, 2014.

International Centre for Prison Studies. (2006, 2011). *World female imprisonment list*. London: ICPS.

Joe Laidler, K. (2009). Correctional services department. In M. Gaylord, D. Gittings, & H. Traver (Eds.), *Introduction to crime, law and justice in Hong Kong* (pp. 185–204). Hong Kong: University of Hong Kong.

Joe Laidler, K., Emerton, R., & Petersen, C. (2007). Bureaucratic justice: The incarceration of mainland Chinese women working in Hong Kong's sex industry. *International Journal of Offender Therapy and Comparative Criminology*, *51*(1), 1–16.

Lee, M. (2007). Women's imprisonment as a mechanism of migration control, Hong Kong. *British Journal of Criminology*, *47*(6), 847–860.

McLaughlin, E., & Lowe, K. (1992). Sir John Pope Hennessey and the "native race craze": Colonial government in Hong Kong 1877–1822. *Journal of Imperial and Commonwealth History*, *20*(2), 223–247.

Reynolds, M. (2008). The war on drugs, prison building and globalization: Catalysts for the global incarceration of women. *NWSA Journal*, *20*(2), 72–95.

Vagg, J. (1991). Corrections. In H. Traver & J. Vagg (Eds.), *Crime and justice in Hong Kong* (pp. 139–152). Hong Kong: Oxford University.

GOVERNMENT DOCUMENTS

Hong Kong Administrative Reports. (1886). Report of the Superintendent of Victoria Gaol for 1885. Government Notification No. 121. Hong Kong, April 3.

Hong Kong Administrative Reports. (1894). Report of the Superintendent of Victoria Gaol for 1893. Government Notification No. 80. March 10.

Hong Kong Administrative Reports. (1933). Report of the Superintendent of Prisons for 1932. Appendix L. March 8.

Hong Kong Blue Book. (1847, 1874–1934). Gaols and prisoners. Hong Kong.

Hong Kong Government Gazette. (1877). Report of the Gaol Committee. Government Notification No. 57. March 8.

Hong Kong Government Gazette. (1890). Rules and Regulations for the Management of the Gaol at Victoria. No. 229. May 31.

Hong Kong Sessional Papers. (1892). Committee's Report on Prison Accommodation. November 15.

